BELMONT UNIVERSITY LIBRARY
BELMONT UNIVERSITY
1900 BELMONT BLVD.
NASHVILLE, TN 37212

Translation and Identity
in the Americas

'In this ground-breaking new book, Edwin Gentzler, one of the leading US translation experts, tackles the important question of the role played by translation in the shaping of the Americas.'

Susan Bassnett, University of Warwick, UK

Translation is a highly contested site in the Americas where different groups, often with competing literary or political interests, vie for space and approval. In its survey of these multiple and competing groups and its study of the geographic, socio-political and cultural aspects of translation, Edwin Gentzler's book demonstrates that the Americas are a fruitful terrain for the field of translation studies.

Building on research from a variety of disciplines including cultural studies, linguistics, feminism and ethnic studies and including case studies from Brazil, Canada and the Caribbean, this book shows that translation is one of the primary means by which a culture is constructed: translation in the Americas is less something that happens between separate and distinct cultures and more something that is capable of establishing those very cultures.

Using a variety of texts and addressing minority and oppressed groups within cultures, *Translation and Identity in the Americas* highlights by example the cultural role translation policies play in a discriminatory process: the consequences of which can be social marginalization, loss of identity and psychological trauma.

Translation and Identity in the Americas will be critical reading for students and scholars of Translation Studies, Comparative Literature and Cultural Studies.

Edwin Gentzler is the Director of the Translation Center and a Professor at the University of Massachusetts Amherst, USA. He is the author of *Contemporary Translation Theories* (2001) and *Translation and Power* (2002). He serves as co-editor (with Susan Bassnett) on the Topics in Translation Series for Multilingual Matters.

Translation and Identity in the Americas

New Directions in Translation Theory

Edwin Gentzler

LONDON AND NEW YORK

BELMONT UNIVERSITY LIBRARY

First published 2008
by Routledge
2 Park Square, Milton Park, Abingdon, Oxon OX14 4RN

Simultaneously published in the USA and Canada
by Routledge
270 Madison Ave, New York, NY 10016

Routledge is an imprint of the Taylor & Francis Group, an informa business

© 2008 Edwin Gentzler

Typeset in Sabon by
Keystroke, 28 High Street, Tettenhall, Wolverhampton
Printed and bound in Great Britain by
Antony Rowe Ltd, Chippenham, Wiltshire

All rights reserved. No part of this book may be reprinted or reproduced or utilised in any form or by any electronic, mechanical, or other means, now known or hereafter invented, including photocopying and recording, or in any information storage or retrieval system, without permission in writing from the publishers.

British Library Cataloguing in Publication Data
A catalogue record for this book is available from the British Library

Library of Congress Cataloging-in-Publication Data
Gentzler, Edwin, 1951–
 Translation and identity in the Americas : new directions in translation theory / Edwin Gentzler.
  p. cm.
 Includes bibliographical references and index.
 ISBN 978–0–415–77451–2 (hardback) – ISBN 978–0–415–77452–9 (pbk.)
 1. Translating and interpreting–North America. 2. Translating and interpreting–South America. I. Title.
 P306.8.N7G46 2007
 418'.02097—dc22

2007022528

ISBN10: 0–415–77451–9 (hbk)
ISBN10: 0–415–77452–7 (pbk)

ISBN13: 978–0–415–77451–2 (hbk)
ISBN13: 978–0–415–77452–9 (pbk)

To Jenny

Contents

Foreword by Susan Bassnett   ix
Preface and acknowledgements   xv

1 Introduction: New Definitions   1

2 Multiculturalism in the United States   8

3 Feminism and Theater in (Quebec) Canada   40

4 Cannibalism in Brazil   77

5 The Fictional Turn in Latin America   108

6 Border Writing and the Caribbean   143

7 Conclusion: New Directions   180

Bibliography   188
Index   205

Foreword

In this ground-breaking new book, Edwin Gentzler, one of the leading US translation experts, tackles the important question of the role played by translation in the shaping of the Americas and looks at the processes currently in play that are bringing the history of pan-American multilingualism back into the public consciousness. Gentzler boldly suggests that where once translation was seen as a rhetorical form that was somehow underpinned by a yearning for some unified original essence, it is now increasingly being seen as a discursive practice that reveals multiple signs of the polyvalence with which cultures are constructed. This change of attitude comes with a reassessment of the history of linguistic suppression and conflict in the Americas. Today there is greater awareness of how many Native American languages have been obliterated, how many generations of African slaves were forcibly deprived of their original languages, and how many immigrants were compelled to speak their native languages in secret for fear of punishment in schools or in the workplace. Rethinking the past of the Americas means re-evaluating the changing patterns of language use and, in particular, re-examining the myth of the melting pot in the light of those plurivocal linguistic histories.

Gentzler's study is divided into an examination of different geographical areas: the United States, Canada, Brazil, Latin America, and perhaps more controversially, the Caribbean and what he calls 'Border Writing'. The rationale for this division makes sense, since not only are there different linguistic histories across the Americas, but research into translation has taken very different trajectories and there is no coherent single perspective. This, of course, is hardly surprising given the very different colonial histories of Latin America and Brazil, and the dominance of English in the United States and Canada for over two hundred years. Gentzler chooses to focus on a particular strand of translation work in each chapter, weaving a fascinating web that will certainly serve as a spur to further research in a relatively neglected field.

In terms of his personal intellectual journey, Gentzler starts by suggesting that this book should be seen as a sequel to his earlier study, *Contemporary Translation Theories* (2nd ed. 2002), a book that provided the first comprehensive overview of emerging trends in the rapidly developing interdiscipline of translation studies. He argues that, when applied to the Americas, deconstruction and postcolonial theories serve as important tools that open up discussion not only about the history of national language policies but also about emerging concepts of identity that are, of course, intimately linked to language. He sees it as essential that any investigation into translation across the Americas should include the three dimensions of translation so well-presented by Emily Apter in her book *The Translation Zone: A New Comparative Literature* (2006) – the geographic, the socio-political and the psychological.

Perhaps the most challenging statement underpinning the rationale behind this book is Gentzler's statement that translation in the Americas "is less something that happens between separate and distinct cultures and more something that is *constitutive* of those cultures." This leads him later on to state that translation is not a trope in the Americas, but a permanent condition, a condition that has nevertheless tended to be disregarded by scholars in the English and Spanish speaking countries. Only in Canada and Brazil does the study of translation flourish, with lively professional associations, conferences, and important publications. The United States and Latin America have been surprisingly slow in developing research into translation or even starting to take translation seriously, and Gentzler offers his own suggestions as to why this might have been the case up to now.

The first chapter starts with a set of questions, principal of which is what translation means for the United States. Gentzler looks at contemporary language policy and tracks the origins of that policy back through to the beginnings of the nation state. He takes as a key text Derrida's *Monolingualism of the Other; or the Prosthesis of Origin* (1998) and builds upon the French scholar's idea that any ideology of homogeneity implies a present but repressed ideology of heterogeneity and difference. So while English is the dominant language of the United States, translation pervades every aspect of the culture because the people who comprise the state come from a wide range of diverse starting points, both linguistically and culturally. In this chapter, Gentzler goes back and examines the earliest period of colonisation, showing how plurilingualism was the norm, as settlers from English, Dutch, French, Spanish, Portuguese and other backgrounds traded with Native American peoples. That history, he suggests, has been largely forgotten, 'at certain costs to the psychic well-being of the nation.' Recognising the role played by translation in the creation of what is the United States today might help a nation troubled by its current difficulties of international understanding.

Turning next to Canada, the book moves from an officially monolingual state to one that is officially bilingual. The Canadian context, particularly from the 1960s onwards, has been the location for one of the major debates about language and the implementation of a policy of bilingualism in which translation played a crucial part. Gentzler notes the wealth of research into translation over the last few decades and the innovative thinking around translation by both scholars and writers. The chapter takes up two particularly strong lines of work in Canada: translating for the theater and feminist translation.

The move to using *joual*, or Canadian street French by writers and especially in the theater, was part of the Québécois movement of the late 60s and early 70s. Translating texts into *joual* served a dual purpose: on the one hand it raised the status of what had been seen as a marginal dialect to that of a literary language, and on the other hand it foregrounded the importance of translation as a means of communicating across boundaries. The second part of the chapter discusses the extraordinary proliferation of feminist translation, both as literary practice and as scholarly activity. Work by Nicole Brossard, Barbara Godard, Susanne de Lotbinière-Harwood and Sherry Simon has had a far reaching impact, both in Canada and around the world. The Canadian feminist translators have developed a new paradigm for translation, in lieu of the old binary dichotomy between source and target, exploring the poetics of no-man's land, and celebrating in-betweenness that cannot be categorised according to traditional methods. The ambivalence of a state struggling to establish and live with bilingualism and its implications is reflected in some of the creative thinking focusing on translation.

There is ambivalence also in Brazil, the subject of the next chapter, but here the tension is between tradition and modernity, the old world and the new. Gentzler starts with a discussion of the so-called cannibalistic theory of contemporary Brazilian translation studies, tracing its evolution from Oswald de Andrade's "Cannibalist Manifesto" of 1928. The cannibalist metaphor, like the Canadian no-man's land, offers a way of thinking about translation that challenges earlier models. Cannibalist translation involves recreating a text, ritually devouring it, preserving its finest qualities and then transposing it into a different cultural context. The work of the De Campos brothers, Haroldo and Augusto, is examined, and Gentzler shows how Haroldo de Campos's extraordinary rendering of Goethe's *Faust* leads to the creation of something that is entirely new, even while being in parts a close, literal translation, which becomes "a hybrid text that both valorizes and kills off its predecessor in precisely the same sense that Oswald de Andrade re-construed his concept of 'cannibalism'."

The chapter sets great store by what is happening in Brazil, even going so far as to suggest that Brazilian work in translation, cinema and literary theory more generally is setting down roots for a new theory of culture that is multilingual, intersemiotic and interdisciplinary. The tensions in Brazilian society, the difficulties of balancing an economy so often in crisis, in a country where some of the inhabitants are living in the rainforest and others in state-of-the-art high rise apartments, is leading to a surge of creative activity in the process of forging a genuinely multicultural nation, where translation is not marginal but fundamental.

The discussion of translation in Spanish-speaking Latin America is completely different, since attitudes to translation and translation research is quite unlike anything that is happening in Brazil. Gentzler has taken an unusual route to discussing Latin American translation, choosing to focus on the wealth of fiction writers and arguing that translation is one of, if not the most important topics dealt with by Latin American writers, more important even than the much-acclaimed magical realism. The chapter accordingly considers the use of the theme of translation in works by Jorge Luis Borges, Gabriel García Márquez and Mario Vargas Llosa, probably the three best known writers internationally.

Walter Benjamin, a key figure for many Latin American literary figures, is used as a theoretical underpinning for the analysis of the novels. Benjamin's theory of translation supplying the afterlife of an original is used to explicate the work of Latin American writers who are seeking both to develop and extend European models and simultaneously create completely new, independent works for a new readership. Translation reveals interconnectedness, happening as it does across and between languages, and fiction writers in Latin America have deliberately created works that continuously remind readers of other works. The library, the labyrinth, the family tree, the forking paths, the undecipherable manuscripts, all images that recur in Latin American fiction, reinforce the significance of translation as a metaphor for the hybrid identity formation.

The last chapter starts with that long-standing, centrally significant American image of the border. The border can delineate a national boundary, but it has also served to delineate the boundary between what is perceived as civilisation and barbarism, between insider and outside, between safety and danger. In this chapter, the idea of border is extended to embrace the Caribbean also, as the border becomes a space where forms of translation are in daily use as traditional notions of standard language cease to hold sway. Language instead is in constant flux, and this can be seen in both the Creole languages of the Caribbean, in Chicano Spanish, Pocho and Spanglish, all language variants that include more than one source. Such languages are, the chapter argues, in a constant state of evolution, and translation is "an ongoing, permanent activity fundamental to the lives and identities" of the inhabitants of these regions.

In his conclusion, Gentzler reasserts his belief that the history of translation in the Americas is a history of identity formation, something ingrained in the very psyche of the millions of inhabitants. He argues that the plurivalence of pan-American translation needs to be seen not only in terms of socio-cultural history, but also in terms of its psychological implications. Having started out by recognising the importance of the cultural turn in translation studies of the 1990s, he ends by suggesting that perhaps the next turn in the field will be a social-psychological one that expands what has hitherto been the dominant functional approach to translation. Using this approach, it might then be possible for scholars to better understand both the significance of translation for individuals in multilingual societies and, ultimately, to look outwards and engage with how translation functions in other parts of the world. He cites Emily Apter's pithy comment that "war is the continuation of extreme mistranslation or disagreement by other means" (2006: 16) and stresses the need for much greater recognition of what happens in language transfer in the dangerous global politics of the twenty-first century. Translation, he suggests, is not a secondary, marginal activity; rather, it is a pro-active potentially liberating activity that stimulates innovation. The examples of how translation has functioned across the Americas serve to stress the importance of the articulation of different narratives of cultural diversity and linguistic independence. The next step is to use the lessons that can be learned from understanding past cultural trauma in order to reach out to new possibilities in a troubled global age.

Susan Bassnett
University of Warwick

Preface and acknowledgements

The formulation for this project has had a long gestation period. After the publication of my first book, *Contemporary Translation Theories* (1993; revised second edition 2001), I found myself lecturing on theories that originated primarily in Europe—translation studies, functional translation, systems theory, deconstruction—and had little time to focus on my first love, American literature. During the 1990s, there was much more research on translational phenomena being undertaken in Europe than in the Americas, and those were exciting times for the field, as all those scholars who have taken the "cultural turn" can attest. My being lost in the explosion of translation theories—new descriptive, communication, cultural, colonial, postcolonial, poststructural theories—is perhaps excusable, given the boom, but all the while I was also traveling in the American hemisphere, too, reading works, talking with scholars, and gaining new insights. This book reflects that period of study, and in many ways also better reflects my own ideas about translation.

I hope that this book may be seen as a sequel to the earlier work: *Contemporary Translation Theories* ended with my reflection on deconstruction and postcolonial theories of translation, which is precisely where *Translation and Identity in the Americas* begins. The nation-states of the Americas are artificial ones at best, carved out of the New World by colonizing powers until the postcolonial movements led the way to revolution and independence across the hemisphere. Thus, deconstruction and postcolonial theories, when applied to the Americas, help uncover theoretical questions regarding definitions of nation, nation-state, and national language, as well as ontological questions with regard to emerging concepts of identity. Such inquiry transitions quite naturally to the translational, transcultural, and transnational theories that follow.

I wish to express my sincere thanks to Susan Bassnett at the University of Warwick, with whom I discussed this book at its earliest stages, and who is a keen student of North American and Latin American literature, women's studies, as well as translation theory. She provided intellectual support, encouragement, and friendship throughout. I also wish to express my gratitude to the hosts at the schools where I have been invited to speak, during which time I discussed many of the ideas which follow. In Brazil, I thank John Milton at the University of São Paulo, Neusa da Silva Matte at the Federal University of Rio Grande, Rosemary Arrojo at Campinas University (later at Binghamton University), Adriana Pagano at the Federal University of Minas Gerais, and Else Vieira at Minas Gerais (later at the University of London). In Canada, I thank Sherry Simon and Pier-Pascal Boulanger at Concordia University; Marco Fiolo, Judith Lavoie, Clara Foz, Paul Bandia, Georges Bastin, and the officers of the Canadian Association of Translation Studies (CATS), who invited me to speak at their annual meeting at the University of Western Ontario; and Annie Brisset at Ottawa University. In the United States, I thank Christopher Larkosh at the University of Connecticut (later at the University of Massachusetts Dartmouth); Jeffrey Green and Rainer Schulte at the University of Texas at Dallas; Marco Miletich at Hunter College; Tomislav Longinovic at the University of Wisconsin–Madison; Marilyn Gaddis Rose at Binghamton University; and Geoff Koby, Brian Baer, Claudia Angelelli, Jonathan Hine, and my fellow officers of the American Translation and Interpreting Studies Association (ATISA). In Mexico, I thank Danielle Zaslavsky at El Colegio de México and Miguel Vallejo at the Universidad de Veracruzana. In Peru, I thank Ivana Suito and Cecilia Lozano at the Colegio de Traductores del Perú, and in Argentina, I thank Astrid Wenzel at the Colegio de Traductores Públicos de la Ciudad de Buenos Aires (CTPCBA). In Europe, I thank Assumpta Camps at the Universidad de Barcelona, Christina Schaffner at Aston University, Mona Baker at Manchester University, Federico Federici at the University of Leeds (now at Durham University), and Lev Zybatow at Innsbruck University.

I thank my colleagues at the University of Massachusetts Amherst, including Deans of the College of Humanities and Fine Arts Lee Edwards (retired) and Joel Martin (current), Chair of the Department of Languages, Literatures, and Cultures Julie Hayes, and Professors of Comparative Literature Maria Tymoczko and William Moebius. I thank my friends at the Five College Crossroads in the Study of the Americas (CISA), including Robert Schwartzwald (now at the University of Montréal) and Jana Braziel (now at the University of Cincinnati), who invited me to teach a section on translation in their "Rethinking the Americas" course. In particular, I want to thank all the graduate students in the MA in Translation Studies and the PhD in Comparative Literature Programs for participation in seminars and engagement with many of the ideas of the book. I thank my staff at the Translation Center, including Shawn Lindohlm, Görkem Cilam, and Adam LaMontagne, who assumed many of my duties to enable me to study and write. Particular thanks go to my colleagues who read individual chapters and gave me feedback, including Sherry Simon, Aaron Suko, Maura Talmadge, and Christopher Larkosh. I am most grateful to Louise Semlyen, Editor, and Ursula Mallows, Editorial Assistant, at Routledge for their belief in this project and for their editorial expertise. My deepest gratitude goes to my wife, Jenny Spencer, who also read numerous drafts and exchanged ideas with me, and to my daughter, Megan, for their continued love and support.

A few acknowledgements are in order. The first presentation of the ideas that were part of the initial formulation of this book occurred at the University of Manchester in a talk titled "What Is Different about Translation in the Americas?" which was later published in *CTIS Occasional Papers*, vol. 2, Manchester: UMIST (2002): 7–19. A small part of Chapter 2 was worked into a presentation titled "Translation Theory: Monolingual, Bilingual, or Multilingual," later published in *The Journal of Translation Studies* (Hong Kong) 9 (1) (2006): 105–124. An early version of part of Chapter 6 titled "Translation and Border Writing in the Americas" was presented at the "Translating Voices, Translating Regions" conference in Rieti, Italy, and was later published in N. Armstrong and F.M. Federici (eds.) *Translating Voices, Translating Regions*, Rome: Aracne (2006): 356–378.

1 Introduction
New Definitions

In *Translation, History and Culture*, Susan Bassnett and André Lefevere officially announced the "cultural turn" in translation studies, suggesting that the translation studies scholar investigate what "the exercise of power means in terms of the production of culture, of which the production of translations is a part" (1990: 5). While this was a provocative thesis at the time, numerous scholars from around the world were approaching similar views; the 1990s resulted in a decade of new investigations that extended beyond the range of linguistic and literary translation and into issues of translation and cultural formation. In particular, translation studies scholars focused on how textual practices were used by governments, publishers, universities, and other institutions of power to manipulate culture, generally in support of, or occasionally in resistance to, the status quo. Translation, often considered a marginal practice, was increasingly shown to be instrumental in the process of developing and maintaining power: which international texts were selected for translation, where those texts were made available—in the marketplace, schools, churches, and government circles—the affordability of said texts, and how those foreign texts were translated or adapted to the receiving culture became fundamental questions for both translation and cultural studies. The mini-boom in translation studies involved increased conference activity, new journals publishing firms, as well as new MA and PhD programs in translation studies.

In 1998, Bassnett and Lefevere published another book, this time called *Constructing Cultures*, in which they argued for cultural studies to take "the translation turn" (1998: 123), moving translation to center stage in cultural studies. Though this argument was provocative and seemingly unrealistic at the time, once cultural studies began studying concepts of linguistic and cultural pluralism, the fragmentation of the literary or cultural artifact, and the multiple histories behind the emergence of artistic objects, the turn to language and translation trajectories was inevitable. Cultural studies has now moved from the national to the international, or, better said, the transnational, and thus translation scholars are well positioned for future investigations. Indeed, those scholars working in only one language and culture, even when positioned in English, French, or Spanish departments,

2   Introduction: New Definitions

are being left behind. With the immigration and importation of multiple groups speaking different languages from a range of social and economic backgrounds, the Americas have proven a fruitful terrain for studying such polylingual voices and transnational discourses. Indeed, translated texts are already referring to at least two different sign systems and cultural traditions; a comparison of source and target texts reveals how meaning travels, making translation an ideal starting point for such a study. Moreover, translations are never perfect; something is always left out, hidden, covered up, well illustrating their fragmentary nature, their failure to travel intact, and, thus, their suitability for cultural manipulation.

In this study, I discuss several new insights and ideas that translation studies scholars in the Americas are pursuing, remaining especially open to sociological and cultural factors. This study builds on research from a variety of scholars in several disciplines—linguistics, philosophy, literary theory, feminism, ethnic studies, and cultural studies—produced in the 1990s and early 2000s, research based on the assumption that translation constitutes one of the primary means by which culture is constructed and is therefore important to any study of cultural evolution and identity formation. One such group especially informs this study: the descriptive translation studies (DTS) scholars, or, more colloquially, the "manipulation school," including scholars such as André Lefevere, Susan Bassnett, Maria Tymoczko, Itamar Even-Zohar, and Gideon Toury. What these researchers are finding is that the definition of translation is a relative term. Perhaps the most revolutionary move in post-Jakobson translation studies has been made by Gideon Toury, who in *In Search of a Theory of Translation* (1980) called for a temporary suspension of more definitions of translation until more data could be collected. He suggested that scholars define translation as any text "regarded as a translation from the intrinsic point of view of the target system" (ibid.: 73), despite preconceived criteria or nonconformity with the original. If any finding is characteristic of research in translation studies in the post-Toury age, it is an overwhelming lack of conformity in translation—mistranslations, pseudotranslations, gaps, contradictions, accidents, numerous shifts both conscious and unconscious, ideological constraints, economic constraints, all seem to be part of the process. This study builds on the post-Toury scholarship and proposes to take it one step further. In addition to studying any text called a translation by given culture, it also considers translation phenomena that occur but may not be defined as such. I suggest that such elements, often covered up, suppressed, or marginalized by that same culture, reveal just as much about translation phenomena as "proper" translation. In her book *Translating Montreal: Episodes in the Life of a Divided City* (2006), Canadian translation theorist Sherry Simon questions the limits of earlier definitions of translation and focuses instead on the conditions conducive to translation, such as the multicultural life in the city of Montreal and the hybrid forms of communication there, many of which take place *after* translation. Indicative of the new directions translation theory is taking in the Americas, she offers a new definition: "I give translation an expanded definition in this book: writing that is inspired by the encounter with other tongues, including the effects of creative interference" (ibid.: 17).

In order to better understand such new trends, this study frequently focuses on minority and oppressed groups within cultures and highlights the cultural role translation policies play in that discriminatory process. Indeed, in the studies of translation phenomena in the Americas, translation studies scholars with critical theory, cultural studies, and feminist backgrounds —including Lawrence Venuti, Carol Maier, Sherry Simon, Barbara Godard, Else Vieira, and Rosemary Arrojo—have proven instrumental in the analysis that follows. As Lawrence Venuti wrote in the introduction to his pioneering anthology *Rethinking Translation: Discourse, Subjectivity, Ideology*, translated texts need to be "submitted to the same rigorous interrogation that other cultural forms and practices have recently undergone with the emergence of poststructuralism" (1992b: 6). This interrogation process is well under way, often led in the Americas by scholars in Quebec and Brazil. In addition, this book considers the use of translation to resist particular social constructions, introduce new ideas, and question the status quo. Aimé Césaire translated and adapted Shakespeare's *The Tempest* into French to combat negative images of Caribbean indigenous peoples; Haroldo de Campos translated Goethe's *Faust* into Portuguese in order to challenge the Christian interpretations of the ending. Such examples suggest that translation is not a neutral site in the Americas; rather, it is a highly contested one where different groups, often with competing literary or political interests, vie for space and approval. Those who win such contests generally find themselves liberated and empowered; those who lose suffer many consequences, including social marginalization, loss of identity, and psychological trauma.

In *The Translation Zone: A New Comparative Literature* (2006), Emily Apter uses the word "zone" to refer to a theoretical space, one that is not defined by language, politics, or nation, but is broad enough to include the aftershocks of translation. She worries that those who decide language and cultural policy also decide translation policy, which in turn affects textual heritage, preservation, and dissemination. Translation policy is also a part of the foreign policies exercised by the powerful economies and larger nation-states for hemispheric goals. Thus, she wants to expand the boundaries of translation studies and to recognize new sites of language contact as battlegrounds on which the survival of languages, and the ethnic and cultural memories embedded within, depend. Her concept of "zone" is conceived as threefold. First, it is a geographical space, similar to a space that a city planner designates a park for multiple uses. Here Apter looks at translation sites: diasporic language communities, border cultures, pockets of print and media spheres, and department and programs in university institutions. She asks what gets translated and, especially, what does not, focusing on caesuras, omissions, transmission failures, and that which is deemed untranslatable. Second, she suggests that the translation zone is a political zone, a medium for social and political formation and reformation. She looks at governmental involvement in domestic policies such as whether a culture will be monolingual or multilingual, or use of standard or nonstandard language. She also looks at international policies, such as translation use in military engagements and foreign policy. Indeed, one of the strengths of the book is the way translation and military policies are intertwined, suggesting the political urgency for more and better translation in the precarious post-9/11 world. Apter's third conception of zone is even more striking, as it focuses on the psychological repercussions of such translational policies. Drawing an analogy to Guillaume Apollinaire's poem "Zone" (1912), which describes a place on the Paris outskirts where bohemians and migrants gathered, Apter discusses this peripheral territory as a psychological space. Here she focuses on the position of the subject within a culture and how one's own self-knowledge, language, and cultural heritage become identified with or foreign to oneself. Adding another new definition to the mix, Apter conceives of translation as a "means of repositioning the subject in the world and in history," and a "significant medium for subject re-formation and political change" (2006: 6).

This study of translation in the Americas emphasizes all three of Apter's dimensions of translation: its geographic, sociopolitical, and psychological aspects. This book is also indebted to and builds upon investigations published in anthologies edited by Anuradha Dingwaney and Carol Maier (1995), Román Álvarez and M. Carmen-África Vidal (1996), Susan Bassnett and Harish Trevidi (1999), Sherry Simon and Paul St-Pierre (2000), and Maria Tymoczko and Edwin Gentzler (2001). The scholarship that informs these works derives largely from poststructuralist and postcolonial theory, including the work of scholars such as Michel Foucault, Jacques Derrida, Walter Benjamin, Gayatri Spivak, and Homi Bhabha. I also speculate on the repressed nature of translation in certain regions of the Americas, turning to scholars such as Jean Laplanche, who uses the term *à traduire* to refer to unconscious, psychological traumas and failures of translation, which I find useful to discuss losses experienced by those subjected to language domination. Indeed, in the chapters that follow I often turn to postcolonial, poststructural, and psychoanalytic thought for perspectives and insight.

This book is not meant to be an overview of the translation histories of the respective regions in the Americas; rather, I focus upon the newest approaches to translation developed in different parts of the Americas over the past thirty years. Also valuable in the development of the ideas that follow has been the work on nation and identity formation, especially by those scholars investigating identity formation in Latin America, such as Fernando Ortiz, Ángel Rama, and Fernando Pérez Firmat. If Susan Bassnett is right that cultural studies has taken the "translation turn," then it should come as no surprise that concepts such "transculturation," coined by the

Cuban anthropologist Fernando Ortiz and elaborated by Latin American literary critics such as Ángel Rama, inform the chapters that follow. Finally, my work also intersects with that of scholars of the "New American Studies," such as Marc Shell, Wai Chee Dimock, Donald Pease, John Carlos Rowe, and Winfried Siemerling, who are investigating American cultures from comparative, interdisciplinary, and "transnational" perspectives. Arguing that the boundaries of the nation-states of the Americas have little to do with linguistic and cultural origins and more to do with political and military impositions, these scholars look at literary and cultural phenomena that extend beyond national borders. Translation is critical to such investigations.

In this book, I divide translation activity in the Americas into five areas: (1) multiculturalism in the United States; (2) theater and feminism in Canada; (3) cannibalism in Brazil; (4) fiction in Latin America; and (5) border writing and the Caribbean. Although the nation-states of the Americas tend to use European languages as "official" languages, those respective languages are by no means original national languages. Rather, they are "translated" languages—that is, "carried across" from Europe to the Americas and imposed, more often than not, via force on the peoples living there. Yet "unofficial" cultures, made up of indigenous roots, repressed languages, and alternative histories unique to the New World, continue behind the scenes. Many minorities are excluded from that power sharing, often because of the very *lack* of available translations and inadequate language policies.

This study also suggests that translation in the Americas is less something that happens between separate and distinct cultures and more something that is *constitutive* of those cultures. In many of the studies of translation and culture of the past two decades, translation has served as a trope or a metaphor for a cultural condition. This study suggests that it is much more: translation is not a trope but a permanent condition in the Americas. What does the word "America" mean? To what does it refer? Its roots are certainly not located in the continents that compose the Americas; rather, "America" is a mistranslation, a word imposed from the outside that has little connection with the lands to which it refers, a word that represents its submission rather than its life. Further, internationally and in parts of North America, the term "America" is often used to refer only to the United States of America, another form of mistranslation, and a cultural imperialism of its own kind. Likewise, what does the phrase "Latin America" mean? Latin America is another mistranslation, referring to Latin languages—Spanish, French, Italian, and Portuguese primarily—translated to and rewritten in America. Latin America thus reflects "original" European cultures and how those displaced languages and cultures have evolved in the New World. Most of the language changes have been derived from cultural incompatibilities that give new meanings to old terms in their new context, another feat of translation. Indeed, such linguistic incompatibilities give rise to numerous difficulties in writing any text about the Americas. For example, how does one refer to the indigenous peoples of the Americas? They have suffered a near-total mistranslation by the Spanish explorers, who, searching for China and India, mistook the Americas for another continent. Still the misnaming continues, to the present. The variety of forms that I use in this text to refer to the peoples living in the Americas upon the arrival of the Europeans is indicative of the problem; I have resorted to a number of strategies, using "indigenous," "aboriginal," "Indian," "Amerindian (or Amer-Indian)," and "Native American" as synonyms, yet find them all unsatisfactory. So many mistranslations of American people, landscape, culture, and artifacts have occurred in the process of the European explorers and colonizers translating and domesticating that which they encountered into their own terms, concepts, and worldviews that any accurate description becomes impossible. Such is the condition of life in the Americas, and why the focus of this study is more often than not upon the misfirings and failures of translation, what such language failure reveals about culture as a whole, and what the psychological repercussions of such misnaming imply.

Despite the fundamental nature of translation in the Americas, translation studies is still an emerging discipline. In both Brazil and Canada, strong translation studies associations exist with regular conference activities and exchanges of ideas. But in the United States, Spanish-speaking Latin America, and the Caribbean, few programs exist, or, if they do, they continue to be housed as subsidiaries of larger linguistics, language studies, or comparative literature departments. No inter-American research group exists, and contact among scholars tends to be erratic. One purpose of this study is to begin a discussion among translation scholars of America to try to discover lines for investigation and to develop a corresponding program of study to better understand the role of translation in the development of cultures in the Americas. I suggest that translation and cultural studies scholars in the United States of America have much to learn from their Canadian, Latin American, Brazilian, and Caribbean colleagues. While European cultures bear the brunt of the language and translational policies that have dominated cultural evolution in the Americas, the new superpower on the block is the United States of America, and its language and translational policies, as I hope to show in the next chapter, reverberate domestically and transnationally.

While this study is informed primarily by interdisciplinary scholarship of the past two decades, the approaches investigated in this book have distinct historical roots, many of which evolve from the most important literary and social movements in their respective countries. The Brazilian cannibalists, for example, date their work back to an avant-garde movement in Brazil in the 1920s in which Oswald de Andrade and other experimentalist writers posited several manifestos, such as *Antropofagia*, to challenge European literary models and to protest against the ongoing mental colonization in

Brazil at the time. In addition to reporting on the recent developments of the respective models, this book explores their different literary and theoretical underpinnings to show how they can contribute to ongoing discussions in linguistics, philosophy, and literary studies regarding the nature of meaning and philosophy of language.

Not only are the strategies covered in this book different from each other, but the more one looks at smaller, regional communities, the more specific the differences become. Yet they also have similarities, one of which is their emphasis on the use of translation as a tool to gain independence from or to form alliances with groups struggling with similar problems. Thus, one central aim of this book is to begin the exploration of the role translation plays in identity formation, which is perhaps the key to understanding how translation functions at the micro and the macro level in the Americas. I perceive a shift in perspective from something that takes place between cultures to something that is itself culture, which has repercussions for the very definition of translation. As postcolonial theorists such as Homi Bhabha talk about culture as "transnational and translational" to refer to a new hybridized condition that is indicative of contemporary culture (1994: 172), so too might translation studies scholars begin to recognize the fundamental role translation plays in the construction of individual identity. I suggest that cultural studies, postcolonial studies, and translation scholars have much to learn from each other. Bhabha's definition of contemporary culture, for example, as one to be seen less in terms of separate and unified nations and more in terms of movement and maneuver that allow new voices to be heard (ibid.: 183), can be very productive for translation studies research. These immigrants, migrants, and refugees are always in the process of translating, both as a means to conform to the ways prevalent in their new locations and as a means to resist assimilationist pressures. The Americas are primarily made up of immigrants, migrants, and refugees, and thus translation operates in the Americas not as an isolated linguistic or literary activity, nor as a postcolonial metaphor or trope, but as a concrete, historical movement with the power to include and exclude. I urge translators and translation studies scholars to participate in those very movements as they occur, producing or investigating those actual texts that create the maneuvers of which Bhabha speaks. I also hope that this book in some small way contributes to that movement.

2 Multiculturalism in the United States

What is translation in the United States of America? What does the term mean for United States residents? How is it conceived socially? Historically? Psychologically? Does it mean the same thing in the United States as in other nations around the world? While the Constitution of the United States guarantees freedom of speech and liberty for all, the United States is also considered a monolingual country, with little perceived need for translation. Yet there are laws making translation services mandatory for non- or limited English-speaking peoples (LEPs), specifically Title VI of the 1964 Civil Rights Act, which prohibits discrimination based upon race, color, or national origin in programs or activities that receive federal financial assistance (Title VI, Sec. 42.101). Programs that receive federal funding are widespread, including the courts, schools (and universities), social security agencies, most hospitals and managed care facilities, numerous social service agencies, towns and cities, police, some banks, and many small businesses, yet regular translation services, with few exceptions, are consistently denied. The problem is invariably attributed to a lack of funding, and while the laws intend well, such unfunded mandates are seldom enforced. The Office of Civil Rights has a backload of complaints raising questions about the law's implementation, but under the Bush regime there has been little impetus to consider translation issues. The issue is largely a sociopolitical one, and has deep roots.

In the United States, translation invariably continues under the radar of "official culture." The country has often been analyzed along the lines of race, gender, and class, but seldom in terms of translation and language minorities. In the United States today, over 150 languages are spoken. According to the 2000 United States Census, over 47 million people, or about one out of five Americans, speak a language other than English at home. After English (215 million native speakers) follows Spanish (28 million), Chinese (2 million), French (1.6 million), German (1.4 million), Tagalog (1.2 million), and Vietnamese (1 million). The number of Russian speakers has tripled in the past decade, and the number of Haitian Creole speakers has doubled. Most scholars agree that these numbers are low, as immigrants invariably are undercounted. As of May 2006, the US Census

Bureau estimates that the Spanish/Latino population has grown to over 42 million, or over 14 percent of the total population, which makes Hispanics the largest minority in the United States, passing African-Americans, who number about 37 million, or 12.8 percent of the population. To survive, these citizens either have to translate themselves into English or translate the English for themselves.

Any consideration of translation and identity issues in the United States must first consider the translational aspect of an assimilationist policy. In theory, the ideology of the country aspires to integrate all incoming languages and cultures into one inclusive, united whole. Yet this melting pot ideology does not match reality. As Wilson Neate argues in "Unwelcome Remainders, Welcome Reminders" (1994), it conceals a sociopolitical repressive aspect: that which does not fit in the homogeneous melting pot is relegated to the margins, excluded, or, in Neate's terms, is referred to as a "remainder," left-over or left out. In terms of translation studies, the term "remainder" has proven useful, appearing in Lawrence Venuti's *The Translator's Invisibility* to help analyze translation in the United States (1995: 216). In terms of translation theory, I suggest that the repression of this remainder by the English-only advocates enables the nation-state as a whole to construct its national identity. Yet that remainder will always return to haunt the dominant majority, accounting for the repetition of the repressive ideology over time.

One of the reasons why there is so much poverty and ghettoization in the culture of the United States is that the parts that do not fit—invariably of a different color, ethnicity, culture, and language—are often cast aside. Examples include Amerindians relegated to reservations, Chinese immigrants centralized in Chinatowns, blacks impoverished in urban ghettos, Latinos relegated to the *barrios*, and many ethnic minorities and non-English speakers, mostly men, incarcerated in a disproportionate fashion. With no national translation policy, there is no policy of mediation, negotiation, communication, or inclusion. In *The American Scene* (1968 [1907]), novelist Henry James reports on his visit to Ellis Island, where he was shocked at the number of immigrants he encountered, visibly disturbed that he must share "the sanctity of his American consciousness" with these non-Anglo-Americans, or, in his terms, "aliens" (James, 1968 [1907]: 85; Neate, 1994: 24). Translators also are implicated in the exclusionary policies. Venuti argues, for example, that many practicing translators unconsciously participate in a similar exclusion-oriented ideology, arguing that they reduce the "foreignness" of the non-English-language texts, absorbing the "remainder" into fluent-sounding, proper English prose.

In this chapter, I suggest that monolingualism always includes multilingualism, albeit in a deceptive way because it hides the very multilingual fabric upon which it rests. As Derrida argues in *Monolingualism of the Other; or The Prosthesis of Origin* (1998; *Le Monolinguisme de l'autre: ou la prothèse d'origine*, 1996), monolingualism cannot exist without the

"Other," in this case multilingualism, just as Derrida, in his earlier work, cannot think of similitude without difference, presence without absence, truth without fiction, semantics without polysemy, a cure without poison, or an author without translation. Monolingual cultures, Derrida supposes, always carry with them their silent, deferred twin, the multilingualism of the Other, as well as that silent but always ongoing process of translation that occurs beneath the surface. Of necessity, the totalizing process of English-only assimilation implies that there is a nonassimilated, non-English process of translation also inherent in the culture, otherwise no such policy would be required. An ideology of homogeneity implies a present but repressed ideology of heterogeneity and difference. While the dominant English-only majority reigns, this centrality is one that is based upon the reiterated marginalization of those who do not conform. Translation, which by definition consists of at least two languages or semiotic sign systems, invariably finds itself located within that which has been repressed in United States culture—that is, in the limited- or non-English-speaking marginalized communities. Translation in the United States is most visible at the "top" (high international government and business echelons) and least visible at the "bottom" (poor, marginalized ethnic minorities), and studies of translation phenomena generally focus on that visible corpus.

In this chapter, I suggest not only that translation pervades every aspect of United States culture, but also that strategically repressed translation plays a central role in the construction of culture and identity. By unpacking translation's hidden role in this process, we can better understand its culturally constitutive nature. Beginning with the hidden multicultural history of the United States, this chapter uses Derrida's *Monolingualism of the Other* to help consider theoretical implications, and then turns to translation studies scholars beginning to explore questions of counterculture and the remainder in translation, including Lawrence Venuti, Carol Maier, and Suzanne Jill Levine. Finally, I look at scholars of the "New American Studies," including Donald Pease, Winfried Siemerling, John Carlos Rowe, and Wai Chee Dimock, who are redefining the field in a comparative, translational format, one that may be open to translation studies investigations as well.

The hidden translation history of the United States

If there ever were a multilingual and multicultural society, the United States embodies it *par excellence*. In pre-Columbian times, multiple First Nations existed, speaking upwards of sixty-five languages, including Navajo, Dakota, Cherokee, Apache, Choctaw, and Zuni. During the colononization process, immigrants arrived from all over the world, certainly from Europe as colonizers, from Africa as slaves, and from Asia and Latin America as laborers, bringing their specific languages and cultures. For centuries after its "discovery" (by an Italian, sailing for the Spanish, landing in Cuba), it was not clear that English would be the national language. The English were latecomers to the United States; the French in the north, the Dutch in New Amsterdam, the Germans in Pennsylvania, the Spanish in Florida, Texas, California, and New Mexico, and the Portuguese in Cape Cod preceded them. The explorations, trading, periods of peaceful coexistence, trust, building, treaties, and even wars required collaboration and communication. Yet the translational history has been largely forgotten, I suggest at certain costs to the psychic well-being of the nation.

The current English-only policy of the United States is a powerful one, dating back to the United States' so-called founding fathers, continuing through the nineteenth century, and ever-present today. John Jay, Thomas Jefferson, and Benjamin Franklin, among others, lobbied for English as the national language. For example, in the *Federalist Papers*, a collection of essays by Revolutionary War leaders supporting the constitution, John Jay talked about "one united people . . . speaking the same language" (Hamilton *et al.*, 1970 [1787–1788]: 6, quoted by Shell 2002: 3). In 1917, Theodore Roosevelt wrote, "we must . . . have but one language. That language must be of the Declaration of Independence" (Theodore Roosevelt, Language Loyalties: 18; quoted by Shell 2002: 8). Two hundred years later, the arguments, even the rhetoric, are still much the same. In 1994, California voters passed Proposition 187, aimed at reducing overall immigration and limiting legal immigrants' access to social services, schools, and hospitals; the bill was later overturned by a federal court. In May 2006, the United States Senate passed a provision making English the national language as part of its tougher immigration laws, only to back off and pass a less binding resolution after further debate. In November 2006, by a nearly three to one margin, Arizona voters passed Proposition 103, a measure making English the state's official language.

Yet, as I argue, the question of translation has never disappeared entirely. The Constitution itself had to be translated into several languages to spread the word to its multilingual citizens, for at the time non-English settlers made up over 25 percent of the population, not including those speaking African and Amerindian languages (considered noncitizens at the time). In some states, the numbers were higher: 40 percent of the people in Pennsylvania spoke German. The historical record shows this language struggle; Anglocentrism was not unquestioned during the country's formative stages. Some of the Revolutionary War leaders argued that independence from the British also entailed linguistic independence. The French supported the American colonists in their war against the British; and French, after all, was the lingua franca of the world at the time. German was the most obvious alternative choice, and an early congressional committee recommended that the laws of the Congress be translated into German. In Pennsylvania, there were many German-language newspapers—the first newspaper Benjamin Franklin published was German—and a German language political party. When a bill was introduced in the Pennsylvania legislature to make German the official language in the Congress, the courts, and the official records of the state, the measure did not fail; the vote ended in a tie (Shell 2002: 7). Another early legislator called for a renaissance of a classical language such as Greek (Charles Astor Bristed in 1855; see Shell 2002: 6). Other proposals for language engineering circulated, including the adoption of Hebrew or the creation of a new Esperanto-like language. The language engineering projects finally ceded to a monolingual English-only policy, the translation policy unofficially adopted was one of nontranslation, and translation subsequently went underground.

Various treaties with Amerindians and with Mexico, such as the Treaty of Guadalupe Hidalgo (1848), invariably support language and translation rights for minorities. Yet an unwritten policy of nontranslation became the norm, enforced, if not by the government, military, or police, then by a vigilante system. Slaves who spoke their own language or who refused to speak English were harassed, beaten, incarcerated, tarred and feathered, sold, or, in some cases, had their tongues cut out. Schoolchildren who spoke their own language in school or even in the playgrounds were verbally and physically abused by classmates, reprimanded, detained, or expelled by teachers, and reports of rape of indigenous-speaking girls were not uncommon. The discrimination against language minorities continues to this day: in the streets, the courts, the jails, the schools, the hospitals, the ghettos, the reservations, the welfare offices, translation policy (or nontranslation policy) is one of the leading political issues at the local level. In every ethnic and linguistic minority community in the United States, you find a committed group of translators working away, often unpaid.

Pre-Revolutionary War: narratives of discovery

The role that translations from American Indian cultures have played in the formation of the identity of the people of the United States has been a neglected area of study. This "native voice" has been erased but also everywhere present—in the landscape, place names, folklore, frontier stories, medicine, community practices, and selected spiritual practices—that are integrally involved in definitions of who United States citizens are and where they live. Walt Whitman, who perhaps more than anyone else gave voice to American English, was fascinated by Indian sounds, names, and references, and they can be found throughout his verse, especially when describing natural surroundings or expressing subjective impulses. The country's debt to Amerindian translators and interpreters extends beyond communication. The Wampanoag Indian named Tisquantum, or better known as "Squanto" by the British settlers, initially a victim of a British kidnapping, seemed to forgive the horror of his abduction and not only returned to translate for the Pilgrims at Plymouth but also taught them how to grow corn, showed them where to fish, and acted as a guide and translator in dealings with other Amerindians. Squanto helped negotiate a treaty between the Pilgrims and the Massasoit Indians, which led to over fifty years of peaceful coexistence.

Translation with regard to Amerindian culture has been a one-way street, with British colonizers translating their culture into Amerindian languages without reciprocating. One reason has to do with the language policy outlined above; another has to do with the fact that most Amerindian literature was oral. While much of this "storytelling" has not been translated, traces of its form and style have crept into the way North Americans tell stories: children's stories, campfire stories, and frontier stories all retain elements of native Amerindian storytelling, a topic that needs further research. In modern and contemporary multicultural studies, traces of Amerindian oral traditions occur within written publications, usually as cultural translations in the form of stories within stories. Beginning with John G. Neihardt's *Black Elk Speaks* (1961 [1932]) and continuing through texts such as James Welch's *Winter in the Blood* (1974), Louise Erdrich's *Love Medicine* (1984), and Leslie Silko's *Ceremony* (1977), cultural translations and representations of such stories increasingly enter the culture, often presented as being passed on orally from ancestors to the young in the private space of indigenous communities. The range and depth of the Amerindian poetic tradition is documented in recent books such as Barry O'Connell's *Song of the Sky* (1993). In anthropology, scholars are reviewing Amerindian artifacts, cultural material, musical instruments, and clothing as well as oral stories, which is leading to a rethinking of the construction of both the Amerindian and Euro-American identities (ibid.: 18). Clearly, much of American culture has been misnamed and mistranslated by the early explorers, conquerors, and settlers, who attempted to make sense out of the "New" World by giving items European names. The Native American writer Gerald Vizenor, author of fictional works such as *Earthdivers: Tribal Narratives on Mixed Descent* (1981) and nonfiction works such as *Fugitive Poses: Native American Indian Scenes of Absence and Presence* (1998), refers to these namings as "inventions" and refers to the current generation of Native Americans as "postindians" (Vizenor and Lee 1999: 84), who have to sort through such rewritings and mistranslations to discover their own history and genealogy. The process, like all searches for origins, is wellnigh impossible, lending a partial and fragmented form to the Amerindian identity. Postmodern or not, clearly these New World translations have affected the self-perception of later Indians and contributed to their marginalization. Nevertheless, to those First Nations peoples who are trying to reconstruct their ethnic origins, reading such translations against the grain becomes fundamental to the reinvention of an American identity, a process, I argue, that can be instructive to the larger culture as a whole.

During the early period of the "discovery" of the Americas, most texts were written in any language but English, making the archeology of such reconstructions linguistically complex. Christopher Columbus, from Genoa, wrote in Spanish with some Italian interference. Hernan Cortés (explorer in the Southwest) wrote in Spanish; Álvar Núñez Cabeza de Vaca (explorer in Florida) wrote in Spanish; John Cabot (explorer in the Northeast) wrote in French; Giovanni de Verrazano (explorer in the Carolinas) wrote in Italian; and Jacques Cartier (explorer in the Northeast) wrote in French, although his works were first published, via translation, in Italian. The Italian version of Cartier's *Delle Navigationi et Viaggi* (1556) was translated into English in 1580, and then *back*-translated into French in 1598. Thus, the very knowledge on which our understanding of the "discovery" of America rests comes not through any native writer or language, but via translation.

Only after reading the translation of Jean Ribaut's *The Whole and True Discovery of Terra Florida* (1927 [1563]), translated from French, did Queen Elizabeth (1533–1603) begin to think about America as a place to establish a colony. The list of translation in relation to exploration of the United States is long; French narratives include work by Étienne Brûlé (explorer of the Lake Superior region), Jean Nicolet (the upper Mississippi), and Samuel de Champlain (upstate New York). Champlain's *Voyages* (1994 [1613]) and *Les Voyages de la Nouvelle France* (1632) are foundational texts that were not translated into English until hundreds of years later. Dutch writings included Adriaen van der Donck's *Vertoogh van Nieu-Neder-land* (1849 [1650]) and *Beschryvinge van Nieuw Nederlant* (1968 [1655]). While many of these narratives have been erased from the collective cultural history of the United States, their presence is felt in the regional communities, and traces of their presence can be found in artifacts, historical monuments, small museums and archives, and among a few descendants who value their cultural heritage. Nevertheless, in terms of a complex definition of translation, one that involves texts and movements that give birth to the transfer of ideas and interrelations of peoples, often open-ended and multiplying without a telos, such texts contain a psychic life, hard to trace but ever-present.

Found in translation: Adriaen van der Donck

To give just one example of such a hidden cultural narrative and its importance to identity formation in the United States, I turn to the case of the Dutch colony of New Amsterdam and its cultural impact not just on New York City but on the whole of United States culture. The area in question represents more than the current financial capital of the country; during its colonial period, New Netherlands was at the geographic heart of the colonies, right in between developing English colonies in New England and Virginia. It included parts of what are now Connecticut, New York, New Jersey, Pennsylvania, and Delaware. Holland was among the most liberal nations in Europe at the time; the Puritans, for example, escaped to Leiden in Holland, living there for twelve years before moving to America. While New Netherlands was founded by the Dutch as a trading post under the auspices of the Dutch West Indies Company, according to Russell

Shorto, author of *The Island at the Center of the World* (2005), over half of its residents were from other parts of the world, including Sweden, Norway, Germany, Italy, Africa (slaves and free), Belgium, England, including those excommunicated from the Puritan colony to the north, and Native Americans, including Montauks, Mahicans, Housatonics, and Mohawks (ibid.: 2005: 2). Thus, New Amsterdam became one of the first multiethnic, multicultural, and multilingual cities in the new world. Shorto suggests that the Dutch Manhattan's influence on the cultural evolution and identity of United States citizens is just as important as, if not more important than, the cultural heritage of the British in New England or Virginia. He writes, "If what made America great was its ingenious openness to different cultures, then the small triangle of land at the southern tip of Manhattan Island is the New World birthplace of that idea" (ibid.: 3).

Historians have told us little of that period; the most an average United States citizen knows is that the Dutch bought the island in 1626 from the Indians for 60 guilders (about $24). Yet extensive records exist: by some estimates over 12,000 pages stored in archives in New York, Albany, and Amsterdam, most of which remain untranslated. Charles Gehring, Director of the New Netherland Project, has devoted thirty years of his life to translating such material (Gehring 1978, 1981, 1995, 2000), so that much of this history is now available in English. Documents that have been translated include political agreements, laws, minutes of meetings, letters, journals, court cases, business documents, shipping records, military records, trade records, and any number of miscellaneous documents about drinking, fighting, thieving, marital infidelities, livestock, and land disputes. I suggest that these translated texts reveal national traits perhaps *more* indicative of the United States' multicultural identity than many foundational texts originally written in English.

The seeds for a multicultural society, freedom of religion, freedom of speech, and other fundamental national rights originated in the multicultural New Netherlands colony. Whereas in the English colony to the north, dominated by the massive influx of Puritans from England in the 1630s and 1640s, only one language was spoken, in New Amsterdam over eighteen languages could be heard. Whereas in the Puritan colony, only one religion was tolerated, in the Dutch colony Protestants, Anglicans, Catholics, English Pilgrims, Jews, Lutherans, Calvinists, and multiple indigenous religions peacefully coexisted. In 1579, the Dutch were one of the first countries in Europe to write into their constitution that "no one shall be persecuted or investigated because of their religion" (Shorto, 2005: 96), and thus Amsterdam became one of the most tolerant and diverse cities in Europe; that tolerance was "translated" to New Amsterdam in the 1600s. The prevailing sense of freedom of religion, openness to immigrants, especially those persecuted in their home countries, and a commitment to equality and diversity may derive more from New York's cultural and linguistic heritage than from its later English colonial period.

One such chronicler, the Dutch-American Adriaen van der Donck, wrote "A Description of New Netherlands," a text that could have been a classic of American literature were there an effective multilingual or translation language policy. Van der Donck, a lawyer who was born in Breda and studied at Leiden, immigrated to New Amsterdam during the summer of 1641, some eighteen years after the founding of the colony. He served as the first lawyer in the Dutch colony, acting as a kind of an attorney general/sheriff (*schout*) for Kiliaen van Rensselaer, a wealthy Dutch diamond merchant living in Amsterdam. Van der Donck, according to Shorto, fell in love with America and went about writing and describing everything. He observed the wildlife, including bears, deer, eagles, turkeys, pheasants, and woodcocks, comparing them with European animals and noting differences in size, shape, and even scent. He wrote about the land, the trees, fruits, nuts, wild vegetables, edible plants, and herbs, some known to Europeans but many yet unknown. Shorto talks of the "sheer exuberance" of Van der Donck's prose, observing that "the man simply fell in love with America" (2005: 131). Van der Donck also was a tireless worker. His first order of business was to stop the illegal black market trading going on in the colony, find employees who had deserted before fulfilling their commitments, and prosecute those dealing with the Indians on an individual basis. He became very efficient at his duties, settling disputes on his own and making decisions on property and improvements, sometimes supporting the colonists against the owners. His writings survive not only in his published memoirs but also in letters, multiple court records, and reports to his employer in Holland. Van der Donck also traveled widely, spending time in the villages of the Mohawks (Kanienkeh) and Mahicans, learning their languages, hunting and fishing techniques, farming and cooking methods, and marriage and sexual customs. The picture Van der Donck paints of the Indians is very different than the earlier Spanish tales of savages and cannibals or the later fearful British reports. In "A Description of New Netherlands," Van der Donck talked of the Indian languages as falling into four groups, with declensions and conjugations that "resemble those in Greek" with "duals in their nouns" and "augments" in their verbs (Shorto 2005: 135). He observed the medicine men, how they can "heal wonderfully with virtually nothing," and how they easily treat venereal diseases that "put many an Italian physician to shame" (ibid.: 136). He studied Indian religions and questioned whether the indigenous peoples could be described as heathens or should be converted to Christianity (ibid.: 137).

Van der Donck's descriptions, the first and most vivid accounts written about the future United States, have largely disappeared from the historical record of the nation. Only one 1841 translation, by Jeremiah Johnson, of a Van der Donck text exists; that translation is but an abridged version and contains many mistakes, omissions, and shifts. For example, according to Shorto, entire passages describing the Native Americans' system of justice, including treaties, contracts, government, and public policy, have been omitted. In light of Van der Donck's legal background and training in Roman and Dutch law, this would perhaps be the *most* reliable portion of the text. The omitted passages show that at least many of the Dutch colonists were well aware of the differing Indian conception of property; Van der Donck wrote that "wind, stream, bush, field, sea beach, and riverside are open and free to everyone within every nation" (Shorto 2005: 137). He also wrote about Indian codes of war, which allowed for safe conduct of messengers and honored treaties and agreements. While many argue that the reason why Van der Donck's texts have not been fully translated is because of the language in which they were written, I suggest that their neglect has been "ideologically" convenient for those who wished to perpetuate the "invention" or image of the savage Indians posited by the Spanish and English settlers.

If one compares the cultural heritage of the Puritan colonies to the Dutch, the picture that emerges is quite different. The Puritan culture of New England has been well documented; the culture was composed of small families, farmers, and ministers, with their single ethnicity, language, and religion, fear of new ideas, and strict ethical and moral code for converting Indians to their beliefs and language. In contrast, in New Netherlands the culture was composed of merchants, traders, and world travelers, with their multiple ethnicities, languages, and religions, openness to new political and philosophical ideas, and tolerance for the indigenous peoples' beliefs. Russell Shorto writes:

> The Dutch—traders and sailors whose focus was always *out there*: on other lands, other peoples, and their products—had always to put up with differences. Just as foreign goods moved in and out of their ports, foreign ideas, and, for that matter, foreign people did as well. To talk about "celebrating diversity" is to be wildly anachronistic, but in the Europe of the time, the Dutch stood out for their relative acceptance of foreignness, or religious differences, or odd sorts.
>
> (2005: 26)

While Shorto romanticizes Van der Donck's importance in the history of New York and the Americas, forgetting the rapacious trade practices, including trading in slaves, his argument that many of the cultural roots of the country are contained in the Dutch-language writings of Van der Donck is persuasive. The part of North America that eventually became the United States was not always English; I suggest that these non-English cultures have their own narratives of discovery, conquest, and colonization that are every bit as exciting as the "canonical" writings of British colonizers, such as William Bradford in Massachusetts or John Smith in Virginia. While they seldom appear in anthologies of United States literature, these alternative narratives are reemerging, thanks to the work of translators such as Charles Gehring. Not only important to the foundational story of the New York region, such material is increasingly crucial to an understanding of United States history.

Translation in colonial British culture

While the early British settlers were not known for the breadth of their worldview or tolerance for opposing ideas, translation also played an important role in their lives and interactions. Sermons, such as Jonathan Edwards's "Sinners in the Hands of an Angry God" (2003 [1741]), served as an important literary genre in British North America. Not just directed at the Puritans, these sermons were also addressed to the natives. In his entry titled "American Tradition" (1998a) in the *Routledge Encyclopedia of Translation Studies*, Venuti cites the royal charter issued to the Massachusetts Bay Company in 1629, which claimed that "the principall ende of this plantation [was] to wynn and incite the natives of [the] country to the knowledge and obedience of the onlie true God and Savior of mankinde, and the Christian fayth" (Morgan 1964: 320; quoted by Venuti 1998a: 306). To be effective, these first sermons had to be translated. John Eliot (1604–1690), author of *A Catechism in the Massachusetts Indian Languages* (1654), translated the Holy Bible into Algonquian—*Mamusse wunneetupanatamwe Up-Biblium God naneeswe Nukkone Testament kah wonk Wusku Testament / ne quoshkinnumuk nashpe Wuttinneumoh Christ noh asoowesit*—as early as 1663.

Translation, though seldom acknowledged, formed an integral part of the heritage of the United States from the earliest days of the development of an "American" voice. During the eighteenth century, not much poetry was written in New England, and the poetry that was written derived less from European models than from the poetics of the Bible in translation. One of the more popular texts among colonial intellectuals was Guillaume de Salluste Du Bartas's *Les Sepmaines* (1578), translated into American English by Joshua Sylvester as *The Divine Weeks and Works* (1605), which served as a primer for the poetics of the Bible, and from which more famous writers such as Edward Taylor derived their craft. In 1626, Virginia colonist and poet George Sandys (1578–1644) completed his translation of Ovid's *Metamorphoses* (1690), one of the first books of literary merit published in America. Perhaps the most widely circulated book of the period was also a translation: *The Whole Booke of Psalmes Faithfully Translated into English Metre* (1640). Commonly referred to as *The Bay Psalm Book*, the text was collaboratively produced by a group of ministers to become the first church hymnal. The Anglo-American translations of the hymns, often a very literal rendering of the original Hebrew put into ballad forms, differed much in style from British translations of the same texts. These translations were political as well as religious, articulating the Puritans' dissent from the Anglican Church as well as from the literature of England. The avowedly plain language and ballad form opposed the more polished and elegant verse forms characteristic of British versions, including translations of psalms made by Sir Philip Sidney and Thomas Carew (Venuti 1998a: 308).

The Revolutionary War: on democracy

One could argue that the "nation" of the United States was born in translation not only because it was a nation of immigrants (and a soon to be decimated indigenous population) but also because the very terms with which it defined itself were translations of ideas of democracy, individual freedom, and liberty that originated in Greece, often arriving in the United States via their translations and mediation through Latin, French, and British English. The works of Greek thinkers translated by British thinkers such as Harrington, Milton, Hobbes, and Locke were widely available in the colonies. The works of French Enlightenment thinkers such as Montesquieu, Voltaire, and Rousseau were also accessible both in the French "originals" and in English translations. Founding fathers such as Thomas Jefferson, James Madison, and Benjamin Franklin were much influenced by French Enlightenment ideas. Jefferson and Madison, classically educated, certainly knew Greek, Latin, and French; Franklin, self-taught, knew French, German, Italian, Spanish, and Latin (Shell 2002: 6). Thus, the Declaration of Independence, the Constitution, and *The Federalist Papers* each incorporated the translated ideas of their creators.

As Alexandra Lianeri argues in "Translation and Democracy in Nineteenth-Century England" (2002), translations of the concept "democracy" were indeed rooted in the ideas, models of thought, and political conceptualizations of Revolutionary War society. Socioeconomic changes in the late eighteenth century—the beginnings of industrialization, the growth of cities, and the formation of the bourgeoisie and working classes—created conditions in the Americas for the transition from a quasi-feudal, religious society, whose members believed in the God-given power of kings and queens, to a modern, industrialized nation-state, whose members believed in a liberal political philosophy.

Lianeri's essay primarily looks at the construction of the term "democracy" in the formation of the nineteenth-century nation-state of England, but her argument also includes a review of translations read and incorporated into eighteenth-century thought in North America, which, in turn, influenced nineteenth-century British thinkers. Her argument is that the concept of "democracy" as instituted in the United States, and later in France and, eventually, England, is a construct produced by plural and often opposed notions that acquired meaning via multiple translations. Translation, thus understood, is viewed as a symbolic code used to construct an imaginary historical tradition that connected late eighteenth-century politics in the Americas to fourth-century BCE politics in Athens. These constructions of democracy, she shows, were expressed not only in translated texts, but also in histories, commentaries, and introductions to the translations. During this period, translation thus was not derivative in any sense, but primary, ushering in the ideas for and traditions of a new form of "nation" for the new world. The power of translation during the pre-Revolutionary War period was massive. Given that monarchies reigned all over Europe, the translation of Greek concepts of democracy threatened the very sovereignty of multiple nations. Translations of Greek texts detailing democratic practices helped articulate a new concept of "commoners," those capable of participating in politics and therefore claiming the right to be "citizens" of the state. The translators, then, authored a new set of terms, a new discourse, upon which to base ideas of the nation-state and what it meant to be a citizen in that state. As such, translation became a primary force behind the American Revolution.

One of Lianeri's arguments concerns the constructed concept of democracy described by eighteenth-century British translators, as illustrated by competing versions of democracy. Thomas Hobbes, translator of Thucydides's *History of the Grecian War*, for example, had a very negative conception of democracy, claiming that the social order would be threatened if it followed the susceptible political judgment of the "common" people (Hobbes 1843 [1629]: xvi–xvii; Lianeri 2002: 6). Hobbes's translation, for example, which contains Pericles's famous "Funeral Speech" in which the Athenian definition of democracy is outlined, had a lasting influence upon British and American thought of the eighteenth and nineteenth centuries. Charles Foster Smith, translator for the contemporary Loeb edition, translates the key passage as follows: "It is true that our government is called a democracy, because its administration is in the hands, not of the few, but of the many" (Thucydides, 1956: 323; Lianeri 2002: 5). Hobbes's version reads, "We have a form of government... which, because in the administration it hath respect not to a few, but to the multitude, is called a democracy" (Hobbes 1843: 8.191; Lianeri 2002: 6). Lianeri suggests that Hobbes's version "appears to distort" the passage because it shifts those in control of the administration of government from the many to the few. She also suggests that these competing versions played a fundamental role in the United States' becoming a "republic" rather than a "democracy." At the end of the seventeenth century, John Locke, British empiricist, further elaborated Hobbes's position, arguing that it was the obligation of the government to protect the natural "property"—the lives, liberties, and estates—of its citizens, who may not be able to govern themselves (Lianeri 2002: 11).

These conceptions of democracy were adopted by the framers of the Constitution of the United States. While appealing to Greek culture as the origin of these ideas, the founders of the United States largely deferred to British translators' understanding of their Greek sources. Political power by the common people was generally viewed as a danger to individual liberty. In *The Federalist Papers* (no. 10, 1778), James Madison wrote, "Pure democracies have ever been spectacles of turbulence and contention; have ever been found incompatible with personal security or the rights of property; and have in general been as short in their lives as they have been violent in their deaths" (Hamilton *et al.* 1970 [1787–1788]: 45; Lianeri 2002: 11). The notion of "republic" thus comes into being as distinct from "democracy," which is why in the United States electors vote for the president, not the common people, resulting in anomalies such as the 1888 election when Grover Cleveland won the popular vote but Benjamin Harrison was "elected" president, or again in the 2000 election, in which Albert Gore won the popular vote but George W. Bush was elected by the electoral college. In theory, those "electors" are to "protect" the common people of the United States from their own interests.

The French Revolution, on the other hand, relied on very different translations of Greek concepts of democracy. The 1789 *Déclaration des droits de l'homme et du citoyen* (Declaration of the Rights of Man and the Citizen) viewed the common man as the ultimate voice for political power in France. The French conception of the "nation," as including the whole of the people, was thus more revolutionary than the American conception. The French Constitution, which granted rights of universal suffrage, provided a much more liberal conception of the term "democracy" and extended the rights of liberty and equality to a wider range of the populace. Unfortunately, these ideas of democratic equality were quickly shattered by the Reign of Terror during 1793 and 1794.

In addition to the canonical texts of the United States by the so-called founding fathers, translation also played a role in the literature of the common man. Translation, rather than being a secondary by-product of the war, was one of the primary forces fueling the revolution and leading to the creation of the newly emerging nation. During the Revolutionary War period, in addition to there being debates in congressional assemblies about the future form of government for the emerging nation, pamphlets circulated in an underground fashion on the streets of the colonies. These pamphlets were usually unsigned and circulated as *samizdat*, for many of the ideas contained within were considered treasonous. The writers used their own and others' translations to disseminate French and Enlightenment thinking to sway the American public against the British. James Otis and Thomas Paine, two sources whose work can be identified, serve as good examples. Otis, author of *The Rights of the British Colonies Asserted and Proved* (1764), quoted his own translations from Rousseau's *Social Contract* (Bailyn 1965, II: 436; cf. Venuti 1998a: 308); Paine's *Common Sense* (1986 [1776]) articulated the more radical French interpretation of the Greek concepts as well as anti-British religious ideas. Paine's audience was primarily farmers, small businessmen, and, once the war started, the common soldiers who did most of the fighting. After the Revolutionary War, Paine went to France to fight for the rights of common man there against the conservative forces of the Restoration. These translations, which served to disrupt the status quo, created conditions for the revolution to follow and could be called more constitutive of the North American identity than some of the canonical works that followed the war.

The Nineteenth century: the North American Frontier

During the nineteenth century, translation played a mixed role in the United States' national development; expansion continued to the west, and explorers such as Lewis and Clark relied heavily upon translators, including the Canadian Toussaint Charbonneau and his wife Tsikikawias, better known as Sacajawea, to carry out the business of trade as well as to negotiate peace treaties. The interpreters invariably colluded with the United States government's interests, but a few actually advocated for the Indians. Lawrence Taliaferro (1794–1871), for example, translator in the Minnesota region during the 1850s, supported the Indians against the traders working for the American Fur Company, who tried to get him dismissed from the Bureau of Indian Affairs (Venuti 1998a: 307). Sarah Winnemucca, an interpreter in the Oregon area, gave lectures in the 1880s reporting the injustices the government was inflicting upon Amerindian people (ibid.).

The nineteenth century was a period in which major writers such as Henry David Thoreau, Ralph Waldo Emerson, and Herman Melville were most concerned with identifying and creating a distinctly American voice—a concern that lasted well into the twentieth century. With such a focus on "original" writing, there seemed little interest in translation. In canonical American literature courses, these writers are often taught as isolationist, with a focus on their meditation on nature, contemplation of the individual, and speculation on the metaphysical, producing a discourse that has developed a sense of national identity. In *Through Other Continents: American Literature across Deep Time* (2006), Wai Chee Dimock shows just how deceptive these national narratives are. Dimock suggests that the Asian influence on Thoreau's essays such as "Resistance to Civil Government" (better known today as "Civil Disobedience") was profound. She defines this form of translation as "slow translation" (ibid.: 15–16), a writing practice that evolves in a complex psychosocial fashion across time and space. The reading experience of the *Bhagavad Gita*, Dimock argues, transported Thoreau to a different level of conception and reasoning, one that survived long after the actual reading experience. Dimock refers to this psychic connection between an Asian culture hundreds or thousands of years old to a New World culture with a short life such as the United States as "deep time" (ibid.: 3), one that binds continents via translation in a complex and subtle web of relations. Thoreau's essay thus restores and extends the *Bhagavad Gita*, rewriting and updating the text and giving it a new context for civil action. Indeed, the "isolationist" movement of early nineteenth-century United States thought may, in some ways, be attributed to a pacifist philosophy that has traveled as a hidden form of translation. Dimock goes on to show how Thoreau's "Civil Disobedience" in turn influenced

Mahatma Gandhi, who claims he read Thoreau when in Johannesburg in the early 1900s and then recommended him to his colleagues fighting for Indian independence, which in turn resulted in one of the strategies of *satyāgraha* (nonviolent resistance) in the campaign for Indian independence. Given that Thoreau's essay also influenced Martin Luther King's concept of civil disobedience and nonviolent direct action during the civil rights protests of the 1950s and 1960s, and the peace demonstrations against the Vietnam War during the 1960s and 1970s, one could argue its continuing centrality to North American cultural identity.

Nineteenth-century authors also believed that the best international writing should be widely available to the reading public. Such was the philosophy behind the fourteen-volume anthology entitled *Specimens of Foreign Standard Literature*, edited by George Ripley (1802–1880). Translators included Ripley himself as well as transcendentalist writers such as Margaret Fuller (1810–1850) and John Sullivan Dwight (1813–1893). These translations proved very influential upon the subsequent thought of American writers, including Ralph Waldo Emerson (Venuti 1998a: 308–309), who, after quitting his job as a Quaker minister, made three trips to Europe, traveling in France, Germany, and England, meeting with many non-English writers and philosophers. According to library records, Emerson knew Latin, Greek, and French, and later taught himself German and Italian. The influence, for example, of Descartes, Kant, and Leibniz, as well as the British English of Coleridge, Wordsworth, and Carlyle, can be found in his subsequent philosophical, religious, and aesthetic poetry and essays, including his major works on American transcendentalism such as *Nature* (1836), *The American Scholar* (1837), and "Self-Reliance" (1841). The influence of Goethe was perhaps most profound. Dimock goes so far as to show that at the end of his life, Emerson was translating from German, including excerpts from Goethe's *West-östlicher Divan* (1872 [1819]), and, via secondary translation, translating the fourteenth-century Persian poet Hafiz (1320–1390) from the German translations by Joseph von Hammer.

While the nineteenth-century American Romantics were seeking enlightenment, the United States was experiencing a tremendous influx of immigrants coming from Europe, primarily Germany, Holland, France, Spain, and Italy. According to the *Literary History of the United States* (Spiller *et al.* 1974), there were literally hundreds of newspapers and journals—over 600 Jewish newspapers alone—publishing news, stories, poems, and letters in dozens of languages. Over 500 Norwegian newspapers and over 100 Norwegian novels have appeared in the United States since the middle of the nineteenth century. A wealth of Swedish-American writers published in Swedish in the nineteenth century in the United States, including novels, poetry, and immigrant journals. Danish-American and Icelandic-American writers were present. Probably the strongest tradition, and the one that best survives to the present, has been the Hebrew/Yiddish tradition, with over

600 Yiddish periodicals published since 1870. Abraham Cahan edited the most important Yiddish newspaper, the *Jewish Daily Forward*, and is author of the Jewish immigrant classic *The Rise of David Levinsky* (1993 [1917]). In addition to well-known novelists, poets, and playwrights, a strong tradition of translation into Yiddish existed in America, including Solomon Blumgarten's, known as "Yehoash," translation of Henry Wadsworth Longfellow's "Hiawatha" into Yiddish in 1906 and his Yiddish translation of the Bible.

While the culture at large was not necessarily pro-multilingualism at the time, it was not certain that English would become the country's primary language. This wide array of papers and journals in multiple languages well represented the multicultural society that lay beneath the attempts to forge an American English culture. German was the primary language in parts of Pennsylvania and in many communities throughout Ohio and the Midwest; French was spoken in New Orleans, in rural communities in New England, and in the newly acquired Northwest; Dutch enclaves still existed in upstate New York; Swedish and Finnish were spoken in the northern Midwest; Spanish predominated in California and the southwest; and both Hebrew and Yiddish were very strong in New York City and other urban areas. Many writers in languages other than English emerged who have not been included in the American canon but whose works were very popular at the time.

Francis Daniel Pastorius, founder of Germantown in Pennsylvania, kept journals and wrote narratives of early German-American life that rivaled those of William Bradford (1590–1657), leader of the Plymouth Colony in Massachusetts and author of *Of Plymouth Plantation* (*ca.* 1650). Most of Pastorius's works have been translated and are available in English (Myers 1967 [1912]), though remain relatively unknown. Friedrich Strubberg, writing under the pen name "Armand," published a score of novels dealing with German colonization, slavery, and the Mexican War, including *Sklaverei in Amerika; oder Schwarzes Blut* ([Slavery in America, or Black Blood], 1862) or *Carl Scharnhorst: Abenteuer eines deutschen Knaben in Amerika* ([Carl Scharnhorst: Adventures of a German Boy in America], 1872). Ideological as well as literary reasons may explain why they have not been translated. Heinrich Balduin Möllhausen (1825–1905) was known as the German James Fennimore Cooper and wrote some fifty novels of frontier life, including *Der Halbindianer* ([The Half Indian], 1861a) and *Der Flüchtling* ([The Escapee], 1861b). Only one of his works has been translated, *Diary of a Journey from the Mississippi to the Coasts of the Pacific* (1858). Robert Reitzel (1849–1898) was perhaps the most distinguished German writer in the Americas; his works have been collected in *Des Armen Teufel: Gesammelte Schriften* ([The Poor Devil's Collected Writings], 1913).

Many of these German-American writers were bilingual and translated their own work, publishing both in English and in German. Between 1840 and 1940, a lively German theater existed as well, especially in New York, producing works both in German and in English translation. In *In Search of a Theory of Translation* (1980), translation studies scholar Gideon Toury argues that translation tends to be primary in young countries, with little literary tradition of their own; it makes sense that new nations rely on translations to import theater pieces. Nineteenth-century German-American playwrights included Geza Berger, Kasper Butz, and Ernst Anton Zündt. Other German theaters existed in towns such as St. Louis and Milwaukee. Chicago was the publishing center for German poetry, with nearly half the poetry written in German published there. Most poetry remains scattered in German-American newspapers, magazines, and small booklets, although some has been collected in anthologies such as Konrad Nies and Herman Rosenthal's two-volume *Deutsch-amerikanische Dichtung* ([German-American Poetry], 1888–1890). Poets included Fernande Richter (pseudonym Edna Fern) and George Sylvester Viereck, who translated his own verse into English.

The Pennsylvania Dutch "dialect" writers also had a strong cultural tradition and publishing record, including translations and self-translations. Well-known Pennsylvania Dutch writers include Henry Harbaugh, Henry Lee Fisher, and Thomas Hess Harter, whose works are still available, and others such as Ezra Grumbine, Matthias Sheeleigh, and Thomas J. Rhoads, whose works, published in small newspapers and journals, have not yet been collected. The dialect stories of Elsie Singmaster (pen name Elsie S. Lewars), who published over 240 stories, were very popular. There is also a considerable body of German dialect poetry, most of it humorous: examples include Carl Münter's *Nu sünd wie in Amerika: Ein plattdütsch Riemels* ([Now We Are (Sinning) in America: Colloquial German Verse], 1878) and Ferdinand W. Lafrentz's *Nordische Klänge: Plattdütsche Riemels* ([Northern Clang: Colloquial German Rhymes], 1881 and 1882). Very little of the German writing has passed into mainstream United States literary history, with perhaps the exception of Willa Cather's *O Pioneers!* (1988 [1913]) and *My Ántonia* (1999 [1918]), which refer to German and Czech settlements and immigrants in the Midwest. Annie Sadilek, Cather's Czech friend to whom she taught English, served as the author's model for Ántonia. Cather was fascinated by the diverse cultures and languages of immigrants to the plains of Nebraska and the southwest United States, and Swedes, Germans, Czechs, and other immigrants are depicted throughout her fiction, although highly Americanized.

French writing during the nineteenth century was based in its cultural capital of New Orleans and included histories, fiction, poetry, and drama, most of it written in Creole French. Charles Étienne Arthur Gayarré wrote a four-volume *History of Louisiana* (1866), with special entries on the French, Spanish, and American periods of domination. Henry Rémy published a *Histoire de la Louisiane*, a journal *Saint-Michel* (1854–1865), and a book on Mexican life, *Tierra Caliente* ([Hot Earth], 1859). Novels include Louis-Armand Garreau's *Louisiana: Épisode emprunté à la domination française en Amérique* (1849). Julien Poydras published two volumes of poetry as early as 1777. Charles Testut wrote histories, romance novels, and poetry, including the abolitionist novel *Le Vieux Salomon* and sketches of fifty-two contemporary Louisiana writers in *Portraits Littéraires* (1858). Other nineteenth-century French-American poets included Françoise-Dominique Rouquette and Adrien-Emmauel Rouquette. French theater, in French and English, was popular in North America and was not restricted to New Orleans; New York and Philadelphia had lively theater scenes, and many of the plays produced were translated and adapted from French. Studies include the *French Drama in America in the Eighteenth Century and Its Influence on the American Dramas of That Period 1701–1800* (Waldo 1942) and "American Adaptations of French Plays on the New York and Philadelphia Stages from 1834 to the Civil War" (Ware 1930). Very little of the French Creole writing and culture has passed into mainstream United States literary history, with perhaps the exception of Kate Chopin's *The Awakening* (1899), now a feminist classic, which was set in New Orleans and Grand Isle and is replete with Louisiana Creole characters and settings. In contemporary multicultural studies, there has been a revival of interest in the French language and French culture in the United States, with new programs such as the proposed French Creole Immersion Initiative at the University of Louisiana at Lafayette or the Creole Institute at the University of Indiana.

Spanish travel writing, oral literature, folklore, and religious drama have a continuous history dating back to the sixteenth century. Again, most of it takes place out of sight, not so much in the metropolitan areas of New York, Boston, and Chicago as in the more rural areas of the Southwest and California, again published in hundreds of Spanish-language newspapers. The fact that Mexico owned much of the land that now comprises the United States Southwest serves to make Spanish writing of this period less "foreign" because it took place on current United States territory. Some bibliographical fieldwork has begun, collected, for example, in *A Bibliography of the Spanish Press of California 1833–1845* (Cowan 1919) and *A Reference Index to 12,000 Spanish-American Authors* (Grismer 1939). In 1977, Juan B. Rael published *Cuentos españoles de Colorado y de Nuevo México: Spanish Folk Tales of Colorado and New Mexico*, an anthology of over 500 oral stories he collected dating back to the first Spanish settlers. In its revised 2002 edition, the *Heath Anthology of American Literature*, to its credit, added a section on nineteenth-century Spanish-American literature, including a series of *Cuentos* (Tales) "retold in English" by Rudolfo Anaya (see Chapter 6), providing another new form for translation in the Americas. Yet much more work needs to be done collecting material and assessing Spanish America's contribution to the development of United States culture. In *Ambassadors of Culture: The Transamerican Origins of Latino Writing* (2005), New American Studies scholar Kirsten Silva Gruesz provides the lead, presenting new research on an array of Spanish-language cultural activity during the nineteenth century, connecting it with travel writing and translations between Latin America and North America, and emphasizing the importance of Hispanic writing for the construction of Latino as well as American identity today.

In short, America during the nineteenth century was a multicultural society, with hundreds, even thousands, of small papers and magazines, all publishing in multiple languages, and translating both from the "foreign" English language into their own and translating their own stories for publication in English journals. The English-only period revived again with the advent of World War I and subsequent movements up until the end of World War II to eradicate the German language in the United States. This entire period remains little researched, yet it was one the most formative periods in the development of the nation's identity. With a new period of multiculturalism, the development of ethnic studies, the New American Studies, and an increasing number of its citizens tracing their family histories, perhaps translation scholars can offer new insights into multilingual and heterogeneous subcultures that once flourished.

Derrida: *Monolingualism of the Other*

Derrida addresses the paradox of monolingualism, with its inherent multilingualism, in *Monolingualism of the Other* (1996/1998). One of his more accessible texts, the book contains much autobiographical information concerning Derrida's linguistic and cultural background; unlike in his earlier work, here Derrida candidly connects his philosophical thought to his own identity formation. The occasion of *Monolingualism of the Other* was a conference in New Orleans attended by Francophone scholars from the Francophone United States, Caribbean, Canada, Belgium, Switzerland, Africa, and France. Derrida attended largely because of his good friend, the Algerian/Moroccan novelist Abdedkebir Khatibi, author of *Amour bilingue* (1990), a book that has engendered much discussion on bilingualism and translation. As both Derrida and Khatibi are Franco-Maghrebian, much of the discussion centered on their growing up in a monolingual culture (French) in which their Arabic, Berber, and, in the case of Derrida, Jewish cultures and languages were suppressed. Access to any non-French language such as academic or colloquial Arabic or Berber was prohibited. The only option for studying Arabic was in the schools, where it could only be studied as a foreign language. Derrida talks candidly about the psycho- and social-pathological trauma endured by people in such a situation, the *unheimlich* feeling of always being an outsider in your home country, as well as the discrimination, beatings, murders, and even state-supported assassinations that took place because of the language gap. Abdelkebir Khatibi does speak of his "mother tongue," which is French, but it is a French within which other language codes—Arabic, Berber, Persian, Spanish, Italian—are embedded, a kind of a secret code that only multilinguals can translate and understand.

Abdelkebir Khatibi, as is well known in translation theory circles, is discussed in the seminal essay on postcolonial translation titled "Translation and the Postcolonial Experience: The Francophone North African Text" (1992) by Samia Mehrez. In the essay, Mehrez discusses the influence that ethnic minorities in North Africa have on translation theory, and her work provides insights for this study of translation in the Americas. The languages of North Africa—varying blends of Arabic, French, Spanish, and Berber, as well as traces of Italian, Greek, and Persian—forge new hybrid language groups that defy translation, notions of equivalence, and ideas of loss and gain via translation. As similar ethnic minorities move to the urban areas of the United States, I suggest that translation theory in these areas will be equally challenged and redefined. Mehrez does not merely discuss the difficulty of translating the language of the Other; rather, the Other invades the space of the Same to create a secret translation discourse from within. Mehrez writes:

> Not that I am referring to a process whereby the language of the Other becomes unrecognizable, or deformed. Rather, the process is one where the language of the Other comes to encode messages which are not readily decoded by the monolingual reader.
>
> (1992: 122)

The trick is to *avoid* assimilation into the dominant language and culture of the language, using translation as a tool not to decode but to evade, expand, enrich, and diversify existing codes of signification.

Certain patterns for using translation as a tool to resist monolingual language policies in North Africa are beginning to emerge. One strategy includes nontranslation: using a strategy similar to that of Ngugi wa Thiong'o from Kenya, who abandoned writing in English for his native language, Gikuyu, North African writers such as Kateb Yacine and Rachid Boudjedra have abandoned French for Arabic. Thus, nontranslation becomes a translation studies category, one of avoiding assimilation by intentionally excluding the speakers of the dominant language. More typical of North African strategies of nonassimilation are those writers who write not in language A or language B, but in a multilingual form, showing how French and Arabic continuously rewrite and inform each other. Novelists such as the Tunisian Abdelwahad Meddeb, the Algerian Assia Djebar, and the Moroccans Tahar Ben Jalloun and Abdelkebir Khatibi have assumed a leading role in redefining translation from the North African context.

While Khatibi uses multilingual writing to destabilize the dominant French language, the aspect of his theory I wish to focus upon is his thinking about translation as a disturbing socio-psychological practice. His polyvalent writing tries to reproduce the "mutilated" memory of his colonized, bilingual life and experience. He writes:

> We well know the colonial imagination: juxtapose, compartmentalize, militarize, divide the city into ethnic areas.... In discovering their alienation such a people will wander, distraught, in the crushed space of their own history. And there is nothing more atrocious than the shattering of memory.
> (Khatibi 1971: 54; quoted by Mehrez 1992: 132; trans. by Mehrez)

Khatibi thus uses translation, multilingualism, and nontranslation as tools to subvert the language and power of the dominant language group. For him, as for all language minorities, translation is an always ongoing process, and cannot ever be separated from any form of writing in any individual language. He writes, "The 'maternal' language is always at work in the foreign language. Between them occurs a constant process of translation, an abysmal dialogue, very difficult to bring to the light of day" (Khatibi 1981: 8; quoted by Mehrez 1992: 134; trans. by Mehrez).

In *Monolingualism of the Other*, Derrida identifies with Khatibi's particular situation in Northern Africa, but his discussion of the institutional insistence of monolingualism and its imposition on non- or limited-speaking citizens applies to other cultures as well. Ironically, the conference took place in New Orleans, where French, the dominant language of the original settlers and *de facto* official language of colonial Louisiana, was long the majority language of Louisianans. With the state constitution of 1913, however, French ceased to be recognized and was officially eliminated from the public sphere as well as indirectly discriminated against in private society; Cajuns were referred to as retarded, hedonists, swamp dwellers, even web-footed. Serious efforts at monolingualism and assimilation have continued through English-only politics to the present; even today, despite efforts of Cajun activists and the creation of the state agency the Council for the Development of French in Louisiana (CODOFIL), the status of French remains quite low. No translation legislation exists, although Cajuns are the second largest minority, after African-Americans, in the region; French can only be studied in school as a foreign language, even though 261,678 Louisianans speak French in their homes and over 1 million claim Francophone origin (Landry and Allard, 1996: 449).

How does translation figure in Derrida's thinking about the binary monolingualism/multilingualism? It is a fundamental necessity, always present, however out of sight or *sous rature*. In the first repetition, elaboration, revision of his initial presuppositions, Derrida posits the necessity of the impossible-forbidden, presence-absence of translation as follows:

> [A] necessity that, however, is there and that works: translation, a translation other than the one spoken about by convention, common

sense, and certain doctrinaires of translation. For this double postulation,

—*We only ever speak one language* ...
(yes, but)
—*We never speak only one language* ...

is not only the very law of what is called translation. It would also be the law itself as translation. A law which is a little mad, I grant you that.
(Derrida 1998: 10; italics in original)

Derrida's thinking about monolingualism of the Other is dependent upon and requires the existence of this ongoing but hidden ("impossible-forbidden") process of translation. The kind of translation Derrida discusses is not the conventional, interlingual type of translation, but another, partially "mad," quasi-schizophrenic, psychosocial kind of translation that underlies any given monolingual cultural condition. Khatibi reinforces this paradoxical form of incommunicable lost form of communication by saying:

> [I]f there is no such thing as absolute monolingualism, one still has to define what a mother tongue is in its active division, and what is transplanted between this language and the one called foreign. What is transplanted and lost there, belonging neither to the one nor the other: the incommunicable.
> (Khatibi, 1985: 10; quoted by Derrida 1998: 8–9)

Khatibi is well aware of the impossibility of "absolute monolingualism," in which the "foreign" languages are embedded. He is also aware of the interaction of the monolingual with the multilingual, both that which can be translated ("transplanted") and that which cannot, the "incommunicable."

Derrida also connects his project of deconstructing monolingual culture to his larger project of deconstructing Cartesian philosophy, or "universal" humanism. This project, as the peoples of all the languages and cultures of the Americas know all too well, is connected to colonialism. Derrida writes:

> All culture is originally colonial.... Every culture institutes itself through the unilateral imposition of some "politics" of language. Mastery begins, as we know, through the power of naming, of imposing and legitimating appellations.... This sovereign establishment [*mise en demeure souveraine*] may be open, legal, armed, or cunning, disguised under alibis of "universal" humanism.... It always follows or precedes culture like a shadow.
> (Derrida 1998: 39)

Here French colonialism in Africa is equated with French, British, Spanish, and Portuguese colonialism in the Americas. Although Derrida's project is largely abstract and philosophical, one can see the political implications of his ideas. In the United States, the English-only movement has largely been within the law and a fairly open process; however, its imposition has been just as unilateral as that of the French in Northern Africa, and its repercussions in terms of cultural loss, not to mention discrimination, degradation, and incarceration, have been comparable. Indeed, the collective extermination of the Amerindian peoples was largely rationalized and justified by claiming the savage and uncivilized nature of Amerindian language and culture.

Indicative of the schizophrenic translational nature of the "United" States culture are the plethora of hyphenated identities such as Cajun-American, African-American, Asian-American, Chinese-American, or even more local hybridizations such as Nuyorican, all of which underscore the difficulty of ever arriving at a unified monolingual "American" identity. Perhaps the disturbing psychosocial nature of the multilingual condition is most visible in its *reverse* construction; those language and ethnic minorities living within the English-only dominant culture know only too well what it means to be identified as carrying out any particular "un-American" activities as insisting upon translation or on bilingual education. There is a kind of madness in this definition of translation, one that implies a continual process of oppression, but one that nevertheless contains an always ongoing process of resistance to that very oppression.

Translation studies and identity formation

When compared to what is happening in countries in Europe, translation studies is in its infant stages in the United States. The American Translation and Interpreting Studies Association (ATISA) has only been in existence since 2002, and its membership consists largely of scholars who teach in modern and classical language departments with little interest in American studies. But the beginnings of a new movement can be seen connecting translation studies to American studies. Scholars such as Lawrence Venuti, Carol Maier, Maria Tymoczko, and Suzanne Jill Levine are increasingly connecting translation phenomena to issues of margin, migration, resistance, and identity. I have mentioned Lawrence Venuti already, whose works such as *The Translator's Invisibility* and "American Tradition" indicate the political/ideological nature of translation and its importance to the construction of culture and national identity. In *Scandals of Translation* (1998b), he directly addresses the issue in a chapter titled "The Formation of Cultural Identities." He argues that translation's greatest effect, and hence its greatest potential cause for scandal, is its participation in the formation of cultural identities (ibid.: 96). He writes, "The identity-forming power of translation always threatens to embarrass cultural and political institutions because it reveals the shaky foundations of their social authority" (ibid.: 97). He then goes on to cite various examples where individual translators, such as St. Jerome, used translation to challenge powerful institutions such as the Christian Church and inspire social and spiritual change. He continues, "Identity is never irrevocably fixed but rather relational, the nodal point for a multiplicity of practices and institutions whose sheer heterogeneity creates the possibility for change" (ibid.: 79). I suggest that the multilingual and multicultural makeup of the culture of the United States allows for openings for marginal discourses, decentering but profoundly affecting the ideas and beliefs embodied in the English-only mainstream.

Such scholars are much aware of the imbalance of power in the United States and the way the English-only majority uses practices of translation and nontranslation to marginalize language minorities. Translation becomes a place for theorizing aspects of minority practices, especially in their efforts to restore a balance of power in language encounters. In the introduction to the anthology *Translation and Power*, Maria Tymoczko and I (Tymoczko and Gentzler 2002) focus on issues of power in translation and suggest that one cannot analyze the transfer of content without addressing the issue of the power relations of the languages involved in the exchange; in other words, "The workings of power are not simply 'top down,' a matter of inexorable repression and constraint; instead, translation, like other cultural activities, can be mobilized for counter-discourses and subversion, or for any number of mediating positions in between" (ibid.: xix). The hegemonic power of English-only discourse plays a role not only externally in global relations and international exchanges but also with regard to internal relations and exchanges with language minorities within the borders of the United States.

In "Toward a Theoretical Practice for Cross-cultural Translation" (1995), Carol Maier talks about the situation in which a translation exchange is characterized by inequities of power, and identity issues immediately surface. Translators quickly learn that certain so-called categories with which people identify—man, woman, white, black, majority, or minority—are constructed rather than universal, and are often relative to the language and culture within which the terms are embedded (ibid.: 31). Maier thus analyzes translations less as a product carrying certain content than as a process revealing certain relations. The "end" of translation, in her words, is less a resolving of language differences than it is a problematizing of identity issues, including the reader's and one's own. The goal becomes to understand not just what the non-English words mean, but what they mean within the culture of the other language, thus opening the way for a new way of conceiving relations in the world.

In a similar fashion, in "Translation, Counter-culture and the Fifties" (Gentzler 1996), I talk about translation in the 1950s and early 1960s in the United States, suggesting that translators such as Robert Bly, James Wright, W.S. Merwin, Denise Levertov, W.D. Snodgrass, and the Beat poets such as Lawrence Ferlinghetti and Gary Snyder, were largely disappointed in contemporary creative writing in the United States, finding it either too formalist or too isolationist. I suggest that these creative writers and translators used their translations of works by Pablo Neruda, César Vallejo, Antonio Machado, Federico García Lorca, Georg Trakl and Gunnar Ekelöf to resist normative, mainstream, established ways of thinking and open new avenues for thought and imagination. Bly and William Duffy thus started a new journal called *The Fifties*, later renamed *The Sixties*, to begin the process of social change. Bly was very conscious of two forms of culture: one he calls the official commercial culture and the other he calls an unofficial, underground movement. It should come as no surprise that Bly was active in the anti-Vietnam War movement in the 1960s, organizing antiwar poetry readings and founding a group called American Writers Against the War. Interrupting normative language with surreal images, parodying the language of official culture, using black humor, Bly and others used translation to poke fun at monolingual America's language and logic. The translations tapped into a psyche of American life, and more often than not undermined elitist notions of the nature of art, poetry, unity, and form. The new form of imaging did not rely on an objective correlative in a T.S. Eliot sense, but was more psychological in nature. The poems and translations often turned inward and uncovered unconscious thoughts and powerful emotions. The translations served not only to import ideas from other cultures but also attempted to inform United States culture and allow citizens to better understand themselves via an alternative culture within the United States.

Perhaps I can best illustrate the multilingual possibilities and the counterculture nature of translation by turning to Suzanne Jill Levine, translator of works by Adolfo Bioy Caseres, Gabriel García Márquez, Guillermo Cabrera Infante, Manuel Puig, and Severo Sarduy, and the translation strategies she describes in *The Subversive Scribe: Translating Latin American Fiction* (1991). In many ways, her theory is similar to Venuti's, and the original title of her book, "Invisible Scribe," is almost identical to that of Venuti's later book *The Translator's Invisibility* (1995). Given that translation is largely a hidden activity in the United States, both want to make visible the behind-the-scene role of the translator. In *The Subversive Scribe*, Levine offers a series of examples of how she went about creatively solving some of the most difficult problems facing a translator—how to translate puns, proper nouns, songs, titles, dialogue, dialects, memories—all derived from process notebooks, prefaces, interviews, and correspondence Levine kept over the years. The book is one of the best texts documenting the creative nature of the hidden process of translation.

Levine's theory is presented not in linear form, but with fragments of insight, initiated by epigraphs at the beginning of each chapter, followed by a bit of expository writing and then by longer examples illustrating problems as she goes. While the book at first appears to be a series of juxtaposed problems, the beginnings of a theory of translation and its connection to identity formation begin to emerge. As writers in exile become more conscious of the mechanisms of their mother tongue by experiencing it from abroad, she suggests, so too do translators become increasingly aware of their language from afar via their search for a home for a foreign text. Levine also relates this search to all writing and identity formation:

> Translation is a mode of writing that might enable one to find one's own language through another's, but then again all writing involves such a search. Perhaps a found style completes the search, but doesn't the original language, intentions, or reality remain eternally elusive?
> (1991: 2)

The topic of subversion in translation is the thread that ties the fragments and examples together, although it is presented to us in multiple synonyms, repetitions, and guises: subversion as "betrayal," as "abusive," and as "uncovering subtexts." As "original" writing can be viewed as a translation of the oral to the written, so too is translation another kind of "original" writing, and Levine's concept of translation first and foremost derives from a Borgesian concept of parodying the authority of the original, as he does in his "*Las versiones homéricas*" ("Versions of Homer") and in "Pierre Menard, Author of the *Quixote*" (see Chapter 5). For Borges, the only difference between the original and the translation is that the translator's referent is visible, a text against which the translation can be compared, and the author's original is invisible or at least unarticulated, the text of so-called reality or some elusive, mediated, perhaps banal, conception of that reality. Borges's "Pierre Menard" parodies the authority of the original by illustrating that each new act of reading, rewriting, translating enters into a dialogue with the "original," causing the original meaning to evolve even if the words are the same, to the point that any original authorial intention is lost. In Levine's words, "Our vertigo upon reading this fiction is infinite" (1991: 5). Translation for Levine thus enters the realm of psychology, philosophy of meaning, reception theory, deconstruction, and parody.

Levine's concept of subversion implies not a reconstitution of any given original, but rather the construction of a parallel fiction, a play, or performance of that story that complements, supplements, and creates similar but new openings for interpretation in its re-versioning. I find such an approach surprisingly applicable to the way translation has functioned historically in North America. While the translated meaning can never be the same, it can produce analogous effects, often by referring to versions latent underneath the original (*sub*versions) that, when allowed to resurface, represent the original through another form. One example may serve. In *Tres tristes tigres* ("three sad tigers"), which Levine creatively translated as *Three Trapped Tigers* in order to preserve the alliteration, Cabrera Infante refers to "*un naúfrago*" ("a shipwrecked sailor"), which Levine translates as

"Badsin the sailor." She justifies this liberty by arguing that *un nuáfrago* in Spanish refers not only to a shipwrecked sailor but also to other, more mythical frames of reference, including the discovery of America (Cuba) by Columbus, Shakespeare's *The Tempest*, and Defoe's *Robinson Crusoe* (Levine 1991: 26–27). While the English version is more "spiced" and more literary, it resounds to the Spanish's "natural" tie to such connotative associations. In a similar way to Borges's Pierre Menard in his rewriting of *Don Quixote*, Levine's reversion attempts to convey "latent truths" inherent but not explicit in the original; her strategy is one of faithful unfaithfulness, allowing for the translator's own creativity and multilingual connections to be heard.

Levine's translations also break new ground by exploring *popular* culture and use an extremely fluent, indeed streetwise, even more localized spoken language, that of Guillermo Cabrera Infante's Havana or Manuel Puig's Buenos Aires. She draws on her native New York City street jargon, Hollywood dialogues, Afro-American speech rhythms, popular fiction, TV melodrama, and regional slang, all the while adding graphic distortion. Here is an example from a piece called "'Los Idus de Marzo', según Plutacro . . . y según Shakespeare, y según Mankiewicz, y según el limpiabotas Chicho Charol" (Cabrera Infante 1974) a short story by Cabrera Infante from his collection *Exorcismos de esti(l)o* (1976) about a shoeshine boy telling his client about Mankiewicz's movie version of Shakespeare's Julius Caesar. Cabrera Infante writes, "Bueno sosio la cosa e quete tipo Sesal no quie sel rey pero si quiere o no quie pero si quiere la corrona" (1974: 35), which Levine translates as, "Well man the thing is that this guy Ceezar don't wanna be king but he really duz or duznt but he really wants the crown" (a Spanish transcription might be "bueno socio la cosa es que este tipo Cesar no quiere ser rey pero si quiere o no quiere pero si quiere la") (Levine 1991: 76). This "slanglish" version draws on several fields of reference, including Black American English, street sense and smarts, melodrama, distortion, and parody, of classical "high art" as well as of daily spoken "fluent" language, to communicate the subtextual elements of the Spanish. One of the goals of Levine's translation strategy is to release the oppressed "Other" from within the United States: the repressed and marginalized multilingual voices of the ethnic minorities not yet part of the political process. Translation thus becomes one avenue by which one can illustrate the processes of coming to know the "other," not just of a foreign culture but of a culture of the "Other" within North America. Levine's translations draw from slang expressions in any number of subcultures in the United States, including synonyms from old thesauruses, etymologies buried in the dictionaries, popular and classical music, folklore, Shakespeare, baroque poetry, burlesque comedy, and the Bible. She seems to show no allegiances to high art, low art, modern, premodern, or postmodern, but she does show allegiance to all those lost discourses that are marginally present in contemporary speech.

Some critics might object to this strategy, suggesting that the supplementariness of the words might reveal more about the translator's imagination than the author's, and, indeed, Levine's imagination is strong. For example, in *Tres tristes tigres*, when Cabrera Infante writes about two girls huddled under a truck watching a couple "making out" on the back porch, he does not say explicitly what the two girls are doing ("*Lo que no le dijimos nunca a nadie fue que nosotras tambien hacíamos cositas debajo del camión*"), only that they are doing some "little things." But for Levine, a "thing" is not necessarily a "thing." For in Spanish, "things" are gendered feminine, and disturbingly so. She recalls that in street-language Cuban, *vaina* also means "thing," and *vaina* shares an etymology with "vagina," both words denoting "sheath" (1991: 169). In a Derridean fashion, Levine lets her imagination run, connecting *La Cosa* (The Big Thing) with *La Muerta* (Death), both referring to "death," the vagina to "hole" and "Hell." She also makes intertextual references connecting *Three Trapped Tigers* to *Infante's Inferno*, where the "vagina" becomes that space of both the decisive (birth) and indecisive, leading to such existential questions such as "Where am I?" of the child (*infante*) inside the womb or the bowels of the earth. So she translates the passage by adding supplementary material: "but what we never told anyone was that we too used to play with *each other's things* under the truck" (ibid.: 169; emphasis mine).

Thus, Levine takes liberties, often expanding the original, making implicit gender and sexual references more explicit. It also moves her translation strategy into the realm of the psychoanalytic. Just as Freud recognized that jokes, slips of the tongue, dreams are pregnant with meanings covered up by more rational thought processes, so too does Levine's translation strategy allow for an openness to the unconscious imagination, allowing, perhaps, for a return of the repressed. In many ways, it is a perfect strategy for translating the "magical realism" of Latin American fiction. It also deconstructs the forms, meanings, and language of contemporary United States culture by means of the substitutions, supplements, and displacements of translation. By opening herself to lateral connotations and repressed meanings, Levine allows openings for the displaced and marginal voices within the United States, allowing readers to glimpse in the translation fragments of the multiple substrata ideas that not only provide subversive pleasure, but are also politically explosive.

Finally, and importantly to this book on identity formation, Levine also addresses how the translations affect *her* identity as a person. First, her translations appeal to the ethnic diversity of the New York Jewish, Irish, and Italian neighborhoods where she grew up, bringing life to parts of her identity suppressed in English. Her mother, for example, spoke Yiddish to her father. By following the path of translation, she accesses parts of her "own" language background from which she has been exiled. I suggest her case is not unusual for a citizen of the United States. All have multilingual and multicultural backgrounds from which they have been distanced.

Second, as an academic (professor of Spanish and Portuguese at the University of California at Santa Barbara), Levine is operating against a kind of double prejudice against both translators and women professionals. Levine's work suggests that translation is just as creative as original writing and that there is no breach between translation and literary criticism, as is often presumed. Finally, and more problematic, is her identity as a woman translating male and sometimes misogynist Latin American writers. Drawing a parallel from her translations to Gertude Stein's or Clarice Lispector's prose, Levine suggests that the narrative strategies of Borges, Sarduy, Cabrera Infante, and Puig parody that very patriarchal discourse they employ. By reconciling fragments of both patriarchal and other modes of discourse, Levine's translations of male machismo Latin American writers can also subvert logocentric discourse and provide openings for a feminist voice (1991: 181–184), a subject to be continued in the following chapter on theater and feminist translation in Quebec.

Translation and the New American Studies

While translation studies is in its infant stages in the United States, the larger field of American studies is increasingly turning toward multilingual and multicultural issues, of which translation forms a part. In "Postnationalism, Globalism, and the New American Studies" (2002), John Carlos Rowe discusses a new generation of researchers who focus on the many cultures of the United States. Rowe cites Werner Sollors's essay "For a Multilingual Turn in American Studies" (1997) and his project (with Marc Shell) at the Longfellow Institute at Harvard to republish non-English works of United States literature as a good example of this new paradigm. Another site for new scholarly and disciplinary ideas is the American Crossroads Project, an American Studies Association electronic discussion group founded in 1995 and maintained by Georgetown University.

In addition, the New American Studies paradigm tends to be comparative. In *Comparative Literature: A Critical Introduction* (1993), translation studies scholar Susan Bassnett lobbied on behalf of establishing a comparative approach to the study of the British Isles; so too do the new Americanists lobby in favor of a comparative approach to the study of the Americas and their points of intersection and interaction. The term "American" thus need not refer to merely the United States; rather, it is to include the different nationalities, cultures, and languages of the New World, including Canada, Latin America, Brazil, and the Caribbean. The scholars of this movement, who include Dimock, Rowe, Gruesz, Shell, Donald Pease, Winfried Siemerling, and Eric Cheyfitz, focus on "points of historical, geographical, and linguistic contact where two or more communities must negotiate their respective identities" (Rowe 2002: 169). Current scholarship tends to be postnationalist, using postcolonial concepts to investigate the development of European imperial systems of political, social, and linguistic domination, especially with regard to the United States' new role as a global power and its own form of linguistic, cultural, and intellectual domination in the hemisphere. The new scholarship is also international in perspective, including the viewpoints of American studies scholars from outside the United States. Thus, Latin American, Philippine, Vietnamese, and, more recently, Near Eastern perspectives on United States texts and culture are welcomed.

The scholars of the New American Studies are inclined to concentrate on border cultures and contact zones within the Americas, which are invariably also sites of translation. Some of the New American Studies scholars' definitions of translation are quite similar to those by translation studies scholars. In *The Turn to the Native: Studies in Criticism and Culture*, Arnold Krupat coins the term "anti-imperial translation" (1996: 32) to refer to the way that contemporary Amerindian writers use fiction to translate their ideas and beliefs into English. Anti-imperial translation is closely connected to concepts of translation well known in translation studies, such as those advocated by Walter Benjamin, who favors a form that imports the foreign into the target text, thus allowing the receiving language to grow. Similar "foreignizing" definitions are found in the work of translation studies scholars such as Lawrence Venuti (1995: 148). Yet there are differences, for the *direction* of the translation differs. For Krupat, anti-imperial translation produces texts that look like novels and short stories, but they are *not* foreign; rather, Krupat suggests, they are *indigenous*, part of *Native American* literature, either literally in the language or figuratively in the cultural knowledge. Winfried Siemerling, who discusses Krupat's work in *The New North American Studies*, suggests that this form of translation involves a "doubling of both 'target' and 'source' cultural practice" (2005: 63). While the language of the Native American text may be English, the translation actually proceeds in the *opposite* direction, adapting and integrating Western forms into Amerindian narrative culture(s). The process of translation for Native American writers/translators is in both directions: from the Native American into English and from the English into Native American. In a Benjaminian sense, then, *both* cultures expand and adapt into each other, forming a kind of oral–literary hybrid that is more indicative of culture in the Americas than any foreignized translation imported into it.

In *Through Other Continents: American Literature across Deep Time* (2006), Wai Chee Dimock, as discussed earlier, introduces several new definitions of translation particularly relevant to this study. Texts such as the *Bhagavad Gita*, read in translation in the West, have proven to have lasting influence, and in Thoreau's case had a personal sociopsychological impact, influencing his own words and actions during the early nineteenth century, which in turn influenced, socially and psychologically, the words and actions of twentieth-century followers. Dimock asks what it means to move across culture and time at epochal speed, with one work influencing another over many generations. She writes, "Translation . . . unites the living and the dead in a gesture steeped in mortality and inverting it, carrying it on" (2006: 16). Again, in a similar Benjaminian fashion, translation restores life to the text and gives it over to future readers. Thoreau, in writing *Walden* and "Civil Disobedience," was "translating" the *Bhagavad Gita*, not necessarily according to traditional definitions, but in terms of carrying the ideas and spirit of the text across languages, cultures, and time; his (re)writings, in some way, effectively reproduced the text, giving it a new context and a new life. Dimock writes, "Translated in just this way, its volatile truth betraying its literal monument, the *Bhagavad Gita* is threaded into an American context unthinkable at its moment of genesis. This sort of threading requires the deepest of time" (2006: 17). With the coining of new and expanded definitions of translation in order to investigate issues of cross-cultural/temporal communication, translation and American studies scholars can contribute much to the very social and political action so fundamental to American cultural life. I next turn to new directions in translation theory in Canada, where translation enjoys an activist role unparalleled in the Americas.

3 Feminism and Theater in (Quebec) Canada

If the United States is officially monolingual, Canada is officially bilingual; if the United States officially covers up its linguistic diversity, Canada "officially" embraces it; and if the United States confidently asserts its melting-pot identity, Canada seems obsessively troubled by the changing nature of its "bilingual" identity. Thus, it should come as no surprise that translation functions differently in the two nation-states. While the United States writes its laws and carries out its policies in English only, Canada, in the wake of the 1969 Official Languages Act, has all its laws translated into French and provides officially certified translators working to implement its guidelines. While the United States has few higher education institutions teaching translation and research translation phenomena, Canada has several bona fide higher education programs in translation, professors conducting both training and research, and several journals devoted to the subject. While the United States has only a fledgling translation studies organization, the American Translation and Interpreting Studies Association (ATISA), which was formed in 2002 and at the time of writing had about thirty members, Canada has a very active Association canadienne de traductologie/Canadian Association for Translation Studies (CATS), founded in 1987, with official bylaws, regular conference activity, annual awards, and an official journal, *TTR* (*Traduction, Terminologie, Rédaction*) supported by the Conseil de la Recherche en Sciences Humaines du Canada (CRSHC) and published at McGill University. Canada even has a journal named *Tessera* devoted to research on experimental and theoretical writing, including translation, of Quebec and English-Canadian feminists, also supported by a grant from the Canada Council and the departments of English at Simon Fraser and York Universities. The *University of Toronto Quarterly* publishes an annual review of literary translation entitled "Letters in Canada." Canada Council Translation Grants, started in 1972, have financially supported translators, freeing them from the demands of the marketplace. Presses that publish translations are also supported by the Canada Council, leading to the growth of many small presses publishing translations. Over 100 novels were translated into English between 1972 and

1984. Poetry translation flourishes. In terms of supporting the practice of translation and supporting translation studies research, the United States has much to learn from Canada.

In this chapter, I give a short overview of the history of translation in Canada, which contains a "nation" within a nation, that is, the French Québécois, who, to a large degree, have maintained their language, religion, and culture for nearly four hundred years. In the past thirty years there has even been an attempt to define a Québécois language that is distinct and separate from standard French. I then provide a section on the sociopolitical climate in Quebec during the late 1960s and 1970s, when translation issues moved to the foreground of the independence movement. This section focuses on a group of playwrights and translators, including Robert Lalonde, Michel Garneau, Jean-Claude Germain, and Michel Tremblay, whose translations of European classics into Québécois French illustrate how translation was used in Quebec in its inhabitants' quest for a separate language, identity, and geographic state. As Québécois as a language is primarily distinguished by its spoken characteristics rather than its orthography, theater provides a good oral medium in which to analyze this evolution. I next turn to a group of women fiction writers and translators, including Nicole Brossard, Barbara Godard, and Susanne de Lotbinière-Harwood, who have been studying and practicing feminist translation in Quebec, this time in a quest to articulate specific women's, as well as Québécois, concerns. Basing their translation strategy on a concept of *écriture féminine* advocated by French feminists such as Hélène Cixous and Luce Irigaray, the Québécois feminists developed a form of translation called *réécriture au féminin* (rewriting in/of the feminine) that has led to a rethinking of how we define translation, and to new openings for translation theory. Finally, I look at the multicultural nature of Canada, suggesting that the intense focus on the bilingual nature of the country and the Francophone question in Quebec have left other language groups, including the indigenous (First Nation) populations as well as more recent immigrants, largely excluded from the discussions characterizing social and cultural policies defining the country.

Canada and the Quebec nation

While the translation history of the United States is yet to be written, several fine histories of translation in Canada exist, and for a more detailed analysis I suggest readers consult texts such as Jean Delisle's *La Traduction au Canada/Translation in Canada 1534–1984* (1987), Sherry Simon's *Le Trafic des langues. Traduction et culture dans la littérature québécoise* (1994), and Jean Delisle and Judith Woodsworth's *Translators through History* (1995). For the purposes of providing background for the chapter that follows, I would like to highlight certain dates and events that illustrate the complexity of the language situation, the reasons why Canada is officially bilingual, and the impact of such a policy on the literary and social formation of the country.

The British colonists were rather latecomers to the Americas; in Canada, the Native Americans, the Vikings, and the French preceded them. The aboriginal peoples lived in America first; to this day, they still occupy the greater part of Canadian land, and over 30 percent still maintain their native language, the three most spoken languages being Cree, Ojibway, and Inuktitut (Driedger 1996: 84). The Vikings arrived in *ca.* 1000 BCE, first exploring and then establishing a small colony in Nova Scotia before, for reasons still unknown, disappearing. The French, however, stayed. French explorers such as Jacques Cartier sailed up the St. Lawrence Seaway as early as 1534, over two hundred years before the first British settlement in Canada. Samuel de Champlain established the first permanent French settlement in Canada in a place in the Montreal region in 1608 (ibid.: 85), which was just one year after the founding of Jamestown in the United States. The first British settlement in Canada was established only in 1757, which is quite late, considering that just a few years later and a little further south, the British-American colonists would revolt against the British crown. Thus, the French were not just the largest but nearly the only European settlers in Canada for over 150 years. With that sort of legitimizing history, pioneering toughness, and continued survival, it should come as little surprise that today in Quebec a very high proportion of people, over 95 percent by some estimates, are of French ethnic origin, and over 80 percent speak French exclusively (Henripin 1993; Driedger 1996: 86). As I hope to illustrate later, this homogeneity and strong sense of nationalism may have served as one reason for the rise of the Parti Québécois in the 1960s, and later as one of the reasons some multicultural Quebec citizens hesitated when voting for independence.

With two competing migrating peoples settling in the region, things came to a head in the mid-eighteenth century. Essentially, there were two immigrant peoples fighting over the same land and the same nation. The French, the older and more established of the two, intended to become a French-Canadian (Québécois) nation; in that same space, the British intended their own nation, a united, Anglophone Canada. In 1763, the French in Canada fell to the British following the defeat of General Montcalm by James Wolfe near the city of Quebec in 1759. The Quebec Act of 1774 allowed the French, who were much the majority, many concessions, including rights to their own language and religion. Tensions continued as British settlements increased, swollen by many loyalists from the former American colonies to the south. In 1867, the British North America Act established what is known as the Canadian Confederation, legalizing the claims of the two colonial powers and establishing language rights for both. In effect, this was the end of over a century of struggle, which was basically a war over language and culture; the United States, during the same period, was settling its Civil War, which was largely over race. Thus, it should come as little surprise that later, in the 1960s, racial unrest should dominate the sociopolitical climate in the United States, and language and translation disputes dominate in Canada. In 1871, the first census was taken in the newly united Canada, showing that of the 3.5 million people living in Canada (Native Americans were excluded, of course), 61 percent were of British descent, 31 percent of French origin; and 6 percent of German ancestry. Yet despite this union, Anglophones and Francophones lived apart from each other; each developed their own communities, social groups, businesses, art, churches and political institutions. The conflicts continued until the 1960s.

Since the establishment of the Canadian confederacy, there have been two significant waves of immigration growth: 1901–1911 and 1951–1961. During the first period, over 1.7 million people immigrated, mostly from Europe. As Canada was losing people to the United States until the turn of the twentieth century, in order to promote immigration Canada offered free land to northern Europeans and, when this did not produce enough immigrants, expanded the policy to include southern Europeans. World War I and the Great Depression halted the flow. During the second period, after World War II, over 2 million people immigrated, again primarily from Europe. With the many European relatives of Canadians unsettled by the war, Canada opened its borders to relatives of citizens and to those who were displaced or refugees. Such immigration policies ensured the dominance of the English speakers and a Eurocentric cultural policy. About 90 percent of immigrants to Canada up until 1961 were of European origin, and most learned English quickly and assimilated into English-speaking Canadian circles. The French-speaking Québécois felt increasingly marginalized.

With the 1960s came a new generation of young people willing to question authority, particularly those in the French minority. The two main resistance movements were the Federalists, led by Pierre Trudeau, Prime Minister of Canada from 1968 to 1983, who proposed that Quebec stay within the confederation, and the Separatists, led by René Lévesque, whose policy was to secede and form an independent Quebec nation-state. In contrast to the melting-pot policy of the United States, Trudeau's goals were to create a pluralistic, federated state, a government allowing for the polyvalent and multicultural groups to coexist and to collaborate to form a fair and just union (Trudeau 1962: 67ff.; and see also Trudeau 1968 and Trudeau 1992). Trudeau was a strong supporter of new legislation called the Official Languages Act, passed in 1969, designed to establish both English and French as the official languages of Canada. Yet despite the Federalists' attempts to build a more inclusive nation, discontent in French-Canadian circles continued to grow.

In 1968, the Separatists and Lévesque formed the Parti Québécois, which slowly grew to become one of the largest parties in Canada. In 1976, the Parti Québécois came to power, and the next year passed a law, Bill 101, declaring French to be the official language of Quebec for the courts, legislature, public service, and even imposing restrictions on the English schools (Driedger 1996: 122). In 1980, a referendum was held in which the citizens of Quebec could choose between the Federalist and Separatist alternatives. The referendum was defeated, with 60 percent voting against separation. Yet the vote was misleading, as over 80 percent of the people in Quebec at the time wanted either some sort of change in the federalist arrangement, or separation. The French Québécois felt increasingly marginalized: Quebec birthrates were dropping; many of the children of new immigrants were choosing English schools, and, especially, perhaps because of the proximity of the United States to the south, Anglophones were dominating in the business world. In 1995, a second referendum was held. This time the vote was much closer, with 49.4 percent voting for Quebec sovereignty and 50.6 percent voting against. Polls going into the election during the last month showed the Separatists ahead. Many of the "allophones" (immigrants who were of neither British nor French descent) and Native Americans, whom the Francophones thought were their allies, voted against separation. Post-election polls showed that while rural areas of Quebec voted nearly two to one in favor of separation, urban areas such as Montreal voted *against* separation by a wide margin (Driedger 1996: 125). In a separate similar referendum held a few days later, the Cree in northern Quebec voted overwhelmingly to stay in the confederation by a 97 percent to 3 percent margin.

For the purposes of this study, who won or lost and by what margin is less important than the nearly even split among the people of Quebec and their clearly divided sense of who they are as a nation. During this period, immigration, language, cultural, and identity politics were closely scrutinized, and translation of all kinds of texts—from the laws of the state to theatre productions on the stage and signs in the stores—played a crucial role. While it is difficult to characterize, I suggest that this new generation of (Québécois) Canadians suffered from a double or even a triple kind of geonational colonization, feeling oppression by vestiges of English and French colonization from within Canada's borders as well as by a growing imperialistic United States on its border to the south. This whole post-1960s period might be characterized by a people struggling to find and maintain their culture and language from the past and to explore new avenues for maintaining and developing their identities in the future. In this search, language issues moved to the forefront, especially the question of which language —French, English, British English, standard French, American English, Canadian English, Canadian French, or Québécois French—people should use to express themselves. The culture as a whole began to distrust institutional definitions of culture, including what it meant to be Canadian, and traditional arts and cultural organizations began to be questioned for their connection to the English-Canadian central government. Instead, participants in the resistance found new and creative ways to articulate their differences, and translation proved a crucial tool in that alternative cultural formation. It is in this context that Canadian French theater and feminist fiction translators began questioning traditional hierarchies, language constraints, and gendered roles. Translation became one of the primary tools with which to intervene and change the culture, and to express one's own independent identity. To better set the stage for a discussion of feminist translation in Quebec, let me turn first to theater translation in Quebec, which well illustrates the social and political background as well as the fertile climate for a whole set of new ideas about translation and its role in cultural (r)evolution.

A translational culture

From 1960 to 1972, Quebec was to all intents and purposes a translational culture. Canada was English, and all the laws, programs, universities, and journals were in English and then translated into French. Ironically, the situation for this period of growth in translational activity was state supported: through the Official Languages Act and Canada Council Grants, the government was attempting another kind of nation building, constructing a bilingual nation and redressing the imbalance of two hundred years of translation that generally flowed from the dominant English into the subdominant French. Translation was conceived as a bridge between two peoples of Canada—as a way to unite the nation and to allay fears of separation and of the disintegration of the nation. What happened instead, however, was a unique reflection on translation as a double-voiced discourse, one which, on the one hand, reflects another culture and carries ideas across borders in order to unite different cultures and, on the other hand, transforms culture, rewriting ideas in a new cultural context that challenge existing hierarchies of power. Rather than solving the uneasy political relations between the two linguistic groups within the nation, translation exposed power imbalances and exacerbated the problem. Translation became a kind of third in-between space, neither English, nor French; it was simultaneously both and neither. Breaking down binary logical thinking and "either/or" categorical thought, translation in Quebec became a mode of articulation in and of itself, ironically not subjugated to either of the dominant languages and cultures the state was forcing on the nation. Surprisingly, rather than mediating between cultures, translation became one of the leading tools for the new construction of a separate "Québécois identity" and for the growth of the Parti Québécois.

Theater translation

The year 1968, when the Parti Québécois was founded, with its independence option, also saw the birth of a new type of drama described as being "Québécois" to indicate its differentiation from standard French. Beginning as an underground, countercultural movement, it rejected French as spoken in France, and instead, similar to Levine's strategy for using New York City street jargon to translate the Spanish of Cabrera Infante's Cuban nocturnal Spanish, used the language spoken on the streets of Quebec. A working-class French as spoken in Quebec called *joual*, a Québécois form of the word *cheval* (horse), characterized a language with its own oral rules and varying degrees of American-English interference, which, during the 1960s and 1970s, came to symbolize the colonized condition of Quebec. The year 1968 saw the first use of *joual* as a literary language in two productions: Éloi de Grandmont's translation of Shaw's cockney dialogue in *Pygmalion* and Michel Tremblay's translation/adaptation of Chekhov's *Les Belles-Soeurs*.

In *A Sociocritique of Translation: Theatre and Alterity in Quebec, 1968–1988* (1996), sociologist and translation studies scholar Annie Brisset traces the parallels between the rise in power of the Parti Québécois and the rise in Québécois translations on the stage. She suggests that one main distinction between the standard English and French cultures of Canada and the translational culture of Quebec is that the people of Quebec were aware of the very markers and cultural codes that invade their culture via copies, imitations, and images of both French and Anglo-American culture. This flood of images, often perpetuated by official translational policies of the nation-state, served merely to continue to colonize the citizens of Quebec and preclude their independent development. In an ironic reversal, Brisset argues that in theater translation in Quebec during this period, translators were not so much concerned with bringing the original across a linguistic border; rather, they were focused on a *rejection* of the original, which not only was a new definition of translation but also, in turn, opened up a space for the invention of a national language. Translators began translating not into standard French but into multiple versions of Québécois French, working-class dialects, *joual*, archaic French, Gaspéan French, all in an attempt to resist a double colonization. In theater, translations into standard French all but disappeared during this period. During the early 1970s, for example, most of the plays in translation produced by La Compagnie Jean-Duceppe used standard French translations. During the early 1980s, the same company staged *no* plays in standard French translations; all nineteen plays performed were in Québécois translation or adaptation (Brisset 1996: 58).

During this period, Québécois translations of canonical European works numbered in the hundreds. Most were "translations" from standard French plays, followed by translations of plays from English. French authors translated were in the dozens, headed by Molière, Georges Feydeau, Eugène Ionesco, and Jean Racine; translations from English included works by Tennessee Williams, Neil Simon, Arthur Miller, Eugene O'Neill, and Edward Albee. Italian, German, Russian, Spanish, Swedish, and Greek translations ensued (Brisset 1996: 39). Italian translations included works by Carlo Goldoni, Dario Fo, and Luigi Pirandello; German translations included works by Bertolt Brecht, Max Frisch, and Heinrich von Kleist. The reasons for the selection of the texts varied according to language, but clearly the canonical status of the plays was paramount, which research shows is indicative of translation in an emerging culture; without a literary history of their own, new and emerging cultures use translation to import and create their own literary history. Other criteria seemed varied: French plays translated seem characterized by their comic potential, perhaps useful to satirize the Quebec situation *vis-à-vis* France. Plays from the United States, on the other hand, seemed chosen because of their tragic value, no doubt to reflect the unequal power relations present in the Quebec culture and the suffering and alienation endured by the Québécois people in relation to their Anglophone compatriots.

In all cases, translation into Québécois was a clear attempt to appropriate European language theater and make it Quebec's own. The language of translation thus became a tool for empowering regional groups and articulating repressed social and political concerns. Éloi de Grandmont's 1968 translation of Bernard Shaw's *Pygmalion*, for example, was one of the first to use the vernacular and Quebec dialects both to break down traditional modes of translation and to question the languages, beliefs, and images imposed upon Quebec by the French and English. Translation moved from the margins of cultural formation to a more central position. Even "original" plays became increasingly about translation; the predominant theme of dramatic writing became translation itself. Jean-Claude Germain's play *A Canadian Play/Une Plaie canadienne* (1983), for example, used forms of translation favored by the colonizer to subvert that very power. Using irony, parody, and other tools, Germain ridiculed the effects of institutional bilingualism. The bilingualism of translation in the play is viewed as *une plaie*, a wound. As opposed to traditional conceptions of translation—that is, as a tool to import the foreign—Brisset suggests that in the Quebec situation the other is seen as a subjugating, hegemonic force, whose presence leads to humiliation and degradation. The struggle in Quebec, and perhaps in other regions of the Americas, is one of how *not* to be assimilated by the other. Translation in the cases of the Americas becomes a form of anti-translation, a rejection of the other that allows space for invention and the creation of one's own identity.

One of the reasons for the success of this form of translation is its very openness to a larger repertoire of translation equivalents. In addition to the standard lexical choices, translators have a wide range of subcodes at their disposal. The translator can choose from dialects, drawls, various vernaculars, high and low registers, archaisms and modernisms, men's or women's language, and various geographical, sociological, and historical variations. Rather than being a passive, self-effacing mechanism of transfer, the translator is very much involved in the selection of language codes. Using such choices, translators can reclaim and recenter codes that have been marginalized by culture. The translators of this generation clearly felt that standard French was incapable of expressing certain experiences and concerns of the Québécois people, and they had to find another language to express those experiences. Different codes were selected, from Gaspesian dialects by Michel Garneau in his translation of *Macbeth* (1978), to the *joual* of the working class in Montreal by Michel Tremblay in his translation of Chekhov's *Oncle Vania* (1983) or "original" work such as *Les Belles-Soeurs* (1972) in the search for that new language that could express the emerging Quebec national identity.

Tremblay, Garneau, and Germain

The most famous of all the Québécois playwrights and translators is Michel Tremblay, whom Brisset (1996: 18) calls Canada's "translator laureate" and whose translations have become "classics" in the Quebec repertoire. For Tremblay, translation and original writing really became one; his first published works were translations/adaptations of works by Gogol, Aristophanes, and Chekhov. Just Tremblay's name on dais or on the cover of the published text ensured a work's success, and indeed sometimes publishers have listed Tremblay the translator as the original author, as in his translation *Le Gars de Québec* (1985), based on Gogol's *The Government Inspector*. Tremblay moved the action of Gogol's play from nineteenth-century Russia to 1950s Quebec, and the "inspector" becomes an imposter government official sent from "Quebec City" to a small Francophone village on the St. Lawrence River. The corrupt Russian government is equated to the insincere Canadian administration, as immediately recognizable by the Quebec audience. The Québécois language solidifies the identification:

MADAME BOUCHARD: Ouan, mais chus sûre qu'y vous a pas dit c'qu'y'avait dit, par exemple, cher. . . . Y'a conté à son ami de Québec qu'y'était tombé sur une gang d'habitants ignorants qui avaient l'air de le prendre pous quelqu'un d'autre pis qu'y'espérait faire une cenne avec vous autres.

[Yeah, but Ah was shoor he didn't tell ya wha' he said, cher. . . . He tole his frien' from Quebec that he stumbled inta a gang of ignoramuses who seem'd ta mistaike hem for sumone else and who were hopin' ta make a dime off a' ya'll . . .]

(Tremblay 1985: 186, quote by Brisset 1996: 72; translation modification mine)

While it is hard to characterize the "true" nature of the Québécois language, characteristics include certainly the fact that it is an uneducated, usually working-class dialect with some rural overtones of American English interference, and orthographic changes, including both phonetic markers indicating differences from standard French pronunciation and markers that have little or no phonetic difference but that signal inaudible language differences nevertheless. Later in this chapter, I show how Québécois feminists introduce a similar orthographic style in order to introduce an inaudible graphic disorder into the language of standard French in order to destabilize it and allow different modes of conception to emerge.

Michel Garneau's Québécois translation of Shakespeare's *Macbeth* (1978) differs from Tremblay's in that the language chosen by Garneau is more of a Gaspesian Canadian French than a working-class Montreal or Quebec French. The Gaspé peninsula is on the east coast of Canada, where French explorers landed in the early sixteenth century and claimed the land for France. Garneau's point is that over time, Canadian French has evolved differently than French in France. The French language he emphasizes in his translation is a language of the first French immigrants, which he implies remains little changed over the past four centuries. Indeed, in a bookstore he found a Canadian French dictionary nearly one hundred years old, and no word appears in his Macbeth translation that does not appear in that dictionary. This lends to his translation a regional Acadian tone that naturally appeals to the Quebec audience, as well as lending an archaic tone to the play, recalling Shakespeare's original Elizabethan English. Lest we forget, Shakespeare was writing his plays at the same time as the French were colonizing Canada.

In translation studies, the first translation of Shakespeare into a culture often coincides with the arrival of a nation or a language into the international community of nations that comprise the global order. Historically, similar examples can be observed in the case of Germany, for example in the translations by Schlegel in the eighteenth century, or, perhaps more analogously to the Quebec situation, in the case of Bedita Larrakoetxe's translation of Shakespeare into Basque during the 1970s, which contributed to the post-Franco revival of Basque language and culture. Garneau's *Macbeth* is the first translation of Shakespeare into Québécois, and it was a landmark event. Brisset devotes a whole chapter to it, arguing that the play resonates to such a degree with the Québec people that Shakespeare *qua* Garneau has become the "Québécois nationalist poet" (Brisset 1996: 109). In this case, the appeal to the Quebec people is both phonetic and metaphoric. Garneau's translation hauntingly evokes both a similar social situation—Quebec's relationship to Canada recalls Scotland's to England— and a geographic national presence—the heath of Scotland/England evokes the association with the *brûlé*, the desolate land of northern Quebec logged out and burned by the colonizing French. The working-class farmers, hunters, loggers, and fishermen who live in that vast rural expanse of Quebec, comprising over 80 percent of the province, identified only too well with the play, which evoked especially their feelings of marginalization and exile. The images Shakespeare used in *Macbeth*—Scotland as a bleeding country, weeping and wounded on a daily basis—recall the images used by Quebec's leading poets, such as Gaston Miron or Paul Chamberland, as the following example from *Macbeth* illustrates:

> Bleed, bleed poor country!
> ... our country sinks beneath the yoke;
> It weeps, it bleeds, and each day a gash
> Is added to her wounds.
> (from *Macbeth*, IV, 3, quoted
> by Brisset, 1996: 147)

Next, we juxtapose Shakespeare's images of the suffering Scotland with lines from Gaston Miron's "L'Homme rapaillé" (1970):

> Mon Québec ma terre amère ...
> avec une large blessure d'espace au front ...
> Je marche avec un coeur de patte saignante.
>
> [My Quebec, my bitter land ...
> with a large wound of space on its forehead ...
> I walk with the heart of my bleeding legs.]
> (Miron 1970: 56–57, quoted by Brisset,
> 1996: 146; translation Brisset)

Miron's "L'Homme rapaillé" is also the poem that invokes the image of *brûlé* as a metaphor for those men and women who populate the small towns and land so characteristic of Canada (ibid.: 50). Finally, we compare the images in Shakespeare with these lines from Paul Chamberlain's "L'Afficheur hurle" (1969), one of the most popular poems among the Quebec independence movement:

> je vis d'une blessure inguérissable ...
> je vis je meurs d'un pays poignardé dans le plein coeur
>   de ses moissons de ses passions ...
> la douleur est mon pays ...
> terre captive par le sang et par les os
> dans le sang et dans les os ...
> étrange terre perdue ...
>
> [I live with an incurable wound ...
> I live I die with a land knifed through the very heart
>   of its harvest of its passions ...
> pain is my country ...
> a land captive of blood and of bones
> in blood and in bones
> foreign land lost ...]
> (Chamberlain 1969: 10ff., quoted by Brisset
> 1996: 151; translation Brisset)

Shakespeare's images used to depict the relations of power in *Macbeth* clearly speak to the people of Quebec in a unique way: the wound, blood, heart, land, country, exile, and despair carry across in an uncanny voice that, via translation, speaks to the identity of the Quebec people in the 1960s and 1970s. I suggest that rather than conforming to some sort of pre-established literary or discursive norm, translation, in this case in Quebec, as in other cases in the Americas, is used as one of the primary tools for writing a people's identity into language, to import new forms of expression, and to creatively rewrite the canon and produce a "national" literary history. It is in this environment of translation, rewriting, rethinking, creativity, and invention that I turn to a new generation of Québécois feminist translators.

Feminist translation

Theater translators were not alone in their search for another language and their quest to not be assimilated by the dominant languages officially sanctioned by the nation-state. Figuring prominently in the complex cultural space of the time was also a rising feminist opposition to patriarchal structures that were characteristic of both the dominant English and French language cultures. In the social turmoil characteristic of countercultural movements during the 1960s and early 1970s, some women began to seize the language and use translation to critique the powerful and often patriarchal structures that predominated. As the translators of theater felt trapped by the "either/or" options presented to them by the official bilingual policies of the state, so too did women of Quebec feel trapped by the options presented them for translation, leading to wide-ranging discussions on translation, identity formation, translation theory, and the construction of meaning. If culture has excluded women and if rhetorical and linguistic systems are part of that exclusion, then translation is implicated in the structures of repression and needs to be rethought. Perhaps the most significant contribution of the Québécois feminist translators has been their ability to reshape the field of associations from which translators conceptualize their options, which in turn has had an impact upon the way theorists conceptualize the role of translation in cultural formation.

If women are always translating from a patriarchal discourse into a discourse that is more suited to articulating women's ideas, then they are already working as translators. This intralingual form of translation is seldom visible, taking place from some position not outside the culture but from within. Thus, as Suzanne Jill Levine had to operate from within American language and forms to find equivalents for the sense of subversion, play, and multiple meanings in her translations of Latin American fiction, so too do the women in Quebec operate from within French and English to expose the limitations of the discourses available and to try to open up other forms that allow for better expression of the feminist ideas articulated by the authors they are translating. Only if they destabilize the cultural identities available within the culture can new modes of articulation emerge. Translation ironically becomes one of the best tools for such countercultural activity. In *Gender in Translation: Cultural Identity and the Politics of Transmission*, Sherry Simon suggests that "this altered understanding of translation as an activity which destabilizes cultural identities . . . becomes the basis for new modes of cultural creation" (1996: 135).

The Québécois feminists, including Nicole Brossard, Susanne de Lotbinière-Harwood, Sherry Simon, Luise von Flotow, and Barbara Godard, were much influenced by French feminism and the writings of Hélène Cixous and Luce Irigaray. While Continental philosophers were discussing the impossibility of escaping the discourse that constitutes all thought and the resulting impossibility of translation, the Québécois feminists turned to the French feminists for input. In the essay "Sorties: Out and Out: Attacks/Ways Out/Forays" from *The Newly Born Woman* (1975; trans. 1986), Hélène Cixous and Catherine Clément graphically describe the problem:

> Where is she?
> Activity/passivity
> Sun/Moon
> Culture/Nature
> Day/Night
>
> Father/Mother
> Head/Heart
> Intelligible/Palpable
> Logos/Pathos
> Form, convex, step, advance, semen, progress . . .
> <u>Man</u>
> Woman
> Always the same metaphor: we follow it, it carries us, beneath all its figures, wherever discourse is organized.
> (Cixous and Clément 1991: 63)

Cixous and Clément go on to discuss the dualist, hierarchical oppositions that characterize literary and linguistic thinking (i.e., speaking/writing; *parole/écriture*; high/low) and philosophical systems (i.e., nature/art; nature/mind; passion/action; master/slave). They argue that this discourse both orders and reproduces thought. The cultural weight of such discourse follows women in such a domineering fashion that it often ceases to be visible. They continue, "Theory of culture, theory of society, symbolic systems in general—art, religion, family, language—it is all developed while bringing the same schemes to light" (1991: 64).

Not only is the location of women in such dualistic thinking disturbing, but the control exerted by the system continues to reproduce itself, and all fields are implicated, including translation theory. Traditional translation theory—that is, translation theory prior to the advent of Jakobson—tended to categorize translations according to the following binaries: primary/secondary; original/copy; producing/reproducing; true/artificial; faithful/unfaithful; author/imitator; father/mistress; dominant/subservient; master/slave. The pervasiveness of this discourse affects even those scholars who attempt to break away from it. In *After Babel*, for example, George Steiner, who tried to avoid such oppositions, fell into heavily aggressive and male metaphors to describe translation: translators "invade," "extract," and capture the "thrust," using possessive metaphors that continually bother women translators (1975: 298; cf. Simon 1996: 144). In "Gender and the Metaphorics of Translation" (1992), Lori Chamberlain looks at the history of metaphors used by (mostly male) translation theorists. She finds that the metaphors are highly sexualized, emphasizing the diminutive, secondary, feminine status of translations, including tropes such as translations as echoes, copies, portraits of originals, or borrowed, ill-fitting clothes. For example, the metaphor *les belles infidèles* has enjoyed popularity dating back to the seventeenth century: women and translation should be either beautiful or faithful. While the linguistic and phonetic resonance of the phrase lends an appearance of validity, Chamberlain is quick to point out cultural connections to issues of fidelity in marriage, to patriarchal structures in society, and to laws and contracts (marriage laws, paternity laws, and copyright laws). Chamberlain suggests that the forms of translation that are *not* beautiful, that tamper with the fluency of the mother tongue, are historically characterized as "unnatural, impure, monstrous, and immoral" (ibid.: 61). Natural law requires a pure, monogamous relation to the mother tongue in order to maintain the beauty of the language and its superiority. Modernist translations—such as those advocated by Venuti—produce illegitimate or "bastard" offspring. Regulations that govern both translation and marriage are seen by Chamberlain as a sign of the father's authority and power, a way of making visible the paternity of the child and thereby claiming the child—or, in the case of translation, claiming it as legitimate property. Thus, the metaphors of translation encode the "production" of originals and the "reproduction" of translations, a discourse that has material effects in culture, as noted by the increase in privilege and pay for authors and the marginal status and low pay for translators.

The extent of the uncritical adoption of such metaphors for translation and for similar binary thinking about the problem extends to contemporary translation theory. Even the more advanced translation studies models developed by Itamar Even-Zohar in *Polysystem Studies* (1990) and Gideon Toury in *Descriptive Translation Studies and Beyond* (1995) use pairs such as adequate/acceptable, source text/target text, primary/secondary, producer/consumer, center/peripheral, and canonical/noncanonical to construct their system of investigation, and translations are categorized accordingly. More "progressive" and cultural studies-oriented formulations by translation studies scholars also remain suspect. Venuti, for example, suggests a rethinking of translation open to gender questions and reevaluations, but he too perpetuates a binary logic by continuing a faithful/free dichotomy, reformulated in his work as "fluent/foreignizing." Binary oppositions are scattered throughout his work—premodern/modern, invisible/visible—and although he favors the foreignizing and visible, which ostensibly would make him pro-feminist, by privileging one of the binary elements, he still perpetuates the traditional paradigm.

The feminists in Quebec have taken another course, one that rethinks translation not as form reproduction or opposition but rather as a form of productive writing in and of itself, meshed or interconnected with "original" writing, thus making such secondary status or such legal contracts unnecessary. As the French feminists developed a kind of writing they called *écriture féminine* to challenge the logocentric male discourse of their culture, so too did the Québécois feminists develop a kind of translation they called *réécriture au féminin* (rewriting in/of the feminine), one that emphasizes difference without binary oppositions or hierarchizing and that celebrates creativity both in translation and in original writing.

Cixous on writing

I quoted earlier from Cixous and Clément's "Sorties: Out and Out: Attacks/ Ways Out/Forays" not just to further delineate the problem of the trap of binary logic that impinges upon all writing in the West but to point out a way to get *beyond* the problem. These authors' suggestion is that women write, from which Cixous derives her concept of *écriture féminine*. For Cixous and Clément, writing does not produce a final, static end result; rather, it produces a result that continues to reproduce, independent of its "author." Through this rewriting, which includes its translation, meaning is not captured but deferred, thereby undermining notions of "representation," "truth," and "originality," concepts that form the basis of Western metaphysical thinking and that fix women in the binary oppositions outlined above (see Cixous and Clément 1991: 168). For Cixous and Clément, the act of writing means "questioning (in) the between (letting oneself be questioned) of the same *and of* the other" (1991: 86; emphasis in the original). Women are viewed as already translators, working (and being worked) in that uncanny space between the "same" (Western metaphysical discourse) and the "Other" (that which has been repressed by that same discourse). They continue, "That is not done without danger, without pain, without loss—of moments of self, of consciousness, of persons one has been, goes beyond, leaves" (1991: 86). Writing thus contains its subversive aspect and is a dangerous activity, both to the culture as a whole and to oneself. Writing produces changes in the culture and in the person doing the work, changing their identity.

In distinction to men's writing, for Cixous, women's writing is not a solitary activity, something done alone, but an activity that brings humans together, "charged with a ceaseless exchange of one with another" (Cixous and Clément 1991: 86). Writing is viewed less as an act of possessing and controlling than as one of giving—one that frees, transforms, and multiplies. In writing, Cixous gives of herself, with nothing expected in return. Such writing continues to develop, to disseminate, independently of its "author" through unlimited readings, interpretations, and translations in differing cultures. Cixous views writing less as an act of putting black ink on white paper, a clash between paper and sign, a cutting, engraving, signature, or stamp of property, and more as an allowing of a ground, a depth, a core, or inner being to surface—a "childhood flesh" or a "shining blood" (ibid.: 88ff.). For example, Cixous often refers to paper—sheets of paper, tracts of paper—as her "sun." For Cixous, *sol/soleil* refers both to the rays of the sun and to *sol* as in solar plexus—the stomach or gut deep inside of women, as in "soil" of the earth. Cixous's sun also resonates with the "soul" of woman as a different kind of spirit, an inner spiritual being. The "sun" is viewed not as some patriarchal, powerful, unified entity divinely radiating down from above but as a feminine light or inner strength radiating from within the body. Cixous and Clément write, "Feminine light doesn't come from above, doesn't fall, doesn't strike, doesn't go through. It radiates, it is a slow, sweet, difficult, absolutely unstoppable, painful rising that reaches and impregnates land" (ibid.: 88). Such a redefinition of terms is indicative of the strategy of *écriture féminine*.

Women's writing also involves a form of play with the language. The metaphor Cixous frequently uses to refer to this activity includes associations with the verb *voler* ("to steal" or "to fly"), as in to steal language in order to make it fly. In her famous essay "The Laugh of Medusa," Cixous writes:

> If a woman has always functioned "within" the discourse of man . . . it is time for her to dislocate this "within," to explode it, turn it around and seize it, to make it hers. . . . The point being not to take possession in order to internalize, or manipulate, but to flash through, to "fly" (or to "commit robbery").
>
> (Cixous 1975: 49; quoted by Kline 1989: viii)

Cixous suggests that women have lived in a kind of an underground in the West and have survived by a kind of stealth (stealing) or flight (as in a thief fleeing). Cixous asks, "What woman has not flown (stolen)?" (ibid.). This stealth activity has been going on for centuries, under the eyes of the male gaze, laws of society, police, bosses, and heads of households. It suggests an evasive conformity or surreptitious behavior that silently, invisibly disrupts. Nancy Kline, translator of Claudine Herrmann's *Les Voleuses de langue* (1976), translated as *The Tongue Snatchers* (1989), writes about this surreptitious activity as follows:

> As Cixous tells it, the woman who writes is a revolutionary, a robber, a guerilla warrior, taking the masculine discourse that surrounds her . . .

possessing it in what is quite explicitly a sexual act, only to rise from the kiss—between the captured masculine tongue and the tongue she has just invented for herself—into flight and further thievery.

(Kline 1989: viii)

This clandestine play with the language, of finding solutions that reveal polyvalence and multiple interpretations rather than final, logical ones is indicative of the strategies adopted by the Québécois feminist translators.

Quebec feminism

A group of feminist authors and translators in Quebec have taken Cixous's concept of writing as a *sortie*, a way out, quite literally and put it into practice. For writers such as Nicole Brossard, author of novels such as *Picture theory* (1982), *La Lettre aérienne* (1985), and *Le Désert mauve* (1987a), translation is not distinguished from "original" writing. Brossard encourages her translators, including Barbara Godard, translator of *These Our Mothers* (1983) and *Picture Theory* (1991), and Susanne de Lotbinière-Harwood, translator of *Under Tongue* (1987b) and *Mauve Desert* (1990), to intervene, to write, to translate from within, and "to go further." As Cixous's project might be described as one of making the feminine visible in language, so the Québécois translators' task might be described as making the Québécois feminist voice visible in a second language. *Réécriture au féminin* is seen as an extension of *écriture féminine* in that it is not seen as a secondary and derivative activity, yet it is also different from *écriture féminine* in that it is more cognizant of the constructed nature of language. Rather than positing sexual difference in language as something given, the Québécois feminists seem to be more intent on exposing the manipulated nature of language, the limitations imposed on a culture for reasons of colonization and/or patriarchy, and creative, possible solutions to escape those limitations in order to create a larger space for inclusion. It is thus specifically to the Quebec situation, rather than to some sort of essentialist, ur-feminine condition, that the Québécois translators address themselves.

According to Susanne de Lotbinière-Harwood, translation of Quebec feminist texts cannot be done behind the scenes; translation needs to be performed up front. In "Taking Fidelity Philosophically," Barbara Johnson talks about translation as a place that unavoidably exposes normally hidden language manipulations: "In the process of translation from one language to another, the scene of linguistic castration—which is nothing other than a scene of impossible but unavoidable translation and normally takes place out of sight—is played out on center stage" (1985: 144). In *Re-belle et infidèle: La Traduction comme pratique de réécriture au féminin/The Body Bilingual: Translation as a Rewriting in the Feminine* (1991), Lotbinière-Harwood suggests that the voice as well as the body of the translator can be seen in translation, and the act of translation productively works to supplement the metaphors of the original. She writes:

When translating, her body bilingual is constantly in motion between the source text, the target-language text-in-progress and the readers she is "entertaining" with her work. Her search for equivalence of meaning keeps her traveling through the standard intertext (dictionaries, reference books) and the feminist one, activating her memory, plumbing the auther's *imaginaire* and her own, making her body one of the most moving/performing bodies in language-centered work of any kind.

(1991: 160)

While the French feminists speculate philosophically and abstractly, the Québécois feminists have a more practical matter at hand, and movements between languages involve physical traveling between cultural spaces as well as drawing upon psychic reserves and memories. The Québécois feminists are negotiating multiple spaces, performing a kind of double translation: English/French and masculine/feminine. The double translation is more difficult in terms of the complexity of the project, but it has its advantages, for the complexity makes it increasingly difficult to be self-effacing. Rather than using writing to expose essential differences between masculine and feminine, the Québécois translators use translation to enlarge the semantic space shared by women and others whose voices have been covered up by the dominant discourse/language/cultural conditions of the given society. Rather than rewriting everything in the feminine, which implies a reversal of roles and the construction of another hierarchy, the Québécois women translators tend to see everything in context, with different kinds of texts —theater, novels, and poetry as well as catalogs, annual reports, legal texts, publicity brochures, and travel writing—allowing for different kinds of liberties (Lotbinière-Harwood 1991: 35). Thus, the feminist project, which began as a women's and translation movement, has evolved into a multiculturalist project and a rethinking of the very definition of Québécois culture open to any number of differing voices.

In Quebec, the expression "*au féminin*" (in/of/about the feminine) was first proposed by Suzanne Lamy in *d'elles* (1979: 61; see also Lotbinière-Harwood 1991: 62) and generally refers to writing in which the feminine subject is conscious of her place in writing. The woman's voice is anchored in a collectivity of women, and the target audience includes and, hopefully, expands that collective. For the Québécois women, there are multiple *écritures*, referring to different kinds of feminist writings. In English Canada, "feminist writing" often refers to both *écriture feministe* and *écriture au féminin*. Yet for the Québécois Canadian feminists, the former implies a prescriptive agenda in terms of ethics, morals, and aesthetics, in which women need to be portrayed positively. The latter implies experimentation with the language, exposure of the conditions for discourse, and the revelation of the constructed nature of the relations between the sexes. Some of the choices need not be practical, and therein lies the play, the fun of subverting male codes with alternatives. According to Lotbinière-Harwood, *réécriture au féminin* does not *reject* one language/discourse for another, but attempts to escape the dominant discourse in order to allow others, letting multiple personalities and voices emerge (1991: 92). Quebec feminists feel trapped by the structures of language/politics/culture, and translation for them offers one avenue through which to circumvent the trap.

In terms of strategies, the Québécois translators are much indebted to Luce Irigaray. In *This Sex Which Is Not One* (1985), for example, Irigaray tries to look behind the way patriarchal discourse, especially in literature, psychology, and philosophy, represents women, and open up the discourse to a variety of images, colors, shapes, and bodies that can be drawn upon for representation. She begins, as most French feminists do, by questioning the (Freudian) conception of woman as having no sexual organ, as defined by their lack of sex or their sex being characterized as merely a hole, an envelope, a sheath to serve the masculine organ (ibid.: 76). Rather, Irigaray sees women as having multiple sex organs: two lips, breasts, vulva, vagina, and uterus. She goes on to suggest that women have sex organs everywhere: face, ears, underarms, shoulders, and thighs. Touching becomes one of the main metaphors to describe women—touching as a sexual, playful activity, touching or connecting with others, and being in touch with oneself.

Touching or caressing also translates into one of Irigaray's tropes to discuss women's writing. Rather than try to repeat exact definitions, to search for underlying concepts, or to have a *telos* or bottom line in mind, Irigaray suggests that women's writing be more a play along the surface without a goal. Because the repression of women has crept into the discourse, especially standard French, women's writing is necessarily aimed at unsetting the linearity of the syntax, the fidelity to certain concepts, and the singularity of the discourse. One of Irigaray's main strengths—she is a linguist as well as a psychologist by training—is her ability to illustrate ways in which the French language has become male-coded and to point out ways to circumvent those very codes. In *Je, tu, nous* (1990), Irigaray reports on her research analyzing the forms of speech used by men and women in daily situations. Her findings effectively show the erasure of women in language in many linguistic constructions, which in turn has led to their marginalization in terms of the society as a whole. For example, she argues that in certain professions in French, no female equivalents exist for certain terms: the word *le moissonneur* (a harvester) is a man; the word *la moissonneuse* (a woman harvester) is not available for the woman, for *la moissonneuse* refers to the tool used by the male harvester. While *Le secrétaire d'État* is masculine, *la secrétaire sténo-dactylo* is feminine, revealing the pejorative social implications of linguistic constructions (1993: 71). This trend is particularly pervasive in terms of French pronouns: the third person plural pronoun, for example, erases the feminine: *ils sont mariés* (they are married) or *ils sont beaux* (they are beautiful) have masculine predicates implying that the subjects are masculine too, even if the pronoun "they" includes women (or feminine nouns). Such erasures have an impact on the way subjectivity is expressed in both culture and discourse, and affect identity formation (1993: 30). In terms of referring to married couples, *Elles sont mariées* is unavailable. Neutral pronouns in French also use the same pronoun as the masculine: *il neige* (it is snowing) or *il faut* (it is necessary), and thus only appear to be neutral. *Je, tu, nous*, the title of the book, ends up showing that the female I (*je*), maternal you (*tu*), and the women's collective (*nous*) have effectively been erased in French discourse, which has had all sorts of cultural repercussions, including, minimally, the loss of vocabularies to express certain matters, the loss of content, linguistic laws that exclude women; cultural laws that demean women, and, perhaps most importantly, according to Irigaray, a loss of relationships to *history*, causing women to lose connections to other women and family members, resulting in a loss of identity (1993: 34).

Irigaray calls for the reopening of the figures—the ideas, substance, subjects, and systems of knowledge—in order to see what may be called feminine. One way to reopen the field is to interrogate those conditions under which the systems are constructed. Systems, she argues, in their striving to be coherent, tend to conceal those conditions under which they are produced. Platonic systems, Hegelian systems, Cartesian systems, and Freudian systems are all implicated. For the Québécois feminists, this would include systems of translation, including traditional systems as well as newer (poly)systems theories. Irigaray refers to systems reproducing themselves as the "specular" economy: the matter from which the speaking subject draws nourishment, the images that makes representation possible, concepts—as defined by philosophy—that allow patriarchal discourses to reproduce themselves (1985: 74). To break this continuum, Irigarary calls for a process of interpretive rereading, listening to the procedures of repression and re-examining the procedures of grammar and their imaginary configurations, metaphoric networks, and silences.

While Irigaray does not address translation itself, one can see how translation might figure prominently in such a rereading. The economy of translation has been instrumental in the perpetuation of the same canonical Western texts; the modes of reproduction for printed matter, films, and photography repeat the imaging process; and the very definition of representation via translation, with its emphasis on sameness, equality, and fidelity, allows for patriarchal discourses to reproduce themselves and travel across linguistic borders. Irigaray asks that women play with these structures to make alternatives visible. While this is often difficult in one language, and women lament the fact that they always have to reinscribe their ideas in the "master's" discourse, foregrounding the play in *translation* is much more feasible, precisely because the "foreign" language can be creatively used to highlight slippages and create openings. The ephemeral nature of translation allows for a style of writing that is tactile and fluid, simultaneously touching figures without capturing them. Translators can use fragments over full figures, metonymy over metaphor, multiple meanings over single ideas, and supplements and tangents over logical, linear thinking.

In *Re-belle et infidèle* (1991), Lotbinière-Harwood reviews some of the strategies Québécois translators use to play with the language, including encoding new meanings with existing words as well as avoiding, or at least using ironically, pejorative words designating women. In her film *Firewords* (1987), Québécois writer Louky Bersianik asks "*Va-tu te faire appeler une cafetière si tu tiens un café?*" (Literally, "Will you be called a coffee-maker if you run a café?"). *Cafetier*, the masculine form, describes the owner of a café; *cafetière* refers to a coffee-maker and is never used to refer to a woman owner. In her translation, Lotbinière-Harwood ironically uses "chefess" in "Are you going to be called a chefess?" (Lotbinière-Harwood 1991: 118). Bersianik continues with "*Quel est le féminin de garçon? C'est garce!*" (literally, "What is the feminine for *garçon*/boy? It's *garce*/slut!"). While at one point in French linguistic history *garce* meant girl, over time its meaning has shifted to the point where today its primary connotation is "slut" or "whore." Lotbinière-Harwood substitutes a similar slippage in English when she translates, "What is the feminine of dog? It's bitch!" (ibid.).

Inventing words also is an important part of the Québécois feminist strategy, such as using phrases such as "auther" rather than "author" or "herstory" for "history." Much of this is carried out through altering standard typography. Again in Bersianik's *Firewords*, Lotbinière-Harwood italicizes "*master*piece" to point out that English has an inadequate repertoire to express female creativity. In her translation of Michèle Causse's "*L'Interloquée*," Lotbinière-Harwood also uses a bold e to indicate the silent *e muet* that is the grammatical sign of the feminine in French. Thus, "*Nulle ne l'ignore, tout est langage*" becomes "No on**e** ignores the fact that everything is language" (Causse 1988: 89; Lotbinière-Harwood 1991: 123). Perhaps most important to the Québécois feminists is the preservation of the intertextual historical references of certain terms. This network is a resource of words, meanings, and references that is continually being resourced in the women's practice of decoding and recoding via translation. For example, in the poem "Rituel," Egyptian-born Québécois writer Anne-Marie Alonzo writes "*pays autres pauvres pays de lames*." Lotbinière-Harwood hears in "*lames*" (literally, "blades") the sharp objects used in clitoridectomies in some parts of Egypt during the past. To keep from reducing her translation to a meaning that predominantly invokes "shaving" in English, she translated, "Remember poor other countries of cutting edges" (Alonzo 1986: 50–52; Lotbinière-Harwood 1991: 127).

Yet the Québécois feminist translators are doing more than merely invoking French feminist typographical changes and resexing pronouns to destabilize male discourse; translation has become a major theme of the fiction and secondary literature itself. Translation is increasingly used to articulate a new theory of culture, one that is more inclusive, more "democratic" for all its citizens, and more open for change and evolution. Whereas in most countries, translation, including feminist translation, continues to be of marginal national interest, in Canada it has become one of the central issues for consideration in the highest literary and cultural circles. To better illustrate the centrality of translation to understanding this new theory of culture emerging from Quebec, I turn to the work of Nicole Brossard.

Brossard: *Le Désert mauve*

If women are always already translators, translating from women's discourse into men's, then it should come to no surprise that translation as a theme and a translator as a character should become central in women's fiction. Nicole Brossard's *Le Désert mauve* (1987a) foregrounds both translation as a topic and the translator as a main character (see Simon 1999: 64–68 and Simon 1996: 158–161). The book is divided into three sections, the first being the fictional novel (a novel within a novel) titled *"Le Désert mauve"* ("The Mauve Desert") by the fictional novelist Laure Angstelle. The second section, titled *"Un Livre à traduire"* ("A Book to Translate"), consists primarily of the notebooks of the fictional translator, named Maude Laures. The third section, which comes with its own separate title page, reveals the simulated "translation" of the book, now titled *"Mauve, l'horizon"* ("Mauve, the Horizon"). Bridging the three sections are short narrative passages narrating the activities of the translator first as she decides to devote a large portion of her life to translating this book by some unknown author and then after she has worked on the manuscript for over a year.

In the plot of the story, a woman named Kathy Kerouac (all the names carry symbolic reference) owns and operates a motel named the Red Arrow Motel in Arizona right on the edge of the desert. She has a lover named Lorna Myher, with whom she lives at the motel, and a 15-year-old daughter named Mélanie, who spends as much of her time on the road as in the motel. Mélanie is a child of the night, who loves to borrow her mother's car, a white Meteor, to drive fast all night long in the desert. The story focuses frequently on Mélanie's thoughts while driving through the night and into the dawn: the fragility of life on the desert and the large open spaces that give rise to thoughts of freedom and eternity. Mélanie is drawn to the shadows, vague outlines, hues, veils, and colors, including the color mauve, hence the title. Two other characters figure prominently as the antagonists who drive the narrative: a mysterious ur-female figure named Angela Parkins, who apparently is a friend of the mother and who frequently comes to the bar at the motel to socialize, and an equally mysterious ur-male guest at the hotel who is silent, calculating, and who possibly shoots Angela in a chaotic final scene.

In *Le Désert mauve*, the plot figures less prominently than the thoughts and imagination of Mélanie. She loves those in-between spaces and works to enlarge those spaces. She loves the dawn and the colors—the grays, the purples, the oranges—between the end of night and the beginning of day. She loves to drive fast, making objects whiz past her in a blur. She likes to drive until dead tired, to the edge between falling asleep and being awake. This is the part of the story to which the translator is attracted. If Maude Laures, the fictional translator, identifies with anyone, it is Mélanie, a young girl, impressionable, pensive, often indecipherable, and full of contrasts. Mélanie is happy, sad, anxious, passionate, hopeful, capable of contemplating complex existential questions, and also capable of youthful caprice.

While Mélanie's charisma dominates the story within the story, the main character of Brossard's *novel* is the translator Maude Laures. In the notebook section in an entry called "Autoportrait," we learn that Laures is between 25 and 30 years old and enjoys the rush of a game of tennis, much as Mélanie enjoys the rush of driving fast. Laures dropped out after three years of attending a women's college, enjoys reading and browsing in bookstores, does not like politics but does like paradoxes. In particular, also similarly to Mélanie, Maude Laures likes the simple beauty of the dawn and the images it conveys. In her translator's notebook, "A Book to Translate," Laures compares the as yet unformed image of the translation to the image of an animal seen from afar—veiled, colored mauve, whose shape, outline, is not yet distinct. Therein lies the analogy to the story within the story: as a coming-of-age Mélanie is attracted to those vague outlines before they take shape, so too is Maude Laures attracted to thoughts, images, words, and paradoxes between two languages, before they take shape. While Laures does not know why she has this desire to translate this book, the reason has something to do with this desire to explore and pursue those vague shapes/thoughts/connections. Well aware of the risks involved, well aware that one phrase can change one's life, Maude allows herself to be drawn into the story and translate it. As Mélanie allows herself to be seduced by the night and travels obsessively through it, so too is Maude Laures seduced by the story and spends the winter months in Quebec traveling recklessly to the other side, into another language. The translation is carried out with a kind of feverish intensity. Laures lets her imagination go, and the notebooks that comprise the second, central chapter grow as she imagines the objects, the places, the characters, and the scenes that take place between the characters. The notebooks end up being longer than the translated story itself.

"Mauve, the Horizon," the "novel" in translation that follows in the third section, is actually not as adventurous or experimental as the reader anticipates after reading the translator's notebooks. Rather than demonstrating the flight of imagination that we were led to expect, rather than adding any supplementary material in a Suzanne Jill Levine fashion or employing any of the feminist techniques to reclaim language in a Susanne de Lotbinière-Harwood fashion, the translation is remarkably "faithful" to the original. Maude Laures does vary the sentence structures, often breaking up compound sentences into two separate sentences or moving a relative clause to another position, but there are no major distortions of meaning, additional material, or deliberate *double entendres*. With a stretch of the imagination, one might characterize the translation as a bit bolder, with selected punchier sentences; Mélanie figures slightly more prominently, Angela Parkins is a bit more excessive and envisioned slightly younger—but even these characterizations might be open for discussion. What is striking is the similarity, faithfulness, and accuracy of the translation.

Brossard is trying to tell us that while the translation appears to be mechanical activity, the amount of work—the imagination and devotion that go on behind the scenes—is enormous. Maude Laures spends one year on the translation from start to finish, the time it generally takes most translators to translate a novel. Given the fact that she may receive no pay, or if she gets the standard rate in Canada—Can$0.06/word, at the time —translating a novel of this length might bring her a couple of thousand dollars, hardly enough to live on. While perhaps most translators do not create written notebooks filled with explorations and extrapolations the way Maude Laures did, they do construct such imaginary scenarios in their minds, crossing over to another's worldview. Laures's notebooks also contain annotations: blue for words with multiple meanings, green for words with sound or tone implications, red for words that need to be verified, black for incomprehensible words, pink for genre clarification, and mauve for temporal unclarity. In addition, the margins are filled with notes and designs that Laures feels might help in the translation process. Brossard's fiction, for the first time to my knowledge, allows the reader to enter that cultural space of translators in their own unique element. Brossard's fiction attests to the intensity of the behind-the-scenes work carried out by translators, and metaphorically reveals the displaced nature of an individual caught between two languages and cultures, such as the entire population of Quebec.

Interestingly, the "translated" story "*Mauve, l'horizon*" is also in French and is not a translation in a traditional sense at all. Brossard clearly wants to highlight the idea that translation can take place across multiple borders, not just between languages. This *intra*lingual translation, while not using any of the Québécois feminist tricks and not distinguishing between Quebec French and standard French, does expand the boundaries of what is normally defined as translation and shows, in a Borgesian fashion, that a retelling of the same story in the same language is always going to be a different story (see Chapter 5). In its own way, it celebrates language's inherent heterogeneity. Translation enters the novel less by the juxtaposition of language and more by the juxtaposition of culture and sexuality. In this motel at the edge of civilization, run by women and with many women guests, the only male figure in the book, "*L'homme long*" ("Longman/ Oblong Man"), comes to represent the foreign. He is the outsider, his arrogance does not fit in, and his devices—the mathematical equations in his writings, the pornography that he reads in his room, the gun that he hides under a napkin—represent a threat to the community. One of the hardest parts in the "translation" is to *not* assimilate the foreign, and in this case the goal is not to assimilate the male figure, who also most of the time is polite and treats people with respect. While Maude Laures is able to capture the chaos, ecstasy, energy, and sexuality radiated by Angela Parkins, whether she captures the foreignness as she translates *L'homme long* into *l'homm'oblong* is debatable.

The other way Brossard introduces translation into the novel is the juxtaposition of the geography, the foreignness of the desert, of its objects, the light, the space, compared with the confinement of the motel, the small rooms, the television blaring, the little swimming pool, and the noisy bar. Here the translation largely succeeds, largely because of the intense identification of the translator with the main character, and the imaging and imagination that went into the process. The cover of the translation "*Mauve l'horizon*" even contains a photograph of the sun rising in the desert, backlighting the cacti and tumblebrush, casting long and mysterious shadows over the desert. While the photo is black and white, the reader can well imagine the array of colors and hues cast. The cover of Laure Angestelle's *Le Désert mauve* contains just the author's name, book title, and publisher, with no graphics.

In fact, color is the main way Brossard thematizes translation, and herein lies the writing/translation "theory" and Brossard's connection to feminists such as Cixous. Rather than focus the novel on the source text and target texts (sections 1 and 3 of the novel), rather than express relations in black/white distinction normally associated with day/night or civilization/nature as represented by the motel/desert, Brossard attempts to expand that middle space—shades of gray and purple that predominate the time between the desert and the motel, and between day and night—by emphasizing the movement, speed, and feelings of traveling between the city and the desert. That middle space, the in-between space when one is thinking not in one language or the other, represents the space of the translator. In "Writing in No Man's Land: Questions of Gender and Translation" (1992), Susan Bassnett cites Nicole Ward Jouve, who writes:

> The translator is a being in-between. Like words in translation, s/he endlessly drifts between meanings. S/he tries to be the go-between, to cunningly suggest what readings there could be in the foreign language other than those the chosen translation makes available.
> (Jouve 1991: 47; Bassnett 1992: 65)

The geographics of the novel set at the border of the desert in Arizona metaphorically resonate for the citizens of Quebec and their cultural condition between French and English in Canada.

One example of Brossard's expanding that in-between space revolves around the metaphors she uses to describe "dawn." They become so enlarged that it becomes hard to think about "day" or "night" as distinct from dawn. Colors emphasized include in-between tones: purples, violets, fuchsias, grays, mauves, pinks, oranges, rust-tones, and flesh tones. Colors are always shifting; primary colors seldom appear. The light of the midday sun is actually portrayed negatively: rather than being characterized as a light that brings clarity to objects, as it is viewed in Western philosophical discourse from Plato on, it is viewed as harsh and brutal, a force that can crush objects and bruise reality. The dawn also becomes a metaphor for other in-between spaces, such as the space between innocence and knowledge (interestingly, Maude often refers to the "original" story as the "innocent" story), between thought and writing, and, most importantly, between "original" writing and "translation." The reader is drawn to the subtle aspects of dawn, how it glimmers rather than directly illuminates, how it "brushes up against our thinking" rather than giving clarity to our thoughts. Multiple dawns are described for multiple occasions: "Dawn in summer, dawn in winter, the dawn on exam days. Jet-lag dawn when thinking hallucinates" (Brossard 1987: 150; trans. 1990: 139). Dawn is also much eroticized, secretive, and fascinating, especially for a young girl like Mélanie. Maude Laures imagines her desire: "Wanting dawn meant making one's way through furtive intuitions which open only at night, meant hoping to know its secret whose meaning, having escaped from the light of day, could only rekindle its appeal" (1990: 140). It also functions as a kind of an escape from reality, but in this novel, "reality" is more construed as an artificial construction—the motel, the bar, the conversations about sports and business. The "surreal," including the flight into the desert, is viewed as somehow more natural, more "real." The "foreign" thus becomes man's construction, and the alien landscape of the desert becomes the normal. Maude Laures writes, "At dawn one can easily have the intention of disappearing, of slipping one's body into the underside of light, very softly" (ibid.: 140). Brossard implies that cultures are heterogeneous, that there are undersides and undergrounds not exposed to light and not captured by writing in mainstream culture, but which are just as "real" as those held up by society. One of those subcultures is the culture of translation, those that can give themselves entirely to the foreign, travel to the other side, and return.

Theorizing feminist translation

Much of the theorizing of Québécois feminist translation has been done in collaboration between and among Brossard herself and her translators. As her fiction indicates a blurring of the boundary between original writing and translation, so too does Brossard seem not to be possessive about her work, encouraging her translators' input and creative ideas in their rewritings.

In a way reminiscent of Venuti's call for translators to reject their self-effacing, invisible status, Québécois feminist translators have embraced their co-creator roles. This dual authorship is energizing and often leads to further discoveries and openings. "Faithfulness" becomes a relative term: while highly faithful to the style, tone, substance, and intent of the "original" text, and extremely loyal and often intimately connected to the author/auther him/herself, the Québécois translators retain license to take liberties with the individual words and phrasing and to "go further" with the ideas, metaphors, and play of the language if they so desire. This creative, free play much resembles Levine's going further with texts by Cabrera Infante, inventing and deviating freely, but in a spirit that is by no means disloyal to the author.

While most translators work alone and are averse to opening their notebooks on translation to the public, the Québécois translators have revealed much of their process work. In "Geo-graphies of Why", included in Sherry Simon's collection *Culture in Transit* (1995), Susanne de Lotbinière-Harwood gives us insight on the process of translation as a theory itself. While most translation theory is aimed at analyzing the translation product, finding the most adequate term, writing it down, and thus stopping the dissemination process, for the Québécois women, translation is aimed at exposing the relativity of language, movement of culture, lack of finality, and arbitrary nature of any specific written solution. For them, this fluid nature of culture (cf. Irigaray 1985: 106) is more revealing of "reality" than any static, objective statement. For example, Lotbinière-Harwood writes:

> As Mélanie drives through the mauve desert in her mother's white Meteor, translator Maude Laures works her way through Angstelle's road novel. This double movement is impressed upon the real translating body, already engaged in dialogic movement with the other by the fiction's structure.
>
> (1995: 60)

Lotbinière-Harwood also reveals her dialogue with the author: "Solidarity with the auther encourages me to take the same risks she did. This implies aesthetic and ethical choices: 'Always choose in the sense of passion,' Brossard urges" (ibid.: 62).

Perhaps the leading theoretician of Québécois feminist writing has been Barbara Godard, translator of Brossard's *Picture Theory* and one of the founding editors of *Tessera*, the Toronto journal devoted to experimental writing, including translation and theory, of both Quebec and English-Canadian feminists. In "Theorizing Feminist Discourse/Translation" (1989; 1990), Godard talks about the double discourse of feminist writing, always in-between, always ambiguously positioned with regard to patriarchal language, connecting it to Bakhtin's concept of the polyphonic text, the one-within-the-other, which works to subvert the monologism of the dominant discourse (Godard 1989: 44–45). Translation for Godard is less a theme or a metaphor for theory, less a tool to deconstruct another theory, and more a material act of resistance and a tool to construct alternative ways of thinking. Godard views translation as a positive, productive means by which women can break out of their silence, gain insight into their experiences, and find a language with which to articulate their ideas. Instead of translation as transparent and the politics of identity as usual, Godard suggests that the focus of Brossard's novel *Le Désert mauve* is about the "process of constructing meaning in the activity of transformation, a mode of performance" (ibid.: 46). Godard notes that Brossard is involved in a collective project with Daphne Marlatt called "Transformance," which is used as a model for feminist discourse/translation in its actions of re/reading and re/writing (Brossard and Marlett 1986; Godard 1989: 46). Godard continually emphasizes that feminist translation in Quebec is production, not reproduction. Translation serves as a way for women to write themselves into subjective agency, to become participants in the creation of culture, not merely reflecting another culture.

Godard also contributed a process piece to Simon's anthology *Culture in Transit* (1995), an essay entitled "A Translator's Journal" in which she discusses the process of translating Brossard's *Picture Theory*. Here we see Godard breaking through, finding not a negative theory of translation but the beginnings of an affirmative theory. Godard writes:

> It is in the "skinscreen" section that Brossard works out most thoroughly her thoughts on dis-simulation (dissemination), repetition, doubling, miming and anti-mimesis. *Picture Theory* explores the "frontiers of fiction" and the way in which this destabilization is worked out as (hi)story, line. *Le désert mauve* dramatizes the activity of translation through the activist/translator, Maude Laure [sic], and explores the subjectivity of the translator, the affective networks that make translation, as reading, a figure of desire. One text touching on another. A reading "with" the text. . . . A narrative of translation, transformation.
>
> (1995: 76)

The transformative process is an open process, and the Québécois women are not about to stop or finalize the process, to arrive. Instead, there is this almost obsessive urge to keep pushing, keep tackling new frontiers, and approaching new subjects. The conclusion of Godard's journal indicates the openness of such a "theory":

> The translating subject as subject of transfer and transformation. Con-figured with the subject/object of/in translation. Essay/on(s).
> Translation, playing with the signifier, the trace, working the in-between. Between I and you. Between texts, languages. Trans/ference incomplete . . .

No final version of the text is ever realizable. . . . As such, translation is concerned not with "target languages" and the conditions of "arrival" but with the ways of ordering relations between languages and cultures. Translation is an art of approach.

The re-visionary process is just beginning. Subject(s) to change. Subject(s) in process. To be continued . . .

(1995: 81)

Godard explicitly shows the Québécois women's lack of interest in theories of translation that are concerned with target languages and final logical solutions. Rather, they are interested in the relations between cultures and the role of translation in contributing to those ever-changing patterns. For them, culture is always changing, in process, or "in transit," hence the title of Sherry Simon's anthology. Translators do not just represent a reflection of that movement but are one of the primary engines of the process.

On Derrida, women, and Quebec

As Hélène Cixous has suggested that women's writing serves as a *"sortie,"* a "way out," a "foray," I suggest that the Québécois women translators have found a way to escape the binary oppositions that characterize translation studies discourse, both traditional and contemporary, and point to new openings. In "The Task of the Translator" (1955), Walter Benjamin talked about the interconnection of translation and writing, translation being a mode of original writing, translation as a birthing process in terms of its giving life to the original, thereby erasing distinctions between the original and the translation. The original lives on (*Fortleben*) in an after-life (*Überleben*) in translation (Benjamin 1969; Derrida 1985b: 178; and see Chapter 5 of this book). Benjamin refers to translation as supplement, as a maturing process, as an abundant flowering—all reconceptualizations embraced by the Québécois women translators.

Derrida's work on Benjamin and translation first reached the Americas via translation in 1985 in Joseph Graham's *Difference in Translation*, which contained the French and English translation of Derrida's "*Des tours des Babel*" (Derrida 1985b). Derrida's essay, however, derives from a long history, developing from a workshop on translation that he had been giving for several years in different parts of the world. One of the first presentations of this workshop is recorded in the "Roundtable on Translation" held at the University of Montreal as early as 1979, published as *L'Oreille de l'autre* (1982b) and in translation as *The Ear of the Other* (1985a). Edited by Christie McDonald, the book is of interest in this chapter not just because it concerns translation but because it also contains a "Roundtable on Autobiography" and an interview with Derrida on sexual identity and the question of women. For Derrida, and for cultural studies scholars in Quebec in the late 1970s, questions about autobiography, translation, and women were all integrally interrelated.

The first section on autobiography, which includes Derrida's essay "Otobiographies: The Teachings of Nietzsche and the Politics of the Proper Name," revolves around questions of how to think about the "empirical" individual versus that which the individual writes. In *Ecce Homo* (1968 [1908]), for example, Nietzsche describes how he became who he was, but he deferred the "meaning" of his texts, suggesting that they would be misunderstood in his time. The text, although signed by Nietzsche, suggested that it would only be understood when future readers connect with him and countersign in their name. For example, he wrote, "When, much later, the other will have perceived with a keen-enough ear what I will have addressed or destined to him, or her, then my signature will have taken place" (Derrida 1985a: ix). In this way, explains Christie McDonald in the preface, the *auto* of the person who writes the biography is displaced by the *oto*, the ear of the receiver, so that it is "the ear of the other that signs," hence the title of the book (ibid.: ix). The section on translation picks up the same question in a similar vein, suggesting that the "original" only comes into being in its afterlife, in its translation and reception in the future. "Meaning" is not inherent in the "original," but changes, modified and augmented by the translation. Referring to Benjamin's "The Task of the Translator" throughout, Derrida and the panel break down notions of translation as reproduction and representation, and instead refigure it in terms of survival, growth, and transformation of both the original and the translation.

The third topic, the question of women, ensues quite naturally from rethinking the subject who writes the autobiography or the subject who writes the original text, which in this case would be a "translation" of one's own life. If that person refigured as "indeterminate" in language—that is, if that person is only determined later by the translators/readers—then the *sex* of that person must by extension be equally indeterminate—that is, only determined by another or in relation to future readers. Questions raised, mostly by Christie McDonald, include: What does this mean for the "person" who writes, for the text that is written, and for posterity? What does this mean for translation? And what does this mean for certain current and future definitions of gender?

Derrida's theories about deconstruction and translation are fairly well known by now, and I do not wish to elaborate here. In this section, I do raise certain questions about the relation of translation to women, identity formation, and Québécois culture raised in *The Ear of the Other*. In that roundtable, Derrida handles questions about philosophy, psychology, and literary theory very well, but he skirts issues of women and Quebec, either not answering or evading the questions. The only Québécois speaker on the panel was Claude Lévesque, a philosophy professor from Montreal, whose question revolved around whether there is such a thing as identity of a language. What is pure language or the same language? Pure French? Can one talk about a language within a language? Lévesque contextualized his question well by describing the Quebec situation, where the people speak a language that has been humiliated, contaminated, dominated, and colonized, despite the attempt by creative writers to affirm its difference. Lévesque talks about several Québécois writers who talk about their distance from the mother tongue, their nomadism, their position of exile within their own culture. He asks:

> What can one say of this curious relation to the maternal language where the latter never appears except as a translation language . . . one that is impossible to situate? Is this relation to language, let's call it "schizoid"—the normally abnormal relation to any language?
> (Derrida 1985a: 143)

Lévesque suggests that this lack of a mother tongue, while a torment leading to silences and paralysis, also might be seen as a chance to reinvent language as if from the beginning, of widening language, opening it for the unknown, thereby breaking with the materialism of language and the paternal laws contained within.

Derrida's answer is tentative. He calls Quebec a "strange" linguistic place, rather than seeing it as showing many characteristics of a "normal abnormal" postcolonial condition. Instead, he talks about the bilingual signage in the streets of Quebec and the different languages spoken in the city. He also remarks that the panelists, with only two exceptions, do not have French as their mother tongue. He does not address the complexity of the question or the possibility of using translation to reinvent language and break with the material paternal order.

The only woman on the panel, Christie McDonald, asks a question interrelating women and translation, suggesting that the couples presented in Maurice Blanchot's *Death Sentence* (1978), discussed by Derrida in "Living On/Border Lines" (1979; see Chapter 6 of this book), might be interpreted as the raising of the possibility and impossibility of writing in the notion of reading as an act of translation. Blanchot's *Death Sentence* is divided into separate stories, but both related by the same narrator. In the first, the male narrator forms a relation with a woman who dies; in the second, the male narrator forms a relation with a woman who happens to be a translator. In a remark in "Living On," Derrida suggests that the two women from the different stories perhaps love each other across the division of the two parts of the text. McDonald is very interested in the relationship between the two women, whom she calls the "most extraordinary couple of all," suggesting that perhaps their mode of communication across the halves of the text is similar to the way a translation sends signals across time and space to touch the original, in the way that Benjamin writes about translation.

In his answer, Derrida runs with the allusion to Benjamin and has much to say about Benjamin's argument about the structure of the original text and its demand (*Aufgabe*) on the translator to ensure its survival (*Überleben*). He connects translation to philosophy, arguing that there is no philosophy unless translation can be "mastered"—that is, its plurivocality controlled, indeed suggesting that the "origin of philosophy is translation or the thesis of translatability" (Derrida 1985a: 120). He goes into a long elaboration of the relationship of the narrator in Blanchot's *Death Sentence* and his relationship to the second woman, the translator. But on the relationship between the two women and how it might be analogous to translation theory, he remains silent, referring McDonald only back to Blanchot.

McDonald does not let Derrida get off so easily, however, and in an interview, titled "Choreographies," which comprises the third and final section of the *The Ear of the Other*, she "interviews" Derrida, giving her the opportunity to follow up her questions regarding women. The interview is actually a written exchange carried out two years after the roundtable. She begins her questioning with a quote from a feminist from the late nineteenth century, Emma Goldman, who once said about the feminist movement, "If I can't dance I don't want to be part of your revolution" (quoted in Derrida 1985a: 163), and then asks Derrida about what constitutes "the feminine." Derrida answers in a series of paradoxes. He sees that feminists are uncovering new bodies of material that have gone unrecognized or misunderstood for some time. One paradox, he suggests, is that having made possible this reawakening of a silent past, feminists will have to renounce an all too easy kind of progressivism in the evaluation of history. If the "liberation" has a history of continuous progress, a variety of stages, with a definable *telos*, then he is skeptical. Derrida connects Goldman's maverick status in the movement and her emphasis on dance to a completely unauthorized history even within the women's movement:

> a history of paradoxical laws and non-dialectical discontinuities, a history of absolutely heterogeneous pockets, irreducible particularities, of unheard of and incalculable sexual differences; a history of women who have—centuries ago—"gone further" by stepping back with their lone dance, or who are today inventing sexual idioms.
>
> (ibid.: 167)

Rather than make any large claims about women, Derrida sees each man and woman as committed to their own singularity, negotiating daily, making compromises between inclusion and individuality, and between joining the "feminist" struggle and allowing for a space for the "madness" of the dance. These negotiations are "sometimes microscopic, sometimes punctuated by a poker-like gamble; always deprived of insurance, whether it be in private life or within institutions" (ibid.: 169). Derrida tends to be skeptical of any "essentializing fetishes" (truth, femininity, the essentiality of woman, or feminine sexuality) and tries to avoid falling into the trap of accepting the basis of economic and ideological structures for a political cause.

McDonald then shifts to the problem of writing the dance, hence the title "Choreographies" of the interview, and the problem of representation of women in writing, and, by extension, the problem of writing/translation itself. Derrida again expresses his reservations about any sort of "new" concept of woman's or women's writing, connecting the distinction between sexual difference to ontological difference, a passage that he thinks can no longer be thought of in terms of binary opposition (original/derived; man/woman). Even some terms that McDonald assumes pertain to women, such as "hymen" or "invagination," Derrida doubts. He also questions modes of writing that resex language, suggesting that such resexualizing must be done without regressing to earlier philosophical conceptions of sexuality (1985a: 181). Derrida does say that no monological discourse, or no monosexual discourse, can dominate future discussions. Returning to the dance motif, he does suggest writing that is open for difference need be a "choreographic text with polysexual signatures" (ibid.: 183). This text might be characterized by its indeterminacy, excessiveness, going beyond the coded marks, grammar, and spelling of sexuality, perhaps approaching a kind of writing in which the code of sexual marks would no longer be "discriminating." Recalling Cixous's opening in "Ways Out," Derrida writes, "the relationship would not be a-sexual, far from it, but would be sexual otherwise: beyond the binary difference that governs the decorum of all codes, beyond the opposition masculine/feminine, beyond bisexuality as well, beyond homosexuality and heterosexuality" (ibid.: 184). He adds:

> I would like to believe in the multiplicity of sexually marked voices. I would like to believe in the masses, this indeterminable number of blended voices, this mobile of non-identified sexual marks whose choreography can carry, divide, multiply the body of each "individual" whether he be classified as "man" or as "woman."
>
> (ibid.: 184)

The paradox of course is that this hypothetical text of Derrida is constrained by what he calls the merciless closure of the two sexes arresting the "dream." But that is the possible/impossible state that characterizes all writing/translation in its repetition/creativity, the same paradox that arrests and closes off Québécois feminist translation as it is created.

Clearly, much more thinking needs to be done to tease out the relationship among identity formation, translation, and feminism. The women writers in Quebec, perhaps because of their ambivalent relationship to English Canada, to French, and to English-United States writers, have made strong contributions to both the theory and the practice of translation and feminism, and have created openings for new directions for theoretical inquiry into translation. While some say that the Québécois theater and feminist movements were short-lived and that their dynamicism has exhausted itself, as has the Quebec movement in general, I suggest that the openings created by the Québécois women and the theater translators will continue to have an impact on the future construction of culture in Quebec and Canada, and on the future of translation and identity formation in the rest of the Americas.

Multicultural Quebec

While the focus of this chapter has been on theater translators and feminists, I do not want to neglect other cultures in Canada. Like the United States, Quebec has always been a multicultural society: various First Nations peoples populate the northern regions; immigrants came from many countries, including Germany, Italy, Greece, Hungary, and Portugal; a large Jewish community exists in Montreal; and, more recently, immigrants from Haiti, China, Northern Africa, and Latin America have arrived. Yet because of the predominance of the bilingual question during the 1960s and 1970s, questions of multiculturalism were occasionally pushed to the side. During the 1990s in Quebec, a great variety of ideas circulated in the theaters, journals, cafés, and universities, in multiple languages, including European ones as well as more recent immigrant languages. The diversity of cultures operating in Montreal between the French and English dominant groups cut across multiple borders, not just in terms of geographic space as immigrant communities grew but also across distinctions between high and low, such as between Francophone theater/cinema versus immigrant theater or street festivals. Sherry Simon's book *Translating Montreal: Episodes in the Life of a Divided City* (2006) well describes the multicultural, diasporic, cosmopolitan nature of the city.

One could argue that much of the success of the diversity is attributable to the success of the openings provided by the theater, literary, and feminist translation of the 1970s and 1980s. As the Quebec independence movement gained momentum, and as Quebec increasingly gained control over its own governance, language policies, and administration planning, many of the Anglophone businesses, government leaders, and, especially, financial institutions, relocated elsewhere, particularly to Toronto, leaving gaps in the community, from jobs to empty apartments, and a general economic downturn that lent itself to opportunities for a new wave of immigrant groups. Some of the Quebec laws advocating tolerance and diversity also no doubt helped this movement, and the nightlife of Montreal, with its alternative communities of prostitutes, street performers, gays, and transvestites, fueled the movement.

Yet as Montreal became increasingly diverse and open, the *political* choices became increasingly restricted, culminating in the October 1995 referendum on Quebec sovereignty. Here the choices were but two: yes or no; Quebec independence or staying in the union. Proposals supporting multiculturalism and diversity were sometimes seen as an attempt by the English to divide the Francophone community and shift the focus away from the "rights" and needs of the Francophone community. Leaders of the Parti Québécois, including Premier Jacques Parizeau, failed to address minority issues. Indeed, Parizeau actually stated one year before the referendum that the "yes" side would not need the allophone vote to win the election, both ignoring the communities' immediate concerns and suggesting that their input would not be involved in planning the future of the new "nation" (Schwartzwald 1997: 206). While the province of Quebec was growing increasingly heterogeneous, the politics was becoming increasingly homogeneous, pushing ethnic groups even further to the margin than under Anglophone rule. When the October 1995 referendum failed by a vole of 50.6 percent No to 49.4 percent Yes, with 90 percent of allophones and Anglophones voting *against* independence, Parizeau came out and blamed the loss on the ethnic vote, further alienating the minorities. However, only 60 percent of the Francophone vote came out in favor of the referendum, indicating the dissatisfaction of many of the members of the Parti Québécois with the party's own policies.

As translation into the vernacular languages of Europe fueled national and religious independence movements—let us remember that at one time, French was considered merely a corrupt form of Latin—so too did translation into vernacular Québécois fuel the independence movement in Quebec. Despite rhetorical claims to the contrary, the reality of election politics in Quebec led to a "no waffling policy," an either/or situation, a French/English future, a nation/province choice, a yes/no vote, thereby leaving no room for movement or maneuver within the language and little place for "other" minorities within the culture. This exclusionary nature of bipolar politics can best be seen by reviewing the Quebec position toward the Native American communities. Just as the Quebec nationalists pushed to draw attention away from the Canadian nation-state to their particular language, cultural, and geographic identity claims, so too did the indigenous populations make similar demands for self-determination and autonomy. The problem was that Native American minorities in Canada make up only 1 percent of the population; thus, the indigenous claims often fell on deaf ears. Just as English Canada ignored the Native American claims for land and self-government, so too did the Quebec provincial administrators ignore past treaties and Native American rights. While asserting their own ethnic and cultural difference and building a state purportedly open for other cultural and ethnic differences, some Québécois nationalists refused to acknowledge competing claims that would challenge their territorial and administrative policies. What began as an issue of bilingualism and translation between two languages and cultures had gotten increasingly messy, with competing multicultural and multilingual claims. The rhetoric of inclusiveness and translation policies of openness did not translate into a politics of inclusiveness.

In fact, in the plans for the development of the Quebec nation-state, the money that was to be used to fuel the industrialization to replace the departing English-owned businesses was slated to come from hydroelectric development in the north of the province, on the lands claimed by the Native Americans. Hydro-Quebec had plans, for example, to invest Can$60 billion in the next decade to build new electricity generating plants to meet future industrialization needs in Quebec and to export electricity to the ever-hungry United States (Salée 1995: 287). These plans involved building dams on major northern rivers and flooding sizable tracts of land where Native Americans live. The Quebec planners were willing to offer financial compensation, to grant hunting and fishing rights, and to concede some administrative control for this privilege, feeling that their proposals were a model of generosity and goodwill.

Unfortunately, the indigenous peoples, including the Cree, Inuit, Atikamekw, and Montagnais, did not feel that way. The Cree and the Inuit signed such an accord in 1975 but were deeply dissatisfied with it, feeling that the Quebec government had not lived up to its promises and that the results of the commercial exploitation had had devastating consequences on their way of life. Unemployment rates were soaring, and economic conditions in the communities were worse than ever. The negotiations with the Atikamekw and Montagnais deadlocked, and relations were strained with feelings of resentment, suspicion, and, at times, racial hatred.

In "Identities in Conflict; the Aboriginal Question and the Politics of Recognition in Quebec" (1995), Daniel Salée argues that much of the problem concerned translation issues, revolving, for example, around different conceptions of terms such as "property." For the Montagnais, land is not anyone's property. Their relationship to land is defined in terms of historical, emotional, and cultural ties. Territory is assigned to a group whose job it is to control and protect the land as well as those who live on it. There is an ethical relation to the land, and issues of collective rights are involved. Ownership involves trust that is higher than any market-based considerations. For the Quebec administrators, the concept of property derives from Western concepts of civil laws, individual rights, and capitalist economic principles. Owners of land have exclusive property rights to develop, exploit, sell as they see fit. The provincial government, while "granting" Native Americans the right of self-determination, remained in control of the definition of the terms and is not giving up its right to legislate land use (ibid.: 288). To the Native Americans, the choice between a French and an English government was no choice at all.

I suggest that some of the problem in "other" regions of Quebec has much to do with translation. If one just translates the terms literally, assuming land is land is land, then misunderstandings naturally arise. However, if one translates culturally, assuming difference and allowing room for maneuver, translation can serve to provide for openings and broader conceptual spaces. Historically, Euro-Americans wrote treaties assuming Western definitions of terms and then let government officials and law enforcement officials decide their implementation. When the language has been disputed, Euro-American courts and militaries have historically decided in favor of the European interpretation. But one could imagine rethinking translation to author a less ambiguous document, spelling out differences in concepts and finding terminology—such as concepts of trusteeship versus ownership—that allow for interaction and coexistence, and respect claims of difference. Herein I think the Québécois theater translators and feminists can help.

The situation in Quebec has well underscored the value of translation as a tool in any ethnic minority's building an identity, and marginalized peoples, be they discriminated against for language differences, ethnic backgrounds, or sexual orientations, can learn much from the Québécois translators and translation theorists. However, the difficult problem remains ahead. At the time of this writing, the future for the Quebec province/nation remains quite unstable. The Sovereigntists, the term currently used for those earlier referred to as Separatists, experienced a setback in the general election of 2007. Certain regroupings will have to take place, and new leaders will no doubt have to emerge. How does one open up that space between conceptual modes of thinking—between French and English, or between the logic of community and the logic of individual rights? What new coalitions and relations are possible? Here language policy and translation will have a role to play, not just to make promises of just and egalitarian societies, but to find a tangible way to construct those very cultures and to find a way out of hundreds of years of treaties and translations that have failed. If culture is always changing and always in transit, and if translation is one of the tools that can be used to reveal cultures' fluid nature, then translation might be viewed as a way out of the impasse created by institutions that have served to create rigidity and distrust. In the following chapter, I look at the case of Brazil, where another group of experimental translators and translation theorists found a way to incorporate the best aspects of European cultures as brought to them by the colonizers, yet to craft a separate and distinct path that allows the indigenous roots, ideas, and culture to flourish as well.

4 Cannibalism in Brazil

"Cannibalism," however increasingly in vogue among scholars as a metaphor for postcolonial studies, in fact derives from a modernist movement that dates back to the early 1920s. Known as the *movimento antropófago* (cannibalist movement), founded by José Oswald de Andrade Souza (1890–1954) in 1928 with the "Manifesto Antropófago," originally published in the first issue of the *Revista de Antropofagia* (de Andrade 1928), the group comprised just one of many avant-garde manifestos characteristic of the age, and intersects with modernist schools ongoing in Europe and the Americas at the time. While readers in the West are more than familiar with dadaism, expressionism, cubism, futurism, and vorticism, movements such as "cannibalism" and other related movements in Latin America, including *Pau-Brasil* (Brasilwood) and *Verde-Amarelo* (Green-Yellow), remained obscure internationally until resurrected by a group of translators such as the brothers Haroldo and Augusto de Campos in the mid-1960s, then by filmmakers such as Joaquim Pedro de Andrade, Glauber Rocha, and Nelson Pereira dos Santos in the late 1960s and early 1970s, musicians such as Caetano Veloso in the 1970s and 1980s, and most recently by critics and theorists, including Else Vieira, Sergio Bellei, Roberto Schwarz, and Nelson Ascher, in the 1980s and 1990s.

In 1920, French painter Francis Picabia (1879–1953) published a "Manifeste cannibale" in a Parisian journal named *Dadaphone* and later edited the review *Cannibale* as part of the Dadaist movement (Nunes 1984: 159; Bary 1991: 36). In his essay "Tupy or Not Tupy" (1987), Brazilian literary and film critic Randal Johnson suggests that Dadaists found cannibalism an aggressive conceit aimed at shocking the bourgeoisie. Futurists such as Marinetti related cannibalism with pre-Columbian rituals. While Oswald de Andrade was criticized for being heavily influenced by European artistic movements (ibid.: 46), to the point that one Brazilian critic, Menotti del Picchia, called the movement *Pau-Paris* (Picchia 1927; see also Athayde 1966), the Europeans' understanding of cannibalism differs from the Brazilians' concept. First, the Europeans were importing a foreign concept and adapting it to their own ideas; thus, the concept of cannibalism conveyed clichéd indigenous images used to shock the Europeans. For Brazilians, cannibalism combined native elements with colonial and postcolonial historical and socioreligious events. Anthropophagia became a vehicle with which to explore the past and raise questions regarding interpretations of Brazilian national and cultural evolution. Second, while cannibalism in Europe was exploited for its negative valences, symbolizing bloody and savage behavior, in Brazil it was more often seen in more *positive* terms, symbolizing the best virtues of the Amerindian race, which has survived despite being conquered. Tracing the blood of the Native American allowed access to multiple ethnic, moral, geographic, and political elements that are also part of the Brazilian identity. Finally, and perhaps most importantly, the difference in the concepts lies in the political attitude toward Europe. While the European metaphor continued to conceive of the cannibal as primitive, lacking civilization, exotic, strange, and foreign, to be subsumed and exploited by European artistic movements, the Brazilian metaphor was distinctly understood as a form of *resistance* to European culture. In Brazil, anthropophagia symbolized an end to the imitation and offered an alternative to the influence of European culture. Copying and importing artistic and sociopolitical forms died; creating new art and sociopolitical movements were born. Thus, the 1920s in Brazil marked the first step in the creation of an original Brazilian national culture and a separate Brazilian identity. Translation, which in the past had served as an uncritical medium by which to import European culture, became one of the artistic tools included in the new devouring process, not as a receptacle for European forms and ideas but as a vehicle to consume European ideas and then to reelaborate them in terms of native traditions and conditions. In sum, it marked the end of mental colonization and the beginnings of an independent identity in Brazil.

From a historical viewpoint, the "cannibalist" movement today is not so much a new, fashionable theory of the 1990s as a theory with a long and complex past. Religious and tribal customs rooted in non-European traditions, including complex references to indigenous leaders, gods, plants, natural resources, and myths, saturate anthropophagist writings and translations. Indeed, the very use of the term "cannibalist" carries a double meaning. First, it refers to the custom of the Tupi Indians (the Tupinambá Indians), one of the largest Native American groups in Brazil at the time of the conquest, of eating conquered warriors in order to absorb their strength. Second, it plays on the European pejorative notions of cannibalism as a barbaric and heretical act, one that continues to shock the so-called civilized (read Christian) Western world. Indeed, much of the entire colonization effort was aimed at civilizing heathens who committed sacrilegious acts; nearly all of the Tupi Indians were killed by the civilizing Christians. This double constitution lends the term its artistic power, allowing for play, parody, and polyvalence in ways that attract, in addition to translation studies scholars, contemporary scholars of both deconstruction and postcolonial studies. Just as Derrida talks about *pharmakon* as referring to both the poison and the cure, so too do the Brazilian cannibalists refer to cannibalism as both problem and cure. By using that which has been historically repressed by European culture and the colonized Brazilian mind, drinking the enemy's blood has become a useful concept, allowing access to modes of thought repressed politically and intellectually. Rather than suggesting that one can ever go back to an ideal pre-Columbian state, anthropophagia accepts aspects of European presence without forgetting native traditions, forms, and meanings.

The Tupinambá Indians who practiced cannibalistic acts were by no means "heathens" or irreligious in any way. In fact, the practice was highly religious, and in many ways akin to the Christian practice of communion, with its symbolic drinking of the blood of Christ. For the Tupi Indians, cannibalism had nothing to do with the European notion, which involves concepts of devouring, dismembering, and mutilation, but instead implied an act of taking back out of love, honor, and nourishment. Only the bravest and most virtuous soldiers were devoured. They would first be taken into the community to live among the families and children of the conquering tribe so that the people could learn virtuous behavior from the captured soldier. The final act of eating the brave soldier was symbolic as well as physical. Cannibalism was seen as a nourishing act in which the positive values of the brave but defeated soldier would be digested and absorbed and become part of the future physical and mental identity of the victorious community.

In his film *Como era gostoso o meu francês* [How Tasty Was My Little Frenchman], produced in Brazil in 1971, Nelson Pereira dos Santos provides one of the best portrayals of the Tupi culture. Dos Santos, part of the Brazil's *Cinema Nova* movement of the 1960s and 1970s, conducted extensive anthropological research on Amerindian tribes of Brazil and consulted historical depictions of such tribes, including one by Hans Staden, a German gunner on a Portuguese ship captured by the Tupinambá, who escaped to write the account *Hans Staden, The True History of His Captivity, 1557* (1929). Dos Santos reconstructed a complete Tupinambá village, with authentic sets and costumes based on paintings of the period. In the film, a Frenchman is captured and mistaken for a Portuguese soldier. He is taken to the Tupinambá village, where he lives with the chief's family, teaching the villagers many things, including how to use European weapons. He falls in love with the chief's daughter and is loved by her in return. Viewers who think his affectionate treatment by the family will help spare his life will be disappointed, for the love felt for the Frenchman only further underscores the village's resolve to carry out the ultimate act of reverence.

For the Brazilian writers, translators, and filmmakers, cannibalism has become one of the primary conceits for illustrating Brazilian cultural difference, bicultural development, and complex and often contradictory identity as a nation. By reinterpreting, rewriting, and translating their own culture, incorporating positive elements from both European and Brazilian traditions but at the same time questioning European sources, these writers have arrived at a theory of translation and identity formation that is historically rich, culturally diverse, and theoretically highly original, anticipating many of the debates characteristic of critical theory in the West today. Brazilian translation scholars emphasize polylingualism rather than monolingualism and complex hybrid cultural formation rather than segregated, nativist, and often xenophobic views. In the course of this chapter, I argue that the anthropophagist translation theorists well understand the double constitution of the cannibalist metaphor and the unique cultural possibilities opened by its advocates, possibilities that allow Brazilians, and by extension, other American subjects, to forge their own independent cultural identities.

The Cannibalist Manifesto

Oswald de Andrade's "Cannibalist Manifesto" (1928) is a complex document: playful, polemical, full of *double entendres*, and rich with indigenous cultural referents. One of its better translations is to be found in Leslie Bary's annotated English version titled "Oswald de Andrade's 'Cannibalist Manifesto'" (1991). In a short introduction, she contextualizes the document, explaining that the Brazilian modernist poet's manifesto was part of other avant-garde declarations of the time, including Mário de Andrade's "Prefácio Interessantíssimo" to his 1921 poetry volume *Paulicéia Desvairada*, and the editorial to the May 15, 1922 issue of *Klaxon* describing the "Semana de Arte Moderna" held in São Paulo earlier that year. Oswald de Andrade had published an earlier manifesto in 1924 titled "Manifesto da poesia Pau-Brazil" ["Manifesto of Brazilwood Poetry"] in which he talked about an "export-quality" poetry that would not copy European models but would find its sources in Brazilian history and popular culture. The *Pau-Brazil* movement opposed erudite and imitative verse that Oswald de Andrade associated with the Portuguese colonists and Brazilian literary elite, and instead looked for a counterweight in native originality and everyday life. Far from generating second-rate copies of Continental art, Oswald de Andrade called for a new, "agile and candid" form of modern poetry (Bary 1991: 35), with an emphasis on youth, new beginnings, originality, and creativity.

The Cannibalist Manifesto of 1928 was a more mature and polemical version of the earlier manifesto, without ignoring the playful aspects. Bary writes:

> The *MA (Manifesto Antropófago)* challenges the dualities of civilization/barbarism, modern/primitive, and original/derivative, which had informed the construction of Brazilian culture since the days of the colony. In the *Manifesto Antropófago*, Oswald subversively appropriated the colonizer's inscription of America as a savage territory which, once civilized, would be a necessarily muddy copy of Europe.
>
> (1991: 35)

Oswald's cannibalization rejects European notions of the idealized savage and instead offers a powerful, multifaceted, highly intelligent yet conflicted subject. Some examples of the tenets from the Manifesto include:

Cannibalism alone unites us. Socially. Economically. Philosophically.

* * *

Tupi or not tupi, that is the question.

* * *

I am only concerned with that which is not mine. Law of Man. Law of the cannibal.

* * *

It was because we never had grammars, nor collections of old plants. And we never knew what urban, suburban, frontier and continental were ...

* * *

We want the Carib Revolution. Greater than the French Revolution. The unification of all productive revolts for the progress of humanity. Without us, Europe wouldn't even have its meager declaration of the rights of man.

* * *

But we have never permitted the birth of logic among us.

* * *

The spirit refuses to conceive a spirit without a body. Anthropomorphism. Need for the cannibalistic vaccine. To maintain our equilibrium, against meridian religions. And against outside inquisitions.

* * *

We already had justice, the codification of vengeance. Science, the codification of Magic. Cannibalism. The permanent transformation.
(Andrade 1928: 38–39, trans. Bary)

The manifesto's points includes citations from Tupi poetry, juxtapositions of magic to logic, questions about progress measured by technology and machines, doubts about patriarchal structures, positive references to matriarchal cultures, redefinitions of concepts such as happiness, and valorizations of cannibalization as a way of absorbing qualities of the enemy, be it one's own, from abroad, or something sacred. Cannibalism is underscored as beginning with the carnal, moving through the sexual, arriving at friendship and comradery, and ending invariably in love and reverence (in its simultaneous irreverence). Cannibalism is viewed as indigenous, always juxtaposed against the "plague of supposedly cultured and Christianized peoples" (1991: 43).

The tone of Oswald de Andrade's manifesto is just as important as its content. The humor, parody, play, and irony become as important to the movement as the ideas. Indeed, the style reflects the meaning; the parody allows De Andrade to positively cite certain Europeans such as Montaigne, Rousseau, Freud, William James, and Herman Keyserline while rejecting others, including Jesuit missionaries such as Vieira and Father Anchieta, Portuguese kings/emperors such as Dom João VI and Dom Pedro I, and intellectuals such as Lévy-Bruhl and Goethe. The line "Tupi or not Tupi" illustrates the parody of Shakespeare, the double and triple meanings, the simultaneous irreverence and reverence, and the reference to repressed indigenous customs, as marked by the voiceless phonetic "p" sound indicative of the "voiceless" indigenous tribes of Brazil, versus the voiced phonetic "b" sound indicative of the commanding "voice" of the European master. Such a rewriting of European classics through the phonetic and cultural background of Brazil results in new meanings and insights unique to Brazil that get woven into a sophisticated translation practice that leads to new definitions of translation as transcreation and transculturalization. This replacement of European cultural icons with native symbols and fields of reference is characteristic of the cannibalist style, a devouring of Shakespeare and revitalization of Hamlet absorbed and transformed through the Brazilian experience. For Oswald de Andrade, the movement retained its youth and innocence while moving to the world stage, leading to a revolutionary movement that asked intellectuals to rethink issues of fascism, capitalism, communism, and imperialism facing the world at the time, and to open themselves up to other versions/visions of societal construction, gender, culture, and progress. While the movement splintered and faded during the 1930s and 1940s, it never completely died. Instrumental to this process of rethinking and the growth of the cannibalist movement as a leading, if not the leading, postcolonial theory of literature and culture has been the contribution of the poets and translators Haroldo and Augusto de Campos.

Translation and cannibalism: Haroldo de Campos

The anthropophagist movement in Brazil experienced a period of recession after its initial flurry during the 1920s. Many factors were involved, including a splintering of factions, with Oswald de Andrade turning to more leftist politics, even joining the Communist Party during the 1930s, and others becoming attracted to more conservative agendas, with some, such as Plínio Salgado, one of the founders of the *verde-amarelista* movement, turning to fascist movements, which were gaining popularity in Brazil at the time. Politically, during the post-World War I period Brazil was full of upheavals, including revolt at the Military School of Realengo in 1922, the outbreak of revolutions that carried to the state capital, São Paulo, in 1924, the rise to the presidency of Getúlio Vargas in 1930, further uprisings in the early 1930s, including those by constitutionalists in 1932 and another by communists in 1935, and finally Vargas's declaration of a dictatorship and the founding of the New State (*Estado Novo*) in 1937. Thus, the *Realpolitik* of the period ran counter to the revolutionary ideas in general and to the *antropófagist* Carib revolution in particular. Those who succeeded in gaining favor with the Vargas government were those modernists who in the end rejected the symbol of the cannibal and who argued that the true roots of Brazilian culture were not indigenous but rather Lusitanian (cf. Johnson 1987: 48). Menotti del Picchia, another *verde-amarelista*, wrote a column called "Let's Kill Peri" as early as 1927, proposing to kill the image of the cannibal as the primary metaphor of the movement and to substitute integration and compromise for revolution and conflict. Oswald de Andrade, while maintaining a critical stance, was more or less forced into the background.

The leaders of the movement to reevaluate and return the cannibalist metaphor to the cultural forefront were the two brothers Haroldo and Augusto de Campos, who rose to fame in the 1950s as concrete poets and translators, began theorizing literature and cultural studies in Brazil and Latin American in the 1960s, and continue to be influential today. At last count, Haroldo de Campos has written twelve books of poetry, eighteen of literary criticism, and fourteen of translations/transcreations, as well as numerous essays on theatre, cinema, and the plastic arts. His theory of literature, derived from his work in translation, and for which he has coined numerous metaphors, including "recreation," "transcreation," "transtextualization," "transparaization," "transillumination," and, most provocatively, "transluciferation mefistofáustica," resurrects and further develops the anthropophagist metaphor. In this section, I focus primarily on Haroldo de Campos's essays from the 1980s, such as "Transluciferçao mefistofáustica" (1981), a postscript to his translation of Goethe's *Faust*, published as *Deus e o Diabo no Fausto de Goethe* [God and the Devil in Goethe's *Faust*], "Transblanco: Reflexión sobre la transcreación de 'Blanco' de Octavio Paz, con una digresión sobre la teoría de la traducción del poeta mexicano" [Reflections on the transcreation of "Blanco" by Octavio Paz, with a digression on the Mexican poet's theory of translation] collected in *Diseminario* (1987), and "The Rule of Anthropophagy: Europe under the Sign of Devoration" (1986). I also refer to Augusto de Campos's introduction to his volume *Verso, reverso, controverso* [Verses, Reverses, Controversies] (1978a), in which he equally links the act of translation to anthropophagy and, by coining the concepts such as "intraduçao" (intratranslation), illustrates the interpenetrating nature of introducing new ideas or forms to any given culture. Else Vieira's work in presenting Haroldo de Campos's ideas to the English-speaking world in essays such as "Liberating

Calibans: Readings of *Antropofagia* and Haroldo de Campos' Poetics of Transcreation" (1999) informs the reading that follows.

The De Campos brothers' theory derives initially from practice; during the 1950s, they, with other writers such as Décio Pignatari and José Lino Grünewald, formed a group called "Noigrandes," an unknown Provençal term Ezra Pound was struggling to decipher in his translation work and which appears in "Canto XX" of *The Cantos* (Gentzler 1993: 192–193). For the De Campos brothers, the term signified poetry (and culture) in progress rather than finished versions. They started a journal also named *Noigrandes* in São Paulo and began making contacts with poets, translators, musicians, and sculptors in Brazil and abroad. Augusto de Campos, Décio Pignatari, and Haroldo de Campos coauthored the text *Teoria de poesia concreta: Textos críticos e manifestos 1950–60* (1975), summarizing the work of the group during its most productive years. Their essays, translations, and original concrete poems, which originally appeared primarily in publications such as the "Suplemento Dominica" of the *Journal do Brasil* (Rio de Janeiro), the page "Invenção" of the *Correio Paulistana* (São Paulo), and the "Suplemento Literário" of *O Estado de São Paulo*, as well as other Brazilian and international newspapers and journals, are included, as we see a theory of poetry evolving into a theory of translation and of culture. The members' translations of authors such as John Donne, Andrew Marvel, Ezra Pound, e.e. cummings, James Joyce, Stephan Mallarmé, William Carlos Williams, Marianne Moore, Christian Morgernstern, and Kitasono Katsue showed an intense focus not only on the content of the poetry but also on the style of the poems. They also published essays by international authors, including work by Pierre Boulez, Walter Kadinsky, Eugen Grominger, Ezra Pound, Edgar Allan Poe, and Max Bense, whose translations and critical essays were similar to those of the Noigrandes group (Campos, Pignatari, and Campos 1975: 175). It was a period of much experimental activity, in which numerous meetings, readings, manifestos, expositions, concerts, and conversations were held about the form, function, composition, and meaning of art. Oswald de Andrade's concepts of absorbing and recreating the best work of the European and North American writers remained fundamental throughout. Foreign authors' methods cannibalized included Ezra Pound's ideogrammic method of translating Chinese and Japanese verse, which was also used for the composition of *The Cantos*; e.e. cummings's methods of nonstandard capitalization, inverted syntax, and phonetic games; Stéphane Mallarmé's methods of subdividing ideas and his prismatic graphic style; and James Joyce's methods of multilayered meanings, multilingual metaphors, and phonetic experimentation.

The creative translation theory and practice of the De Campos brothers in the 1950s evolved into a theory of cultural evolution and identity in the 1960s. The discourse shifts from the influence of European theories to an increased interest in the language and ideas of Brazilian-born writers, including Oswald de Andrade and Mário de Andrade (not related). In 1967,

Haroldo de Campos published *Oswald de Andrade – Trechos escolhidos* [Oswald de Andrade: Selected Passages] and in 1973 *Morphologia do Macunaíma* [Morphology of *Macunaíma*, a "novel" by Mário de Andrade], an assessment of the style of two most important anthropophagistas of the 1920s in Brazil, resulting in the elevation of cannibalism from a literary method to a critical cultural intervention. According to translation studies scholar Else Vieira, the timing of this evolution was not accidental (1999: 102), for it is at this moment that the term "Third World" started to be used with increasing regularity internationally, but with little recognition of cultural specificities. As the Cold War intensified (the Cuban missile crisis occurred in 1962) and as binary oppositions, such as socialist/capitalist and developing/developed, increasingly dominated discussions of global situations, concepts of "Third World" became reified and theories of pluralities and heterogeneity began to disappear. Choices offered to Latin American scholars seem limited to those of the progressive left, heavily invested in communist movements, or those of capitalism, heavily invested in free economic models. Both derive from non-Latin American sources. Vieira cites Haroldo de Campos as arguing that cannibalism "does not involve a submission (an indoctrination), but a transculturation, or better, a 'transvalorization': a critical view of History as a negative function (in Nietzsche's sense of the term), capable of appropriation and of expropriation, de-hierarchization, deconstruction" (Haroldo de Campos 1986: 44, quoted by Vieira 1999: 103). As Oswald de Andrade's cannibalism differed from the cannibalism of the European Dadaists, so too does Haroldo de Campos's cannibalism begin to distinguish itself from its European and North American influences.

This rethinking of cannibalism begins with a rethinking of Brazilian identity in light of widespread notions of what is progress in the new modern world. Haroldo de Campos begins his essay "The Rule of Anthropophagy: Europe under the Sign of Devoration" (1986) with a reflection upon Octavio Paz's essay "Invention, Underdevelopment, Modernity" (1973). Paz takes issue with both Mexican and European critics who use the word "underdevelopment" to describe the situation in Latin American culture. "Underdevelopment" connotes notions of social and economic progress in the North that Paz would like to question. He writes:

> Aside from the fact that I am very much averse to reducing the plurality of cultures and the very destiny of man to a single, industrial model, I have serious doubts as to whether the relationship between economic prosperity and artistic experience is one of cause and effect.
> (1973: 19, quoted by Haroldo de Campos 1986: 43)

Certainly, writers such as Paz, Neruda, Borges, Fuentes, García Márquez, and De Campos, despite the economic status of their respective countries, do not consider their artistic work as in any sense lacking. In the case of Brazil,

Haroldo de Campos turns to Oswald de Andrade's *Antropofagia* as a "philosophical-existential" vision, enabling one to rethink the national in its relationship with the international. Rather than the idealized version of the "noble savage," Oswald's vision, according to De Campos, is that of a "bad savage," one that devours white texts and ideas. No longer a passive consumer, indoctrinated by European ideas and values, Oswald de Andrade's consumer is active, using European ideas not to replace their own but to fortify and renew their own ideas and images. This idea of an active consumer serves as a metaphor for the active process of translation—not as a slavish reiteration of the source text's ideas and forms but as creative participation in the authoring of the translated text, crafting a text that will speak to specific readers in a particular receiving culture. In sum, what Haroldo de Campos and Octavio Paz call for is a new model for studying Latin American culture that does not subsume all writing under some sort of generic definition of the "other" or "developing" that applies across cultures but rather allows for real and specific cultural differences in real and specific cultural conditions.

The concrete poetry phase, especially the translation work, of the De Campos brothers was instrumental to the revitilazation of the cannibalist metaphor. As Oswald de Andrade "Brazilwoodized" Italian futurism and French cubism, so too have the De Campos brothers "Brazilianized" many modern European canonical texts. Haroldo de Campos writes, "With Concrete Poetry, the difference (the national) came to be the operating space of the new synthesis of the universal code. More than a heritage of poets, this is the case of assuming, criticizing and 'chewing over' a poetics" (1986: 51). The Brazilian concrete poets changed the direction of the dialogue. Rather than merely an old pattern of simple cross-cultural influence from the old world to the new, a whole new process is opened up. The Brazilian authors, who in European eyes represent a "minor" culture, appropriated the entire code and reclaimed it as their own. Haroldo de Campos talks of the European modernist tradition as an "empty shoe" just waiting for a new subject to step into (ibid.: 52). When the Brazilians moved into this space, revitalizing it first and foremost via translation, all sorts of new possibilities opened up.

For Haroldo de Campos, the translation process is always creative, much like original writing. Translation reorganizes the signs, sounds, and images of the text, therefore leading to new insights and possibilities of thought. This view of translation has led to a rich theory in which Haroldo de Campos incessantly develops new metaphors to describe the transtextual process by which he absorbs and transforms. For example, in his translations of the Hebrew Bible, he talks about how he "Portuguises" the Hebrew language and "Hebrewizes" Portuguese. For example, in order to capture the original's ability to combine the high written word of God with the familiar and colloquial of man, de Campos transtextualizes the Hebrew by invoking the style and rhythm of Brazilian writers such as Guimarães

Rosa and João Cabral de Melo Neto, who have incorporated popular speech in novels such as *Grande Sertão* and plays such as *Autos* (cf. Vieira 1999: 105–106). Similarly, in his translation of "Paradiso" from Dante's *Divine Comedy*, Haroldo de Campos develops metaphors of "transillumination" and "transparadisation" to describe his process of translation. In his translations of Homer, he derives metaphors of "transhelenization"; and in his translations of imagist Chinese poetry, he refers to the process as "reimagination." But in his translations of Goethe's *Faust* we find his most symptomatic and aggressive metaphors. Extending the cannibalist metaphor, translation here is viewed as a "transfusion of blood" (1981: 208) and the process is described with its most provocative (sac)religious connotations, using metaphors such as "transluciferation mephistofáustica."

Deus e o Diabo no Fausto de Goethe (1981) is a curious book, for it contains in equal parts translation, literary interpretation, and translation theory. The first third of the book is a literary translation of the final scenes of Goethe's *Faust, part two*, beginning with the graveyard scene just after the death of Faust, followed by the battle between Mephistopheles and the angels for the spirit of Faust. Faust, of course, has made a pact with the devil; in exchange for fulfilling his desires for lust and power, Faust has agreed to sell his soul. In this final scene, however, a reversal occurs. The sworn agreement is not fulfilled; Faust is abducted by God's angels, leaving Mephistopheles wondering to whom he can appeal for justice. For most critics, the scene suggests that despite human weaknesses and curiosities, Faust's inherent noble character surfaces, that his ceaseless drive for knowledge and understanding saves him from eternal damnation. The ending parallels the Christian belief that although all humans may be sinners, there is always the possibility of final redemption. De Campos, however, is a "bad" savage, and he rejects this interpretation, as he explains in the next section of his "translation."

The second and the largest section of *Deus e o Diabo no Fausto de Goethe*, comprises two longer essays. The first, titled "A escritura mefistofélica" [Mephistophelian Writing], covers the various influences and versions of *Faust*, and the second essay, titled "Bufoneria transcendental: O riso das esferas" [Transcendental Buffoonery: The Smile of the Spheres], interprets and explains De Campos's reading of *Faust II*. The first essay covers well-known source material, including the popular folk legend from the sixteenth century, through early versions such as Johann Spiess's *Volksbuch* of 1587 and Christopher Marlow's *The Tragical History of Doctor Faustus* of 1588 as well as multiple other popular German versions in oral, puppet, and popular theater versions (Campos 1981: 73–74). De Campos's point is that Goethe himself freely translated and cannibalized earlier versions of his classic. In the case of the Gretchen scenes in *Faust I*, Goethe was even accused of plagiarizing a song of Ophelia occurring in *Hamlet*, Act IV, Scene 5, which Goethe freely admitted in a conversation with Johann Peter Eckermann on 18 January 1825, asking rhetorically why he should not be able to do such a thing (Haroldo de Campos 1981: 75). De Campos connects Goethe's unabashed literal incorporation of source material from Shakespeare to his concept of translation as "plagiatropy," which he developed in the 1960s during his work on Oswald de Andrade and expanded upon in 1978 while teaching at Yale (Haroldo de Campos 1981: footnote 75–76; see also Vieira 1999: 107); are related both to his cannibalistic theory of translation. As great writers draw on the best writers in their own national tradition for source material, so, too, do translators draw upon the best material in source language traditions, but then incorporate that material (in the bodily sense) into the best of their own traditions. For De Campos, the term "plagiarism" (derived from *plagiarius*) invokes etymological corporeal roots such as man stealing, kidnapping, and blood consuming), as well as more oblique postmodern connections such as parallelism, obliqueness, and parody.

De Campos also selected Goethe's *Faust* to translate because it destabilizes any set notion of a unified original. Goethe worked on the *Faust* tragedy over a period of sixty years, beginning with his interest as a student in Leipzig, through the pre-Weimar publication of *Urfaust* in 1773, then a renewed interest during his Italian trip (1786–1788), resulting in *Faust: Ein Fragment* in 1790, and finally the first definitive version *Faust, erster Teil* in 1806 at the height of his classical period in Weimar. *Faust, zweiter Teil* follows some twenty-five years later, in 1831, completed before his death and published only posthumously. Haroldo de Campos points out that the work must be a hybrid and contradictory work, containing an amalgamation of ideas developed during different periods of Goethe's life. De Campos discusses Goethe's Romantic *Sturm und Drang* period, his travels in Italy, his more conservative classical period in Weimar with his friendship with Schiller, and his subsequent period as a government official in Weimar, by which he effectively destabilizes any set notion of a unified "original" or an inherently single national influence. With images of Satan borrowed from the Gothic and the Middle Ages, love scenes and witch scenes inspired by *Macbeth* and *Hamlet*, wedding scenes and *Walpurgisnacht* scenes borrowed from images of Roman and Italian carnivals, *Faust* for Haroldo de Campos contains multiple intertextual fragments interwoven to take on a dynamic polyphonic and multilingual quality. Mephistophelian writing and translation thus entails, for De Campos, elements of plagiarism, parody, polyphony, and carnivalization, all of which he highlights in his translation, thereby contradicting the "higher" spiritual and aesthetic aspirations emphasized by most critics.

"Transcendental Buffoonery," the second essay of the second section, carries Mephistophelian writing to higher power and more fully explicates the selection of the text presented in De Campos's opening chapter. In contrast to the many critics, including Eckermann, who tend to see *Faust II* as proving a Catholic/Christian salvation from sin (invariably viewed as a thirst for knowledge) committed in the first part, or others, such as Adorno and Benjamin, who see a utopian/Hegelian transcendental resolution of competing dialectical opposites, De Campos seems less inclined to resolve or synthesize Goethe's conflicting ideas. De Campos picks the final scene beginning with the *Grablegung* [Internment] precisely to juxtapose images of grotesque humor and divine sublimation. For De Campos, Mephistopheles and his band of fallen angels, who are guarding the grave of Faust, play out a "medieval mock mystery" of "impetuous buffoonery." Their blasphemous cries and obscene gestures, while lending drama to the high seriousness of the scene, recall comic-erotic parodies and precisely the popular verse forms that inspired Goethe in the first place. The scene begins with the "Lemuren," [Lemurs], nocturnal hybrid half-man, half-spirit creatures of the dead, who are derived from Roman mythology and who, in the translation, are comically complaining about the poor quality of the tomb they themselves are digging for Faust. The section translated continues through Mephistopheles's soliloquies, called "ravings" by critics because Mephisto blasphemously calls the good angels witches and devils for going back on their word, but which De Campos points out are highly rational arguments about how unjust such a last-minute pardon, reneging on the original pact, was. In his translation, De Campos also highlights the homoerotic passages of the love Mephistopheles exudes for his co-hosts as well as the perverse love he feels for the androgynous adolescent angels, further complicating Christian and Western philosophic interpretations. The erotics continue to the conclusion, where Faust ascends not to some sort of Father in Heaven, but to the *Ewig-Weibliche* [eternal feminine], a kind of a "Triumph of Venus." Here De Campos sees Goethe parodying the patriarchal Christian belief system ingrained in nineteenth-century German culture, something that was less clear during Germany's preclassical period. He also reads Goethe as parodying himself, or at least the figure he had become in German society; Goethe died in 1832, less than one year after finishing *Faust II*. De Campos's *Faustus*, rather than concluding with a positive, quasi-Olympian hero, remains full of ambiguities; rather than ending with resolutions, the conflicts remain open-ended and enigmatic. The comic, the "buffoonery," and the carnival aspects do not get sublimated into some sort of higher order but remain contemporaneously present, ironically smiling upon our hero to the end, hence the title of de Campos's second essay. In De Campos's translation, the trace of the diabolic remains unerased.

The third and final section of *Deus e o Diabo*, titled "Transluciferação mefistofáustica" [Mephistofaustian Transluciferation], is actually a postscript, but, as with much translation theory, in such "marginal" prefaces and postscripts lie key pronouncements regarding translation. The unique addition to the theory that Haroldo de Campos brings to bear is the acceptance of the "satanical" element in translation: whereas most translation theories tend toward the passive on the one hand or toward the angelic/transcendental on the other, de Campos claims that translation should not be submissive to or sublimate the original. Rather, translation needs to break with the straitjacket of a theory based upon some sort of ur-metaphysical presence and admit to its diabolic enterprise. Translation, according to de Campos, is always a hybrid activity: it invariably transgresses the limits of signs and the seemingly natural relation between form and content. Basing his theory upon Walter Benjamin's "Task of the Translator," who reverses the hierarchy between original and translation, suggesting that it is only via translation that the original lives on, that without the translation the original would cease, thereby making the original beholden to the translation, De Campos pushes Benjamin's thought one step further: translation, according to De Campos, is less an act of synthesizing or an act of resolution of the contradictions than a radical operation of transcreation ("operação radical de transcriação," 1981: 18) that creates new, tangential lines of communication. De Campos describes these offshoots with metaphors of flashes of light, sparks flying, a volatile process culminating in a text that "usurps" the original (ibid.: 180). While attracted to the Benjaminian argument liberating translation from its subservience to the source text, De Campos remains skeptical of Benjaminian concepts of both "pure language" and the messianic overtones of his theory. Distancing himself from metaphysical concepts that constrain thinking about translation, Haroldo de Campos turns to theories such as those of Derrida and Nietzsche to develop a theory that foregrounds the pragmatic intersemiotic operations of translation without the metaphysical overtones (ibid.: 180). The primary process, according to De Campos, is one of reinscribing or reprojecting the language and the poetry in a *different* tradition, during which the translator is viewed as a choreographer, one open to the play and possibilities of language (ibid.: 182). The translucideration metaphor picks up on the fires ignited by the sparks flying; "Mephisto," too, etymologically contains the root "photo," but in a malevolent sense. Herein lies the cannibalistic notion extended by De Campos: translation is viewed in a similar fashion to some of Ezra Pound's translations, as a transfusion of blood from the original to the translation (cf. Kenner 1954; Campos 1981: 208; Gentzler 1993: 20), giving nourishment not to a copy but to a free-standing, independent, new work of art. In the process, translation ends up usurping the original, or, as he phrases it in the conclusion to the essay, "obliterating the original," killing by devouring the European source. De Campos concludes the essay with "A essa desmemória parricidea chamarei 'transluciferação'" [I call this parricidical dismemory "translucideration," 1981: 209], killing off the Western canonical father/author as well as the divine inspiration empowering that figure.

The process of obliteration occurs by rechanneling the source material through the language, art, and customs of the target culture, in this case Brazil. The title of De Campos's translation is indicative of the process: *Deus e o Diabo no Fausto de Goethe* not only draws attention to his juxtaposition of both the heavenly and the diabolical in his translation but also connects

Goethe's work to Glauber Rocha's film *Deus e o Diabo na Terra do Sol* (literally "God and the Devil in the Land of the Sun," but translated as *Black God, White Devil* in the English version of the film), familiar to all Brazilians (Vieira 1999: 106). Thus, the image of Goethe's *Faust* is filtered through contemporary Brazilian cinema before the reader even gets to the text. Additionally, Haroldo de Campos's name appears on the cover of the book not as translator but as the author, calling into question traditional notions of the concept of the "author." The book actually has two cover pages: the first again lists Haroldo de Campos as the author, this time as giving a reading of the poem accompanied by a transcreation of the poem. Only the second cover page cites Goethe as the author, and then, in smaller print, lists De Campos as "transcreator."

The translation itself is remarkably true to the original. In fact, if anything can be said about the translation, it is that De Campos is *more* faithful to the original than many previous translators: he works hard to capture the meaning, the rhyme, the alliterations, the tone, the puns, and the neologisms. The carnival aspect of the final scene is present in the original, though often omitted in translation. The erotics, especially Mephisto's homoerotic inclinations, are also manifestly present in the original, though seldom highlighted in translation. However, De Campos does freely adopt the best of the Brazilian literary tradition to find a parallel style, and Brazilian readers quickly recognize verse forms and everyday speech of writers such as João Cabral de Melo Neto or the neologisms and verbal play of the concrete poets. Indeed, one of De Campos's goals, similar to Pound's goals as a translator, was to find the right persona for his translation. In this sense, his notion of parody, plagiarism, parallel text, and his complex sense of national identity come into play. As Goethe drew upon Germanic culture for roots and allusions, so too does Haroldo de Campos draw upon Brazilian traditions. Going back to the Brazilian poet Sousândrade (1833–1902), the father of creative translation in Brazil, who would insert verse forms of Camões, Francisco Manoel de Melo, Antonio Ferreira, and others in his translations, Haroldo de Campos (1981: 191) finds a Brazilian voice for his persona, one nourished by Goethe but nevertheless retaining its own identity. Thus, the translation is both a new work and a translation, authored by de Campos but based on Goethe. *Deus e o Diabo no Fausto de Goethe* both is and is not an original work: while often a quite literal translation from the original, it is new in the sense of becoming a hybrid text that both valorizes and kills off its predecessor in precisely the same sense that Oswald de Andrade reconstrued his concept "cannibalism."

Herein lie the roots for a new theory of culture that is multilingual, intersemiotic, and interdisciplinary, leading to multiple cross-cultural connections, some of which flow from the Old World to the New, and others of which flow the opposite direction. In music, Pierre Boulez comes to Brazil and meets various writers and painters, discussing art, poetry, as well as music in the process. As the magazine *Noigrandes* was read in Europe and the United States, influencing musicians such as Stockhausen and John Cage, who "prepared" the piano, allowing percussion to enter the realm of classical piano, so too have the De Campos brothers' theories of translation begun to reach postcolonial studies scholars internationally. Many of the theories developed in Brazil *precede* their similar development in Euro-North American critical circles. For example, theories of intertextualization in Brazil preceded those by Kristeva and others in Europe. Theories deconstructing the original and challenging metaphysical presence were being worked out in Brazil before, or at least parallel to, similar theories in France by the *Tel Quel* group. In fact, deconstruction arrived in Brazil long before it arrived in the United States. The elevation of Mephistopheles to a kind of antihero to the positive European tradition and the further development of the cannibal metaphor into a parricidal disremembering that transmutes meaning and values allow, in an ironic fashion, for new openings, especially for ideas and forms taking shape in cultures outside of the Eurocentric traditions and canons.

Derrida and De Campos

Much within the artistic impulses and experiments with language behind Haroldo de Campos's work derives from modernism, yet because of his breaking down of boundaries between European and New World oppositions, many have come to think of him as a postmodern thinker whose ideas often complement and precede those of Continental philosophers such as Jacques Derrida. The two were familiar with one another's work; both participated in a series of seminars held in Montevideo, Uruguay, in the fall of 1985 and collected in the anthology *Diseminario: La desconstrucción, otro descubrimiento de América* (1987). Derrida presented a paper called "Nacionalidad y nacionalismo filosófico" followed by Haroldo de Campos talking about "Más allá del principio de la nostalgia (Sehnsucht)" and then "Transblanco: Reflexión sobre la transcreación de 'Blanco' de Octavio Paz, con una digresión sobre la teoría de la traducción del poeta mexicano." The seminar ostensibly was to introduce deconstruction to the Americas, and other participants included Emir Rodríguez Monegal (perhaps his last conference before his death from cancer in 1985), J. Hillis Miller, and Geoffrey Hartman. But, as became clear in the subtitle of the conference—"Another Discovery of America"—deconstruction had already arrived in the Americas. Topics addressed in the seminars quickly turned to issues of nationalism and identity, and, perhaps surprisingly to some critics, translation, led by Derrida's opening remarks.

During the 1980s, critics tried frequently to get Derrida to take a position regarding nationalism and with regard to Marxism. However, due in large part to the predominantly binary thinking involved between First and Third World, between developed and underdeveloped countries, the role of the superpowers, and the plethora of Cold War dichotomies, Derrida invariably declined. In Montevideo, he broke his silence on both topics. It is of vital interest that he approached both topics through the theme of translation. His talk "Nacionalidad y nacionalismo filosófico" discusses nationalism not from the perspective of social or historical studies but from the perspective of translation, specifically the translation of the languages of philosophy. Thus, Derrida deals with the same cultural and philosophical issues using the same vehicle—translation—to displace and destabilize traditional notions about nation as Haroldo de Campos does in his work on literary and cultural theory.

"Nacionalidad y nacionalismo filosófico" begins with what Derrida calls the scandal of philosophy, namely that it presumes to consider itself essentially a universal and cosmopolitan field, one that is not interested in national differences and social idiosyncrasies, or, if it is, only under certain provisional and "inessential," often accidental, conditions (1987a: 27). This position is doubly ironic when philosophy, deemed to focus on universal truths, must cross linguistic boundaries in order to validate its claims. For Derrida, this dual constitution—uninterested in national differences yet at the same time dependent on national differences—raises the question of what is the language of philosophy. As De Campos has found by translating modern European poetry, a concrete poem or a surreal poem in Europe does not have one universal meaning; when translated to Latin America, because of its incorporation into another idiom with a new range of sounds and semiotic associations, the meaning necessarily changes.

Derrida's raising the question of what is the language of philosophy leads naturally to the question of what is a national language. Does philosophical thought have a natural, national language? Or does it transcend national boundaries? This in turn leads to speculation on the question of what is a nation, and the audience has arrived at Derrida's topic for his essay. The concept of nation is further problematized by Derrida's raising of questions about what constitutes a people, a race, or a state. Even if one could answer any of Derrida's questions about nationality with clarity, the problem of philosophy's natural idiom is still not resolved. The paradox for Derrida revolves around the idea that even in today's world, with an increase in communication between institutions, schools, and national languages, and an increase in the quantity and quality of translation, he finds that the limits of nationalities and the divisions between nation-states have never been more prominent. While interchanges have resulted in more deformations and hybridizations, the search for national identity, for affirmation of existing boundaries, the revindication of existing nationalities is always present. Even deconstruction, he points out, with its strategies of breaking down such positions, has been absorbed into national politics: Derrida critically cites the numerous examples in which deconstruction has been affiliated with Eastern religious practices such as Zen or connected with Chinese nationalist thought (1987: 30–31).

According to Derrida, there are no guarantees that one can ever finally determine that entity often referred to as "national identity." The topic of the essay, and the topic of the discussions of deconstruction in Latin America held in Montevideo, question the existence of the concept of "nation." Derrida shifts his focus to begin to look at the history of the concept of nation in philosophical discourse and the translation of the concept across borders. By looking at international roots of definitions of the term "nation," one discovers regional differences and the indeterminate nature of the concept. Deconstruction, while not offering a solution to the problem or an alternative politics, does displace and disorganize the question to the point that fundamental assumptions regarding nationalism and/or regional ontologies disintegrate. The problem for Derrida concerns those authorities —the sciences, the humanities, and, especially in the context of this essay, the field of philosophy—because they tend to separate the international and the intranational from the national.

In the paradoxical situation of today, when, in light of increased international communication, often via translation, pretensions of national identity seem increasingly impenetrable, Derrida finds it helpful to begin asking questions such as: When did such an insistence upon nationalization begin? What is the urgency today? How do nationalization movements today differ from those of the past? Of the sixteenth century? Of the eighteenth century? After the two world wars? While cultural studies scholars in Latin America embrace such questions, many professional European philosophers resist such questioning, which invariably leads to the instability and the arbitrariness of concepts such as nationality and nationalism. In his Montevideo essay, Derrida "discovers" the Americas, where borders defining nations have shifted constantly, ethnic backgrounds are varied and multifarious, regional groups have different interests than federal governments, and language identification is more closely affiliated with the colonizing power than with the autonomous, "independent" state. His findings coincide with new investigations of translation phenomena in the Americas, which this book attempts to sketch, and how they function differently in the Americas.

The philosophic concept of nationalism, as traced by Derrida, goes back to German roots. He cites Johann Gottlieb Fichte's work, including his *Addresses to the German People* (1808), as an example of the rise of the concept of liberal nationalism that predominated in Europe during the nineteenth century. In Fichte's work, Derrida sees the definition of the nationalist as patriotic and cosmopolitan assuming universal proportions. Concepts such as nation (*Staat*), people (*Volk*), origin (*Ursprung*), Federal Republic (*Bund*), and consciousness (*Bewußtsein*) not only become ingrained in German thinking but are exported, especially in philosophical circles, as universal concepts, influencing not only nineteenth-century revolutionary thought in the Americas, but also the French Revolution of 1848 and the establishment of the Second Republic. They continue to exert influence on a series of German revolutions in the latter part of the nineteenth century, resulting in the Frankfurt Parliament, which favored German unification. Important concepts regarding what is German (*Heimat/ Deutsch/Land*) and what is foreign (*Fremd/Undeutsch/Ausland*) also arose during this period and continued to influence discussions of nation and identity, with disastrous geopolitical results in the twentieth century.

According to Derrida, the first person to begin to question such definitions was Karl Marx. In *The German Ideology* (1947 [1845]), Marx and Engels find suspect reasoning that allows any philosopher or politician to discuss the concept of a country or a nation that "represents" or "identifies with" any sort of universalized individual human who has come to embody this "people" (*Volk*). Instead, Marx questions not only those humanists who universalize concepts of liberal nationalism but also those socialists who claim some sort of universal socialism, especially those who idealize certain North American peoples for their "progressive" legislation. For Derrida, the paradox of North America is that while resisting European invasions and purporting to be a place for freedom and liberal democracy, a form of reactionary nationalism has developed in the United States, reminiscent of the early nineteenth-century German nationalism.

For Derrida, because the very definition of North American liberal democracy is one derived from translation (see Chapter 2), by borrowing such philosophic concepts from the revolutionary thinkers in Germany and France, the United States has also translated the metaphysical structures underlying such concepts with their universal applications. Thus, the resistance to European forms of nationalism becomes one of the most powerful affirmations of the very philosophical concept of nationalism, hence the title of Derrida's essay (1987a: 46). The goal of translation is to import difference, in this case to devalorize certain notions of European nationalism and identity, but borrowing the terms as well as the assumed universal notions carried by the terms means that what ends up being translated is more of the same.

This philosophic discussion of translation, philosophy, nationalism, and the Americas is continued by Haroldo de Campos in his contribution to the Montevideo seminar. In the essay "Más allá del principio de la nostalgia (*Sehnsucht*)" [Beyond the Nostalgia Principle (Desire)], De Campos discusses key philosophical and aesthetic terms as they occur in the work of Georg Lukács's *Theory of the Novel* (1971) and Walter Benjamin's "The Task of the Translator" (1969a). As the philosopher, according to Lukács, in the process of seeking some transcendental unity, posits some sort of archetypical fatherland, nostalgically desiring a reconciliation of the heterogeneous traits into one homogeneous whole, so too does the translator, according to De Campos's reading of Benjamin, posit a messianic moment of transparency in the process of translation (1987: 135–136). Benjamin's concept of a "pure language" and the "language of truth" accessed through translation, is viewed in much the same way as Lukács's concept of the "philosophic genius" in which "totality" is revealed. In an era of modernism and a crisis of thought concerning any sort of higher religious or philosophic order, philosophers, as translators, read between the lines of the text of culture or a work of art to arrive at some sort of "other" text, some sort of restitution of the human in the Garden of Eden.

De Campos calls this grasping for unities in the face of the modern condition a "metaphysical gesture" and a "theological resurrection." Benjamin, resisting the notion that the translation needs to be subservient to the original, posits another form for translation, one which accesses that hidden relation of all languages to each other, their occult complementary and integrated nature before separation into a multitude of vernaculars. The "task of the translator" thus is to access this "pure language," translators thereby being liberated from slavishly adhering to the source text, and allowed to reveal the occluded transcendental signifier. De Campos calls this task "angelic" in keeping with his messianic/cabalistic interpretation of Benjamin.

This theological movement in Benjamin's work, as well as the idealistic, neo-Platonic gestures in Lukács's work, is juxtaposed with what De Campos calls "the Luciferian usurpation" (1987: 143–144). Beginning with the antihumanism, negative theology, and negative anthropology of writers/philosophers such as Heidegger, de Campos detects a kind of "anti-communication literalism." He sees traces of this literalism in certain ironic passages in Benjamin, for example in his emphasis on the "monstrous" translations of Hölderlin. Here, rather than seeing some sort of messianic/angelic revelation of some transcendental signifier, De Campos sees Benjamin as surreptitiously favoring the demonic translator, the one who "threatens" and even "ruins" the original via a strict adherence to the literal over the transcendental. Translation becomes the ultimate act of hubris for the Luciferian translator, transforming the original into a translation of a translation, similar to Derrida's concept of *différance*, in which all original writing occurs an infinite movement of difference (Campos 1987: 144). De Campos writes:

> Sería ésta—así la llamó—la última *hubris* del traductor luciferino: transformar, por un instante, el original en la traducción de su traducción. Reponer en escena el origen y la originalidad como "plagiotropía": como "movimiento infinito de la diferencia" (Derrida) y reproponer la mímesis como instancia de la producción de esa diferencia.
>
> [This would be the so-called ultimate hubris of the Luciferian translator: to transform, in an instant, the original in the translation of its translation. To restore in the scene the origin and its originality as "plagiatropy," as "an infinite movement of *différance*" (Derrida) and to restore mimesis as a first stage in the production of this difference]
>
> (1987: 144; translation mine)

The connection of De Campos's thinking about philosophy, translation and his *Deus e o Diabo no Fausto de Goethe* should be becoming increasingly clear. The irony below the surface of Benjamin's essay recalls Borges's use of Western fiction forms to ironically question the metaphysical assumptions behind the scenes of most European novelists (see Chapter 5). If metaphysical philosophers can discern an intertext between the lines that recalls Platonic forms and ideas, so too can the Luciferian translator read between the lines to discern the fragmentary and heterogeneous nature of the original and use those semiotic markers to equally destabilize any notion of a unified language, nation, or cultural heritage of the present. By adhering to the literal, the translator can access multiple symbolic relations among the signs, their fragmentary nature, "in ruins" as it were, which preclude the possibility, however philosophically or theologically ordained, of their transcendental and harmonious reconstitution. The "monstrous" literal translations of Hölderlin point to the possibility of constructing another history for Latin America, not one characterized by linearity and homogeneity but one as a series of ruptures and open to the possibility of transgressive translation and new intersemiotic configurations in the future. By avoiding the culturally transparent equivalent and instead transplanting the terms, "cannibalizing" them, the translator allows the words and symbols to take on new meanings. Translation for De Campos is viewed as a medium that does not correspond to religious or philosophical writing; rather, it is more similar to original writing, just as inventive, spontaneous, and irreverent. The goal is a re-version, a reinvention, of the source text, reconstituting the movement of signs in one multilingual culture in another, equally multilingual culture, transcreating the original even at the risk of adding phonetic, syntactic, and/or semantic connotations that resonate differently and highly creatively in the target culture.

Other cannibals

While Haroldo de Campos is perhaps the leading translator and theoretician of the anthropophagist movement, there are many others who subscribe to a similar poetics of translation. Haroldo de Campos's brother Augusto de Campos is closely identified with the movement in both theory and practice. In the text *Verso, reverso, controverso* (1978a), Augusto de Campos presents his anthropophagized translations, including translations from Provençal poets, Ezra Pound, Andew Marvel, John Donne, and William Blake. The preface is often cited, wherein Augusto de Campos gives his version of cannibalism, a very organic form of devouring with love, of getting inside the skin of the original. He writes, "My way of loving them is translating them, or devouring them, according to Oswald de Andrade's anthropophagic laws" (ibid.: 7). He quotes his own translation of an Andrew Marvell poem, "To His Coy Mistress" (ibid.: 7). The influence of Ezra Pound is everywhere to be seen: in the preface, introduction, authors chosen for translation, and style of the translations themselves. Augusto de Campos continues, "Translation for me is a persona. Nearly a heteronym. To get into the pretender's skin, to re-pretend everything again, pain by pain, sound by sound, color by color [*dor por dor, som por som, cor por cor*]" (ibid.). While aware of the strong emphasis on the artistic and formal aspects of the poetry, however, Augusto de Campos does not lose sight of the historical and political implications for Brazilians. He criticizes those Brazilian artists and bureaucrats who look to the future and have cut themselves off from the past. He continues, "poetry, by definition, has not a homeland. Or better yet, it has a larger homeland. . . . But if someone says that all this has nothing to do with 'our roots,' it is another lie" (ibid.: 8). As the Brazilians have assumed and consumed European art and sociopolitical models, they also have altered—reversed—those very models, adapting them to apply to the conditions of Brazil. Such moves have not been without controversy, hence the title of the collection. This translation/ manipulation of European art and ideas has led to new and creative insights, which Augusto de Campos sees as being as original as the so-called "original" writing: "New egg in the old [*Ovo novo no velho*]." In Portuguese, the word for egg [*ovo*] is "inside" the word new [*novo*] novo. Boundaries between original writing and translation disappear; which writers are selected for translation and how they are translated very much forms the identity of the Brazilian people, both their past and present.

By bringing such writers as Blake or Marvell into Portuguese, by placing them in the tradition of Brazilian writing, indigenous voices and images cannot help but interpenetrate the original, creating a hybrid form. Augusto de Campos introduces the term "intradução" [intra-translation] on the title page of *Verso, reverso, controverso*, a term that combines "introduction" and "translation," suggesting a kind of translation from within (cf. Vieira 1994b: 433). The term is followed by a text with two scripts, one the Provençal of Bernart de Ventadorn, and the other in Portuguese by Augusto de Campos. Rather than being on separated pages facing one another, however, the texts are interlaced, mixing the Portuguese into the Provençal, interpenetrating one with the other. The concrete poem is and is not a translation, more a hybrid text illustrating the cannibal theory of translation in which the European text is, literally, lovingly absorbed by the Brazilian Portuguese.

In his essay "O texto e sua sombra: Teses sobre a teoria da intradução" ["The Text and Its Shadow: Theses toward a Theory of Intra-translation"] (1989), the poet, translator, and literary critic Nelson Ascher elaborates Augusto de Campos's concept of "intradução," discussing the problem of translation in terms of the similarity or identity of the translation to the original. Ascher traces the problem back to the book of Genesis and the resemblance/difference of man (the translation) to God (the original). For Ascher, because God has no history and because of the impossibility of ever replicating God, the history of translation lies in the analysis of the difference between the original and the translation. Additionally, the concept of original ideas is in itself a theological and metaphysical construct. Translators invariably find themselves working between the world of ideas and the world of shadows (their translations). With the crisis in philosophy in the modern world, with questions being raised about metaphysical ideas, Ascher argues that the contemporary philosopher and translator is increasingly preoccupied with the world of shadows, the world of differences, as manifest in the material, concrete, world of everyday reality (ibid.: 143). For Ascher, it is precisely those areas called "mistranslation," whether simple errors or unconscious lapses, that are of primary interest because it is this area of mistranslation that gives the translated text its own identity and allows it to have its own history (ibid.: 145).

Ascher likes Augusto de Campos's concept of *intradução*. In Portuguese, *dução* means to conduct, to convey, to transport. *Tra* means traverse, transverse, or across. The *in*, however is trickier, for it functions primarily as a prefix of negation in Portuguese, yielding nontranslation, but combined with *tra* to form *intra* it conjures up the idea of penetration, yielding the polyvalent term of antitranslation/translation from within. Traditional translation theory, with a theory of carrying across, over, and above, suggests translation of an original into another original; the cannibalist conception suggests a subverting from within as well as a translation transporting one inside oneself to something that by definition is unreachable, unattainable (see Chapter 7, particularly Laplanche's concept of the *à traduire* as the unconscious). Augusto de Campos's term implies an operation antithetical to translation, searching for identity not in the area of sameness but in the area of difference. Brazil, implies Augusto de Campos, discovers its identity not in the similarity of its artistic ideas and expressions to those of the European masters but in the differences of its ideas and expressions. Only through extremely close readings and a different kind of fidelity—not to some universalized metaphysical concept or underlying Platonic idea that easily carries across cultures, but by a careful internal analysis of what can and cannot be said in any given discourse in any given period, looking at both the light and the shadows—can one discover the material from which to describe one's own history and identity (Ascher 1989: 151).

Perhaps the most important writer associated with the cannibalist movement was Mário de Andrade, author of *Macunaíma*, officially published in 1928, although earlier versions circulated. Macunaíma, the title character/(anti)hero, is a black-skinned native from the Tapanhumas group in the rainforests of northern Brazil. On a trip to São Paulo with his brothers, he wanted to stop and take a bath in the River Araguaia, along which they are traveling. However, they cannot bathe in the river because of the man-eating Caribe fish; instead, they choose to bathe in a nearby pond. While they are bathing, Macunaíma's skin miraculously changes from black to white, a "translation" not of a text but of the man himself.

This transformation enables Macunaíma to undergo a variety of experiences in the industrial capital, passing as a Euro-American, while at the same time retaining his indigenous perspective and vernacular speech. Most of his experiences are negative as he confronts a variety of rogues, greedy businessmen, corrupt government officials, and tempting women, all of whom Macunaíma mocks in a humorous yet merciless fashion. Disillusioned by "civilization," he returns to the jungles of the north, where he dies and is transformed into a constellation of stars. The book has enjoyed an uncanny literary history, recalling a wealth of popular legends and myths, consumed, digested and transformed in what at best might be termed a parody of the European realist novel. The text has tapped into the psychic nature of Brazilian identity for both the literary elite and the popular masses.

Drawing frequently upon the tropes of translation, Mário de Andrade is especially insightful in articulating the complex relationship of Brazil to Europe. He is invariably included as an anthropophagist in literary historical discussions; however, while he was a contemporary of Oswald de Andrade (though not related) and was familiar with Oswald's futurist poetry, he claims not to be affiliated with the cannibalist movement. An early hand-circulated edition of *Macunaíma* actually was available almost two years before Oswald de Andrade's "Cannibalist Manifesto" (cf. Suárez and Tomlins 2000: 96), indicating the temper of the times. The text has undergone multiple revisions since, with official editions published in 1928, 1936, and 1944, and other private editions in circulation. Full of innovations and contradictions, the book is hard to characterize as belonging to any fixed literary movement or style, but the cannibalism motif has certainly resonated strongly in the subsequent decades. In his film adaptation of *Macunaíma* (1969), Joaquim Pedro de Andrade increased the emphasis on cannibalism, viewing it as the primary force underlying all social relationships from Brazil to its European colonizers, and even to Brazilians' relations with other Brazilians. The film not only was a critical success but became one of the Cinema Nova's first truly popular films at the box office, showing the appeal of cannibalism as a coded language of revolt against the military dictatorship.

Other cannibals associated with the movement include José Celso Martinez Corrêa, who in the play *O rei da vela* [The Candle King] (1937) critiqued multiple forms of capitalism and authoritarianism, as well as parodying all theatrical styles. During this period, Dos Santos released *Como era gostoso o meu francês* (How Tasty Was My Little Frenchman, 1970). Márcio Souza in *Galvez, imperador do Acre* (1976) (The Emperor of the Amazon, 1977) satirized a real historical event, Brazil's taking possession of the Acre territory. Nearly all the characters of the novel are foreign, including a Spanish leader, French opera singers and prostitutes, and a British scientist named Sir Henry Lust, who collects Indians' genital organs. In *Utopia selvagem: Saudades da inocência perdida* [Savage Utopia:

Longings for a Lost Innocence] (1982), Darcy Ribiero cites Oswald de Andrade's *Manifesto Antropófago* in his allegorical satire of Brazilian society, weaving many different forms of literary discourse into his "fable." In his film *O homem do Pau-Brasil* [The Brazilwood Man] (1982), Joachim Pedro de Andrade again pays tribute to the life and work of Oswald de Andrade. Two actors, a man and a woman, play the role of Oswald, with the woman playing his "female" side. At the end of the film, she overcomes his dominance and takes charge of his erect phallus (a pun on the Portuguese word *pau*) before embarking on the path to the matriarchal, Caraíba revolution (cf. Johnson 1987: 55–56).

In addition, the movement has been adopted by Brazilian poet-songwriters such as Caetano Veloso and Gilberto Gil, who are associated with the "Tropicalismo" movement, a revolutionary movement begun in the late 1960s to oppose Brazil's military dictatorship. Its music is meant to be shocking, combining electric guitars, violent poetry, traditional Brazilian music, rock and roll, avant-garde, innovative Brazilian jazz rhythms, and translation. The movement led to a crackdown by the dictatorship, and Gil and Veloso spent two months in prison, four months under house arrest, and two years in London in exile. In December 1991, Veloso produced a CD in which the opening song incorporates a translation of a John Donne poem in which Donne (following *Hamlet*) writes that "time is out of joint." Rather than suggesting that there is some sort of universal meaning to the phrase that can be translated intact across time and cultures, Veloso, by inscribing the phrase in the Brazilian situation, suggests that it takes on a new meaning in a different historical paradigm, and what ensues is referred to by the critic Else Vieira as a new and "reverse moment of universalization" (1994a: 66). Veloso first sings the refrain in Portuguese and then retranslates the phrase back into English and then into French, Spanish, and Japanese, setting new chains of translations of a translation in motion, this time with the "original" coming not from England but from a South American source. This is not the first time that Veloso has translated John Donne poems in his work; in a previous record, he translated John Donne's "Elegy: To His Mistress Going to Bed" into Portuguese and set it to Brazilian music and rhythms. Earlier, Augusto de Campos, when translating John Donne's "The Apparition," incorporated a passage from a popular Brazilian song into the middle of the translation (cf. Vieira 1994a: 66; Arrojo 1986: 138).

Cannibals and criticism

The Brazilian critic Else Vieira is one of the leading theorists making connections between the cannibalist translation movement in Brazil and postmodern and postcolonial theory in other parts of the world. In her essay "A Postmodern Translational Aesthetics in Brazil" (1994a), she makes the connection not only between the power dynamics of European culture versus

Brazilian culture as represented by the power of the original text versus the translated text but also with the refusal of the Brazilian translators to adopt a model of translation preferred by European culture (ibid.: 65–66). Translation thus is seen as a site of tension between Europe and the Americas, with not only the authority of the source text being called into question but also the very model for the study of translation. Rather than a one-way flow of information and ideas from the source culture, generally the colonizer, to the target culture, generally the colonized, Vieira uses the anthropophagists to show that the flow of ideas and information is a *two-way* flow, to and from both cultures simultaneously. If, for example, Haroldo de Campos highlights the Mephistophelean and demonic nature of Goethe's *Faust* rather than the transcendental and angelic, and if his "angels" metaphorically represent indigenous antiheroic characters, the text takes on new meanings, which in this new postcolonial world resonate back across the borders already traversed and, in turn, influence the international reception of Goethe's work elsewhere. For Vieira, in her attempts to sketch a postmodern theory of translation, the very terminology, such as "source" and "target" texts, gets called into question, for in some cases the target text becomes another source and, especially with the cannibalist translators, the source text becomes the target. Vieira also turns to Walter Benjamin and Jacques Derrida to call into question the definition of the "original" and the relationship of the translation to the original. Translation, in her view, is just as creative, although expressed differently, as the original; in addition, the original is seen as a translation, another kind of intersemiotic reworking of existing signs. Finally, Vieira calls into question the notion of the self-effacing translator. Rather than minimizing one's own identity and one's own traditions, the cannibalistic translators actually are encouraged to let their voice be heard and, especially, to incorporate indigenous traditions and literary forms in the translated text. Translation, thus, in Vieira's definition, as with De Campos and others before her, becomes a truly polyphonic site, one which by nature is inscribed in multiple sign systems and frames of cultural reference. In her essay 'Towards a Minor Translation," Vieira uses the metaphor of "grafting" to describe the process: "Original texts are not merely cast in another language, they continue to live by being integrated into another literature—they are grafted and live on in mutation" (1995a: 148). This metaphor allows her to measure translations not by exclusions and errors but by continuities and creative additions, or, perhaps better expressed in Derrida's terms, supplements. The goal for Vieira is less one of independence, in more traditional narratives of nationalism and identity formation, than one of interdependence, which she feels is more characteristic of the hybrid postcolonial situation in which Brazil finds itself, and one that is more indicative of the postmodern age.

Roberto Schwarz, one of the most respected critics of Brazilian literature, author of *Misplaced Ideas: Essays on Brazilian Culture* (1992), takes a differing view, suggesting that Haroldo de Campos's move from *antro-*

pofagia to transculturalization and transluciferation reveals the failure of Brazil's modernizing project, especially the failure of the intellectual elite of the country to construct their own identity. Indeed, much recent social as well as literary criticism regarding Brazil is characterized by commentary on the increasing failure of the culture to achieve the modernism and the industrialization of other Western nations. Rather than integration and interdependence, Schwarz sees disintegration and deeper and deeper dependencies, especially in the realm of economics, employment, and technology. Schwarz sees the goal of modernizing via a cannibalist process of blending the rural Brazilian with the urban European as largely unattainable, as another kind of utopian, elitist desire out of step with the realities of the situation.

Schwarz suggests that the cannibalist writers and translators belong to a cultured, Eurocentric elite cut off from the working class and Brazilian indigenous rural populations. Schwarz addressed Oswald de Andrade's poetry directly in an essay titled "The Cart, the Tram and the Modernist Poetry," included in the volume *Misplaced Ideas* (1992). On the one hand, Schwarz provides an insightful reading of one small poem by Oswald de Andrade about a horsecart stuck on a tramline and the reactions of the driver and the lawyers to the incident, pointing out the confrontations between industrialization (the tramlines) and the primitive (horsecart), the cosmopolitan (the lawyers) and the indigenous (the driver). Yet his conclusions are a bit harsh, for Schwarz finds Oswald's poetry "easy" and "illusionary," allied to the discourse of conservative modernization, prefiguring cosmopolitan bourgeois culture, and, in sum, a kind of "critical jingoism" (ibid.: 111). He views Oswald de Andrade's theory as equally unsuccessful, offering only an "allegory and quasi-theory of Brazilian national identity" (ibid.: 116) and later "a certain admixture of unreality and childishness" (ibid.: 123). Schwarz is even more damning regarding the verse of Augusto de Campos. In an essay titled "A Historic Landmark" from the same collection, Schwarz again gives a perceptive reading of the concrete poem "Póstudo" [Post-everything] by Augusto de Campos and published in the arts section of the *Folha de São Paulo* (1985). The adjectives Schwartz uses to sum up the work and the theory are even more pointed, including terms such as regressive, dogmatic, ignorant, and banal. Schwarz finds Augusto de Campos selfishly interested in only "blowing his own trumpet" and "owing nothing to anybody" (ibid.: 192) rather than commenting, actually rather sadly and generally, on the end of the age of the proliferation of poststructural theories.

Schwarz suggests that his own views on culture, which are expressed in more materialist terms than those used by the literary cannibals he critiques, are more relevant to the conditions of what he refers to as the "real world" than to those of the "misplaced" realm of ideas and identity. It should come as no surprise that Schwarz's primary area of literary interest is the nineteenth-century realistic novel, and the theorists he prefers tend toward

Marx, Lukács, Benjamin, Brecht, and Adorno. It also may not be surprising that, although raised in Brazil, Schwarz was born in Austria and spent much of his professional life living and teaching in Paris. To be sure, the forces of globalization and multinational capitalism weigh heavily upon developing nations, resulting in both economic booms and poverty and exploitation for many, thereby complicating anyone's sense of what it means to be part of a nation, whether one counts oneself as part of the cultural elite or the working classes. Nevertheless, when compared to the rest of his work, Schwarz's assessment of the Brazilian cannibalists seems less well argued, often unduly personal and vitriolic, and out of touch with accumulating data offered by translation studies scholars, cultural historians, musicians, filmmakers, and postcolonial studies critics.

Yet Schwarz is not alone in his critique of the "elitist" nature of the De Campos brothers' theories of translation. In his essay "Brazilian Anthropophagy Revisited," Sérgio Bellei makes similar claims. He suggests that the anthropophagists have a kind of split consciousness, being aware of both the "superior" European culture and the material backwardness of their own culture; the "purpose" of the anthropophagists, according to Bellei, was to dissolve the borders between the two (1998: 91–92). While most critics see the cannibal manifestos as being aimed largely at disruption and often aggressively promoting a change in relations with regard to the power dynamics of colonization, Bellei focuses rather on the continuity with the past and Brazilian cultural traditions. Citing the Brazilian critic Antonio Candido, Bellei emphasizes the theme of traveling and encountering between two cultures, and this movement between the two worlds is characteristic of the "American man" (ibid.: 98). Traveling was for Oswald de Andrade a way of understanding and feeling "the Brazilian nation." Bellei cites Candido as follows: "Hence, in his [Andrade's] work, there is a certain reversibility between Brazil and Europe, which points to the significance of traveling as an experience of the spirit and of the national consciousness" (Candido 1977: 54; Bellei 1998: 98). For Bellei, thus, the anthropophagists continue the theme of the cultural encounter between the powerful and the oppressed on the frontier, similar in many ways to an earlier generation of Brazilian Romantic writers.

Bellei is particularly critical of Haroldo de Campos's theory of open multilinguistic hybridization, which he sees as an easy way of juxtaposing the underdeveloped with the developed on an equal playing field. For Bellei, this is offensive, for it dismisses real material conditions and historical stages of evolution. It also reaffirms aesthetics as an autonomous cultural practice cut off from real social practices. Bellei characterizes de Campos as arguing that the world is a vast multicultural banquet in which "everybody eats everybody else" (Bellei 1998: 106). For Bellei, much depends upon who eats whom, and, as the anthropophagist movement moves through the 1950s and the work of the De Campos brothers is exposed to even more postmodern interpretations, he finds that question of power gets deleted from the theory. Thus, the evolution continues, from the Romantic, through the avant-garde, to the postmodern, all detached and splitting the art from the social realities, another kind of art for art's sake. Bellei concludes his essay by arguing that "As in Campos, texts are here only 'multilingual hybridizations' existing in a pure spatial dimension deprived of any historical depth" (ibid.: 108).

Not all contemporary scholars are so critical. In his essay "Tupy or Not Tupy" (1987), Randal Johnson traces a different history, seeing cannibalism as a critical metaphor for the cultural relations between First and Third World nations, perhaps even more relevant today than in the 1920s. Johnson sees cannibalism very much in terms of rejecting images of passive, submissive Native American consumers and instead of favoring the more aggressive images of the cannibal foregrounded by contemporary Brazilian translators, musicians, and filmmakers as outlined above. The history he traces goes back to the early days of colonization and the trauma induced by the colonial repression, and continues through the religious conversions perpetuated by the Jesuits, the economic oppression carried out by the European-Brazilian governing elites, and the military dictatorship of the 1960s. Many poets, artists, musicians, and later filmmakers continually resisted European assimilation and dependent relations throughout Brazilian history. Johnson sees the movement as very much alive in the irreverent sense of humor, the satire, parody, and critical evaluations of social relationships, particularly in the filmmakers from the 1960s to the 1990s (Johnson and Stam 1995: 362). In his 1969 introduction "Cannibalism and Self-Cannibalism" to his film *Macunaíma*, Joaquim Pedro de Andrade claims that at that time the dominant, conservative social classes still controlled the power structure and that nothing had really changed since the 1920s. He writes:

> The present work relationships, as well as the relationships between people—social, political, and economic—are still basically cannibalistic. Those who can "eat" others through their consumption of products. . . . Cannibalism has merely institutionalized itself, cleverly disguised itself. The new heroes, still looking for a collective consciousness, try to devour those who devour us.
>
> (Johnson and Stam, 1995: 82–83)

Johnson thus sees cannibalism as very much alive and, in contrast to Schwarz and Bellei, very much socially and politically engaged. He writes, "Initially then cannibalism is a form of resistance. Metaphorically speaking, it represents a new attitude toward cultural relations with hegemonic power" (1987: 49). This new relation is aimed less at either/or solutions than toward the creation of a new national identity with its own artistic forms. This form of cannibalism is connected to reversing the power relations between the Old and New World and a reevaluation of the image of the indigenous peoples of America, largely constructed through translation, which need now to be largely *reconstructed* again through another round of translation. While resonating with oppositional politics, contemporary cannibalism satirizes those very same oppositional categories, and, on occasion, the author's own cannibalistic position—one self-reflexively using literary forms and discourses from previous traditions—in the text itself.

The political struggle has not ended just because certain theorists claim that such texts exist only in spatial dimensions. What critics such as Bellei, Candido, and Schwarz seem not to see are the political ramifications of a marginal culture constantly bombarded by Euro-American culture. The question of what constitutes the Brazilian nation and identity is more complex than ever, and the translational dimension, with the international media and multinational capitalism, is only increasing rather than decreasing. What Johnson, along with many contemporary Brazilian cinematographers, translators, and musicians, seems to accept is the fact that throughout its history, Brazil has received, translated, and critically adapted a number of European and, more recently, North American intellectual and artistic movements. Using humor, irony, and multiple cultural referents, they have nevertheless kept a sense of Brazilianness alive by undermining claims of universality and destabilizing institutions of power. Although consumers, the Brazilian cannibals have not been uncritical consumers, which perhaps more than anything else has allowed for indigenous, national traits to *not* be consumed. Whatever Brazilian identity might be, it is not something fixed, inherent, or universal in and of itself, but is constantly evolving and changing, nourished by international as well as national ideas. Rather than convert to European values and ideas, or merely juxtapose indigenous ideas with European ones, Brazilian anthropophagists use the European ideas in an emancipatory fashion in the creation of new cultural identities, ones not separated from but embedded in multiple cultural traditions.

The process of rethinking nation and identity, however, begun in Brazil in the 1920s by Oswald de Andrade and others, continues to be a difficult question today, perhaps increasingly so in light of the enhanced communication technologies, which make the cross-cultural exchange of ideas even easier than in the early modernist period. Questions of translation —which texts to select, what strategies to use when translating them, how to adapt them to the changing Brazilian market—are the same ones applied to the market economy—which products to select, what strategies to use when importing them, how to adapt them to the changing Brazilian market. The act of consuming is often a very creative process, more akin to construction, shaping, and collage than to imitation. How consumers read, shop, deal with their employers, and play, may be less "materialistic" than critics such as Schwarz and Bellei imagine. Through this process of selecting the best of another culture, adapting and consuming it, and then making it one's own—in short, through a process of transculturalization—

Brazilians may be better suited to adapt to the new world order than other cultures caught up in a more traditional North–South divide.

Translation, thus, for critics such as Johnson and Vieira, is viewed as more than a secondary literary activity; rather, it comes to exemplify Brazilian cultural philosophy itself. The cannibal metaphor becomes the very site for original artistic expression and one of the primary tools for expressing one's own identity and independence. This independence creates new cultural conditions that allow for the possibility of rethinking one's own past, such as the function of Baroque writers and musicians in the Brazilian context, which in turn leads to a rethinking of the Baroque period in Europe as well. This new internationalism and two-way flow of ideas lead to the poetry/music of "popular" musicians such as Caetano Veloso and Gilberto Gil, whose initial major defender and theorist was Augusto de Campos, cinema by filmmakers such as Joachim Pedro de Andrade and Glauber Rocha, whose works echo both Oswald and Mário de Andrade, and to translators such as Haroldo and Augusto de Campos, whose work intersemiotically connects to that of filmmakers such as Rocha and songwriters such as Veloso as well as canonical European writers. In sum, cannibalist translation, both as a theory and as a cultural practice, can help Brazilians as well as Americans in other parts of the New World better understand their international roots as well as their growing interrelations with other transnational cultures. Cannibalist translation, as a model of cultural evolution, can show all Americans a way of taking at least partial control of the construction of their own identities.

5 The Fictional Turn in Latin America

As theorists in Brazil have turned to poets such as Oswald de Andrade and Haroldo and Augusto de Campos for ideas on which to base a theory of translation, much of the rest of Latin America has turned to its fiction writers. Translation has not become a subject for postgraduate research in Spanish-speaking universities in the Americas, nor has there been much conference activity, with perhaps the exception of recent conferences in Argentina and Peru. As far as governments and universities are concerned, translation remains primarily a technical activity, considered more a vocational skill than a creative activity, and the training programs that do exist focus primarily upon practice rather than theory. Economics plays a role here, too, as many universities simply do not have the research funds equivalent to those of their American neighbors in the United States, Canada, and Brazil, although United States institutions on the whole remain largely indifferent to translation studies (see Chapter 2). This state of affairs within the academy, however, belies the fact that among Latin American fiction writers the theme of translation has figured prominently in investigations of culture and identity. In this chapter, I suggest that translation is perhaps the *most* important topic in Latin American fiction, more important even than the widely circulated magic realism theme featured by most (North American) scholars. In this chapter, I look at the work of writers such as Jorge Luis Borges, Gabriel García Márquez, and Mario Vargas Llosa, tracing their use of translation as a theme and showing how understanding translation becomes a key to understanding both the fiction itself, and, by extension, the cultural formation in Spanish-speaking South America. I also show how this appreciation of translation's presence in the novels and stories of Latin American authors reciprocally informs the field of translation studies. Translation in South America is much more than a linguistic operation; rather, it has become one of the means by which an entire continent has come to define itself.

The Brazilian translation studies scholar Else Vieira was the first person to recognize this trend. In an essay titled "(In)visibilidades na tradução: Troca de olhares teóricos e ficcionais" [(In)visibilies in Translation: Exchanging Theoretical and Fictional Perspectives] (1995–1996a), Vieira coins the phrase the "fictional turn" in translation studies to refer to this phenomenon. She writes, "Denominaria esta etapa o *fictional turn* dos Estudos da Tradução" [I call this stage the *fictional turn* in translation studies] (1995–1996a: 50). Drawing on the discourse of translation in the writings of fiction writers such as the Brazilian novelist Guimarães Rosa, referring to theories such as those of Charles Sanders Peirce, Jacques Derrida, and Luce Irigaray, and situating her work in line with translation studies scholars such as Susan Bassnett, Nelson Ascher, and Lawrence Venuti, Vieira develops a theory of translation that challenges mimetic theories that emphasize fidelity to the source text. Instead, similar to her reading of Haroldo de Campos's translation work (see Chapter 4), she shows how translation is invariably a *creative* activity: translators are never totally invisible, but rather always writing themselves into the texts they translate. In "O espelho" [The Mirror] (1962), for example, Rosa ironically plays with scientific notions of *mimesis*, not only invoking the ability of the mirror to reflect reality but also incorporating various indigenous superstitious beliefs associated with mirrors, moving his realistic fiction closer to the realm of magic realism. Vieira suggests that there is always a reciprocal play between invisibility/visibility, covering/discovering present in every fictional work as well as every translation, which Vieira sees as empowering for the translator.

As this book reflects upon issues of translation and identity formation, it should come as no surprise that fiction becomes a source for theoretical inquiry. As a medium for recording a culture's evolution, fiction narrates a culture's history and traditions as well as individual characters' experiences and growth. In Canada, novelists such as Nicole Brossard in *Le Désert mauve* (1987) used translation in her fiction to articulate multiple borders—both language and gender—that her characters need to negotiate in their lives, as well as to enlarge that in-between space where Canadians in general, and Quebec women in particular, whether Anglophone, Francophone or bilingual, find themselves culturally situated (see Chapter 3). In Brazil, novelists such as Mário de Andrade in *Macunaíma* (1928) used translation both figuratively and physically to show how indigenous peoples of the Americas are enmeshed in a web of linguistic and racial codes that define and constrain their very existence (see Chapter 4). In both cases, the fiction writers, with their focus on the topic of translation, engendered theories of translation that also apply to a theory of cultural identity formation.

A group of new translation studies scholars are emerging who examine the relationship between fiction in translation and translation theory. Rosemary Arrojo looks at fiction as a source for translation theory in the works of Latin American writers such as Jorge Luis Borges and João Guimarães Rosa, and then expands her corpus to include Central Europeans Franz Kafka and Dezső Kosztolányi (Arrojo 2002). Adriana Pagano (2002) analyzes the work of Julio Cortázar, who not only uses translation as a theme in many of his works, but also includes characters who are translators themselves. Christopher Larkosh (2002) dwells upon the work of several Argentine writers and translators, including Borges, and Victoria Ocampo. Anibal González (1989) rereads Gabriel García Márquez's novel from the perspective of translation, with multiple fascinating new insights. To their pioneering studies, in this chapter, I add my own readings of Borges, García Márquez, and Mario Vargas Llosa, focusing on how the topic of translation in fiction can inform both translation theory and theories of identity formation.

Beginning with Borges

The study of the fictional turn in translation studies must begin with Jorge Luis Borges, whose fiction is everywhere concerned with the theme of translation. For Borges, translation is more than a metaphor for the cultural conditions of the twentieth century; it is the determining aesthetic characteristic of all writing from antiquity to the present. He began addressing the question of translation and writing as early as 1926 with an article in the newspaper *La Prensa* titled "Sobre las dos maneras de traducir" [On the Two Ways of Translating]. In 1932, he wrote a prologue to the translation of Paul Valéry's novel *The Marine Cemetery*. That same year he issued his first major essay on translation titled "Las versiones homéricas" [The Homeric Versions], included in his collection *Discusión* (1989c [1932]) (cf. Larkosh 1996: 25). Borges's insights are further developed in the essay "Los traductores de las 1001 Noches" [The Translators of *1001 Nights*], first published in the volume *Historia de la Eternidad* (1989d [1936]). Borges's thinking about translation culminates in the story "Pierre Menard, autor del Quijote" [Pierre Menard, Author of the *Quixote*], collected in his *Ficciones* (1989a [1944]). I suggest that Borges's foregrounding of translation is inherently present in all of his writing, including later fiction such as the stories included in *The Aleph* (1989f [1949]).

In addition to translation, the theme of identity formation is crucial to understanding Borges's work. Argentina during the early parts of the twentieth century was a nation in formation, with many of its citizens having been born overseas, or first-generation immigrants. In Buenos Aires, where the recent European immigrants—mostly from Spain, Britain, and Italy—met with the rural population—mostly earlier immigrants and indigenous peoples—many languages were spoken, and traditions could be traced back to diverse cultures. Fiction writers and intellectuals during this period, including José Ingenieros, Ricardo Rojas, and Manuel Gálvez, were obsessed with forming a national literature and tracing the nation's history, language, and traditions. Borges, born into this cultural and intellectual climate, found that certain sources for such thinking were far from unified and stable. That he developed a form of parody/essay to satirize such *ficciones* (fictions), calling into question the unity of such diverse groups of immigrants and migrants, might come as little surprise. In the early twenty-first century, as scholars increasingly question the category of nations and/or nation-states as a map, or territory, for thinking about culture and identity, it also should come as no surprise that scholars turn to Borges for their reconceptualizations.

In "The Homeric Versions," Borges talks about translation in terms of his conception of the labyrinthian nature of all literary studies. In this essay, he includes multiple avatars often cited by critics of translation, including "Ningún problema tan consustancial con las letras y con su modesto misterio como el que propone una traducción" [There is no problem as fundamental to letters and to its modest mystery as that proposed by a translation] (1989c [1932]: 239); "La traducción, en cambio, parece destinada a ilustrar la discussion estética" [Translation, on the other hand, seems to be destined to illustrate the aesthetic discussion] (ibid.: 239); and, most significantly, "El concepto de text definitivo no corresponde sino a la religión o al cansancio" [The concept of a definitive text does not correspond with anything but religion or weariness] (ibid.: 239).

Borges calls the notion of the inferiority of translation a superstition rather than fact. *The Odyssey*, argues Borges, is a veritable international library of works in both prose and verse, ranging from the couplets of Chapman to the authorized version by Andrew Lang, from the classical drama in French by Bérard to the ironic novel by Samuel Butler. The myriad versions of Homer in English translation illustrate the heterogeneous nature of writing and reveal perhaps more about the diverse characteristics of the translators than anything unified about the "original." According to Borges, it has become difficult to know what belongs to the poet and what now belongs to the tradition of language. Borges next looks at various passages as translated by different translators, including "literal versions" such as those by Buckley, archaic versions such as those by Butcher and Lang, or more oratorical versions such as those by Pope. The versions are characterized by the strategies and motives employed by the respective translators: Pope's use of luxurious dialects and spectacular discourse; Chapman's ardent, passionate lyrical verse; and Butler's aversion to the visual and emphasis on the facts. By the end, Borges is wondering not which version is most faithful but what translation has to do with faithfulness at all. Ironically, though, in a network of intersemiotic connections and differences, *all* of them have come to represent Homer. Over the past two decades, translation studies research also demonstrates that fidelity is an impossible standard; all translators make choices, favoring one artistic or ideological feature over another, and their translations reflect such preferences. In many ways, Borges's theory precedes translation studies in dissecting basic concepts such as faithfulness and equivalence with his much more humane and ironic stance regarding fidelity. His work also connects translation to history and identity formation, for it is by their collective, intersemiotic *history* of translation that the contemporary cultural representation of Homer is formed.

Borges's reading of Homer also destabilizes certain notions of literary tradition, especially ones that attempt to provide a single literary tradition, clean separations between national literatures, and neat theories of how cross-cultural communication takes place. Borges's *Odyssey* is a collage of French, Spanish, and especially English translations, all consciously and unconsciously intersecting and informing each other. In the essay, Borges quotes Chapman and Pope, but in Spanish, not in English, further complicating the process of ciphering any "original" intent. In many ways, such single-nation literary tradition, be it English, French, or Spanish, is already fiction. What better vehicle to illustrate this network than a paradigm of translations? One could argue that Borges's entire work is a kind of a detective story aimed at uncovering this network of deception and at complicating simplified notions of authorship, language, and nationality.

Borges continues his reflection on translation with its connection to identity formation in "The Translator of *1001 Nights*," his most extended essay on translation. Many of the themes raised in "The Homeric Versions" resurface in "1001 Nights," including the lack of any fixed original, the performance quality of the translations, the influence of national literary traditions on the process, and, of course, the subjective idiosyncrasies and even personal vendettas of the individual translators. Borges first comments on the obscurity of the source text: derived from various oral tales from a variety of cultures and historical periods, the Arabic version—*Qitab alif laila wa laila*—generally is *not* the source for European translators. Rather, the source text is actually the translated text, or a series of translated texts. Jean Antoine Galland's translation into French in the early eighteenth century, published in twelve volumes from 1707 to 1717, which became the canonical European version for years to come, includes both translations from the Arabic text and, according to Borges, an additional supplementary text by an "obscure consultant" (1981: 74), a Maronite whom Borges calls "Hanna," not wanting to omit the author's/translator's name. It is this (infidel) Christian outsider in the Arab world who brings us stories such as "Aladdin," "The Forty Thieves," "Prince Ahmed and the Fairy Peri-Banu," and "The Sleeper and the Waker," invariably attributed to the Arabic original. Galland's translation thus becomes the ur-text in the West for *1001 Nights*, and no translator who follows can omit tales that he included, although, according to Borges, none since mentions this obscure co-author Hanna.

Borges's "The Translators of *1001 Nights*" (1981) traces the translation work of four translators: Edward Lane, the British translator who lived five years in Cairo and offered a puritanical version in the 1840s; Richard Francis Burton, the legendary English world adventurer, who offered a more eccentric version in 1885; J.C. Mardrus, another French translator, whose 1899 embellishments and Gallicisms prefigure later cinematic versions; and finally the more sober Enno Littmann, the fourth of a series of German translators, whose translations in 1923–1924 have become, for many

European Orientalists, the definitive version. Borges comments how *none* of the translators covered in his essay, nor other well-known translators of *1001 Nights*, including Coleridge, Stendhal, Tennyson, and Edgar Allan Poe, uses the Arabic as the source text; rather, Galland has become the standard. In addition, Galland's text has also become the source for later translations into Arabic and Hindustani, reversing traditional translation studies definitions of source and target texts (see Larkosh 1996: 39). While in this book, I do not touch upon the impact of such back-translations on identity formation in Asian and African cultures, other scholars, such as Tejaswini Niranjana in *Siting Translation* (1992), have made such connections. Borges, however, being from Argentina, was well aware of the colonizing process of cultural importation and translation by North American and European Latin American specialists interpreting and explicating Latin American culture to Latin Americans.

Borges's essay is uncharacteristic of typical translation criticism; rather than focusing on fidelity and equivalence, he emphasizes instead the differences, digressions, and accidents. Many of the embellishments and contrasts by the translators he cites are not due to mistakes or errors but instead are attributed to the literary traditions and values of the respective cultures of which the translators form a part and to which they contribute. Burton's translations, with their energy and eloquence as well as their vulgarity and imperfections, were inconceivable, according to Borges, without John Donne's obscenities, Shakespeare's myriad vocabularies, Swinburne's archaisms, and the British colonial arrogance of the age. In Mardrus's translations, Borges sees *Salammbô* and La Fontaine, the *Mannequin d'osier*, and the *ballets russes*. In Littmann's versions, Borges finds the erudition of an age of German folklorists, a probity and honesty that is consistent with the scientific nature of scholarship of the period. Ironically, far from being critical of the subjective interpretations and deviations from the "original," Borges finds that much of the meaning is captured in those digressions. The texts in his mind are much about magical operations, fabulous scenes, battles, dawns, lovers, comedy, palaces, kings, and gods. The supernatural plays a role as well as the natural, and the more sober and puritanical translations, perhaps more linguistically correct, miss something, in Borges's opinion—that is, the *pleasure* of the text. Despite their flaws, the more poetic versions of Galland, Burton, and Mardrus transform the mysteries and suspense because the writers draw on genres and literary devices that develop the fantastic in their own traditions. The more literal versions of Lane and Littmann, according to Borges, lack the imagination, resorting to literal equivalences and linguistic equations. Borges suggests that he would like to see the German version rethought precisely because Germany also possesses a grand tradition of the fantastic. He wonders, in the conclusion, what Kafka might have done if he had translated and intensified the tales in line with the more creative German tradition.

The process of drawing upon the *local* in the target culture in translation has a long tradition in Latin America, as can be seen from the anthropophagist tradition in Brazil (outlined in Chapter 4). Borges shows, however, that this cannibalist tradition is not limited to Latin America but present in European translation traditions as well. For example, while Borges admits that Galland's versions are the "worst written" and the "most fraudulent" (Borges 1981: 74), readers at the time felt that these versions captured the pleasure, astonishment, and bedazzlement, indicative more of French literary taste and of an exoticization process of translated writings from "the Orient" at the time. Lane's version is more erudite and "corrects" Galland's indiscretions and poetic licenses, but for all Lane's knowledge and scholarship, Borges feels that the latter's version is a mere "encyclopedia of evasion" (ibid.: 75), reflecting British morals and modes of responsibility at the time. Lane not only would delete offensive passages but would add notes such as "I suppress a repugnant explanation," or "Here a line too coarse for translation" (ibid.: 75), which, in a Freudian way, draw more attention to the purported offensive passage than its mere omission.

For Borges, Burton's version epitomizes the drawing upon all resources available to capture the richness and color of the original. Burton's persona is clearly present in the translations, as is his desire to distance himself as much as possible from Lane. He circumvented the censorship problem in England by publishing his version as a single private edition limited to the Burton Club members. In some ways, the audience of the original oral tales —roguish, prone to exaggeration, appreciative of remote, adventurous tales—had much in common with the Burton Club members. Burton's version adds copious notes explaining everything from jails, food, legends, colors, deities, horses, politics, dress, and, of course, obscenities, in the Islamic culture, which he personalizes with his own direct experiences. His vocabulary is as prolific as his notes, adding all sorts of archaic words, slang, dialects of sailors and prisoners, neologisms and foreignisms, usually derived from French and Arabic, in the translated English text. Borges, rather than criticizing these foreign-sounding and hybrid terms, praises them: "Each of those words may be just, but their intercalation implies a falseness. Not a bad falseness, since those verbal antics—and others, syntactic—divert the sometimes wearisome course of the *Nights* (1981: 81). J.C. Mardrus's translation, which draws similar praise from Borges, also resists the prosaic and literal. Mardrus enhances the wonder by drawing on visual cues, adding adjectives, similes, and metaphors to increase the splendor and the "magical." Borges writes, "With a persistence not unworthy of Cecil B. de Mille, he [Mardrus] strews about viziers, kisses, palm trees, and moons" (ibid.: 83). Mardrus continues to embellish, adding obscenities, comic interludes, circumstantial details, and visual markers. Borges suggests that Mardrus is translating not the book's words but the book's scenes, perhaps more in line with painting or film adaptation than translation.

Thus, the mounting infidelities in the differing versions, which for Borges are indicative of the labyrinthine intersemiotic network in which all literature is embedded, draw him to speculate on the larger topic of translation theory. In the infidelities arise the personal traits that give translations their character. In the local traditions arise the vocabularies and images to give life to the stories of the original. Translation for Borges is a heterogeneous activity, and the best translators draw on a broad repertoire of personal experience and literary knowledge to convey and contribute to the source text. In the case of *1001 Nights*, Borges seems to prefer those versions that heighten the fabulous, the magical, and the fantastic, those versions that expand the language of the source and target culture by creatively coining neologisms and foreignized terms, and those translations that reveal the personality of the translator as well as the "original" author. For in Borges's mind, the two are indistinguishable: translators are authors; translation is as creative as original writing; and disorder is as acceptable as order. Because *1001 Nights* has no known source text, as its origin is scattered across various cultures, dialects, and performances, all versions are to a certain degree "un-authorized," or, indeed, found only already in translation.

In fact, the themes of the stories themselves foreground deviation, supplementarity, and deferral. At the center of the story's intrigue is the fact that the narrator, Shahrazad, is a storyteller/translator, who embellishes at will, delaying the end so that King Shahiyar, the authority figure, does *not* put an end to her life for her alleged infidelities. Each story thus adds to its own telling; there is no set original with a beginning, middle, and an end. The telling of the story with its inventions and deviations becomes an ironic act of resistance to the king and the authority of the state, all the more reason for a Latin American writer such as Borges to foreground not the original but the translation, not the fidelity of the translators but their infidelities. Borges's clever story has an air of innocence and accepted literary criticism to it; yet underneath it contains a parody of traditional translation studies, Eurocentric literary histories, Arabic studies in Germany, and institutions of literary authority. Extended interpretations also allow for seeing it as a Latin American rebellion against the colonizing European monarchies.

While "Translators of the *1001 Nights*" contains a covert parody, in "Pierre Menard, Author of the *Quixote*" the parody is played out on center stage. Perhaps because of its earlier availability in English translation, included in the pioneering anthology *Labyrinths* (Borges 1962), translated by Donald Yates and James Irby, it has become Borges's most discussed text in translation circles. The story itself is rather simple. Pierre Menard, a fictional writer, scholar, and translator from early twentieth-century France, decides to "translate" Cervantes's *Quixote*. He does not want to translate another version of the Quixote, but he wants to write the definitive version of *the* Quixote by becoming Miguel de Cervantes, knowing Spanish equally well, becoming Catholic, fighting against Moors or Turks, and forgetting the entire history of Europe between 1602 and the present. Menard's goal was not to translate or interpret, but to *reproduce*, word for word and line for line, the very words of the original. The parody of course is a critique of translation theories that call for translators to totally identify with the author and to transport themselves across three hundred years of history as if the intervening years had not happened. The impossibility of anyone totally giving up their own identity to such a degree—the impossibility of ignoring the intervening ideas and events and how they shape a translator's life—is manifest to all the readers. Borges's critique extends to literary interpretation, philosophical thought, and even to theological exegesis.

The parody reaches its peak toward the end of the *ficción*, when Borges begins a comparison of the two identical texts, and yet claims that Menard's is actually superior to Cervantes' original. While Cervantes' local color often reflected the "reality" of the land during the early seventeenth century, Borges suggests that Menard must elude the now much-changed local color of the twentieth century. Menard had to articulate and defend ideas that often were the opposite of those he personally held. Borges concludes that "Cervantes' text and Menard's are verbally identical, but the second is almost infinitely richer," satirizing in the process translation theories that claim that the original is invariably superior to the translation, no matter how good the translation is. Borges, in his playful style, quotes a passage illustrating the curious discourse with which Don Quixote discusses the subject of arms, letters, and history. Twice Borges cites "truth, whose mother is history, rival of time, depository of deeds, witness of the past, exemplar and adviser to the present, and the future's counselor" (1989a: 94) Borges argues that the first version, written in the seventeenth century, is merely transparent praise of history, whereas the second version, although word for word the same, is, in light of intervening philosophical thought, much more complex. History in the latter version becomes not what happened but what we judge to have happened. Citing the work of William James, Borges claims the latter version to be "staggering" and "brazenly pragmatic" (ibid.: 94). Borges's fiction not only parodies traditional translation theories but also anticipates translation theories governed by reception theories, discourse theories, and target-text approaches. He ironically shows how every translation, even in its fidelity, is always different, just as every reading of a text by different readers yields a unique interpretation, not right or wrong but different, conditioned by historical and cultural factors of the culture.

Once one begins to trace the translation theme in a few stories, one sees the thread in other Borges stories. "The Library of Babel" (1998c) echoes the labyrinthine nature of all writing, the impossibility of any two books ever being alike, the arbitrariness of systems design to classify texts by their content, and the unlimited creative possibilities of language. In the library of Babel, while the books are organized in an orderly, hexagonal fashion, the texts are all written in random and accidental combinations of letters that seldom make any sense. No scholar can break the code or discover the original. No one can even be certain that the central text is Spanish. The point Borges seems to be making is a Joycean one: all texts, even originals, are multilingual, embedded in wild semiotic systems and modes of inscription that challenge the possibility of ever understanding the ideas and the language of the source. In Borges's library, the accident is not the foreignizing term, the alienating construction, or the non sequitur; rather, the "accident" becomes the line that appears to be fluid, transparent, and homogenous. For Borges, all of literature, even the clearest and most unified texts in standard Spanish (English, French, etc.), resemble hybrid texts and translations. Borges's perspective on the Spanish language is indicative of one held by writers in Latin America, in which the Spanish is always infused with multiple languages and dialects, preserving archaic and Arabic traces, adding new and native American terms, and combining with English and Portuguese to form new hybridized terms.

In the "The Garden of Forking Paths" (1998d), Borges further develops this concept of infinite possibilities of language. The story refers to a Chinese spy for the Germans in World War I, who is also the great-grandson of a famous Chinese astronomer, writer, and architect named Ts'ui Pên. While pursued by an English agent, the spy flees to his ancestor's home to discover a unique kind of labyrinth: a novel. Whereas fiction is the West is generally governed by linear time and characters making choices that eliminate other possibilities, in Ts'ui Pên's fiction characters can simultaneously choose all the alternatives. The result is chaotic: each decision results in multiple forkings and possibilities, all of which are followed; sometimes the different paths converge, yet often they do not, resulting in an infinite variety of rhetorical possibilities, offering multiple possible endings. Enemies become allies, allies enemies; some live, some die. The analogy to translation is clear: so too does translation involve forking paths, opening up often infinite creative opportunities based upon initial decision. If one decides to translate a word or a sentence in one fashion, that decision sets up a paradigm for the rest of the text; however, if that same word took an even slightly different turn, the resulting text would be correspondingly different. In "On Matching and Making Maps: From a Translator's Notebook" (1988), the Dutch–English translator James Holmes makes a similar argument.

A small body of scholarship is beginning to grow that thinks about Borges's fiction as a source for translation theory. In the first chapter ("In the Place of a Theory of Translation: Translating Migrant Sex with Borges") of his dissertation (1996), Christopher Larkosh discusses the themes of translation, migration, and sexuality in the work of Borges. Larkosh draws heavily on Borges stories that focus on translation, such as *1001 Nights*, outlined above. But he adds discussions of migration; Hanna, the translating migrant who adds to Galland's first French edition, becomes a more central character in Larkosh's discussion. He goes one step further, opening up questions of sexuality and its relation to translation. As Shahrazad reveals sexual secrets, temporarily seducing the king to avoid punishment, so too is translation seen as a form of revealing secrets of another culture in an attempt to seduce the reader and to broker internal cultural differences.

In "Writing, Interpreting, and the Power Struggle for the Control over Meaning: Scenes from Kafka, Borges, and Kosztolányi" (2002), Rosemary Arrojo explores themes of control and authorship versus escape and labyrinths in Borges's story "Death and the Compass." In this detective story, the detective Erik Lönnrot pursues the criminal Red Scharlach ("*red*" refers to "net" in Spanish; "Scharlach" recalls "Shahrazad" or "Scheherazade"), whose maze ends up overwhelming not just the detective but Scharlach himself. The labyrinth, in a typical Borgesian fashion, becomes both a form of protection and a trap. Arrojo explores the architecture metaphors—the symmetries, repetitions, the devices, and ornaments, including a two-faced Hermes (the Greek word refers to "interpreter")—relating them to the authors' and most translators' attempts to reconstruct forms and control meanings, but more often than not weaving a textual maze subject to the inevitabilities and excesses of interpretation.

The theme of the sexuality of translation and the trauma induced by its impossibility reaches its culmination in Borges's story "Emma Zunz," also from Borges's collection *The Aleph* (1989f [1949]). Emma, daughter of a German immigrant named Manuel Maier (formerly Emmanuel Zunz), seeks to avenge the wrongful accusation of embezzlement made against her father, which in turn led to his exile and death. To do so, she constructs an elaborate plan of allowing herself to be raped, going to the accuser's home, shooting him, and then telling the police that he had molested her and that she had had to kill him in self-defense. While the plot is a fairly straightforward detective story, the complexity revolves around translating *memory*, Emma's thinking and acting logically while suffering tremendous rage, grief, fear, and fatigue. So too does the narrator/author figure find it difficult to narrate such horrible events, telling a story that involves experiences that have such an air of unreality about them. In "Z/Z: On *Midrash* and *écriture féminine* in Jorge Luis Borges' 'Emma Zunz'" (1997), Bernard McGuirk uses a complex methodology blending translation, psychoanalysis, and feminist theory to discuss Borges's story and its themes of translation, representation, re-representation, memory, trauma, and action. Because of the impossibility of "translation" or explication of such a story, and because so much of the story is mental rather than descriptive, McGuirk derives an interpretive strategy aimed at reading what cannot be said because of the limits of language and narration. The implicit meaning in the story, according to McGuirk, gives voice to the marginalized, immigrant, Jewish women's culture of Buenos Aires during the 1920s and 1930s. For example, in Emma's last name, "Zunz," McGuirk translates Hebrew connotations, deleting the vowel, and arrives at "zhn" as in "to play the harlot"; "znh" as "to reject as abominable"; "znv" as "to attack from the rear"; "zvz" as "a silver coin, a fourth part of a shekel"; and "zzm" as "a people from east of the Jordan," echoes that are always present for the Jewish reader but lost for most Western readers. So too are the textual echoes, the full range of meanings, covered up in translation. The full "meaning" of the original is thus only accessible by the bilingual/bicultural translator/reader, recalling Samia Mehrez's argument in "Translation and the Postcolonial Experience: The Francophone North African Text" (1992). For the stories of oppressed peoples, people living in exile at the margins of culture, such as Jewish exiles, it is not the literary meaning but precisely that excess of meaning, the haunting memories, that carries the most significance for their lives.

In a similar vein, Susana Romano-Sued focuses on issues of trauma and translation in Borges's story "Averroës' Search" (1998f), also from the 1949 collection *The Aleph*. In "Duelo y melancolía en la traducción o la travesía imposible hacia la equivalencia" ["Grief and Melancholy in Translation or the Impossible Voyage toward Equivalence"], Romano-Sued (1999) sympathizes with Averroës, a Muslim scholar from Córdoba during the height of Moorish Spain, who was translating/interpreting Aristotle's *Poetics* into Spanish, the "vulgar" dialect of the Muslim masses of the region. The problem was that he knew no Syrian or Greek, and therefore he was working from a translation of a translation. He also struggled over words such as "comedy" or "tragedy" because no Moor—since theater was prohibited in Islamic culture—had any idea as to their meaning. Borges imagines Averroës *imagining* theatre without ever having seen a play. For Romano-Sued, the story well illustrates the impossibility of ever achieving equivalence, the impenetrability of different systems of thought, and the painful, sad struggles of translators, peoples, caught between different sign systems. Yet Romano-Sued suggests that Averroës, in his search for the radical other—in this case a form of representation prohibited within Muslim culture—creates something new, thereby creating a space or condition for an Other to appear. She suggests that Borges's story, in its act of thinking about translating the Other, illustrates the difficulties not just of the translation process but the writing process in general, the act of "autopoesis" (ibid.: 84). For Romano-Sued, as for the Quebec women discussed in Chapter 3, the act of translating is an act of writing and one of the tools for Latin Americans, especially Latin American women, in light of the cultural oppression and *los desaparecidos* [the disappeared ones], to write themselves into history.

García Márquez: *One Hundred Years of Solitude*

While Borges wrote about translation in his essays and short fictions, translation assumes a major position in the novel with Gabriel García Márquez's *One Hundred Years of Solitude* (1998). In Borges's work, translation is considered from a literary-historical, psychological, and philosophical framework; in García Márquez's work, translation, or the lack of awareness of the implications thereof, becomes a major sociohistorical and material factor in the development of Latin America. Márquez scholarship has been dominated by magic realism readings and sociohistorical readings. The topic of translation remains remarkably effaced, especially when one considers that the *main* stucture of *One Hundred Years* is that the story of the Buendía family is (fore)told in Sanskrit in manuscripts written by Melquíades, and that the work itself is a *translation* of those manuscripts by Aureliano Buendía/Babilonia, the last of the Buendías.

In many ways, Márquez's great work echoes Borges: the Babylonian multilingual nature of the world; the impossibility of knowing things with certitude; the futility of the language and social constructions erected to control culture and/or nature; the desperation and uncertainties people find themselves in, especially when living in exile; and, perhaps most importantly, the mirrors (mirages) people construct that actually further distance themselves from their own roots, their own identities. The condemnation of the Buendía family to "one hundred years of solitude," despite the "greatness" of the patriarch José Arcadio Buendía, and the "heroism" of Colonel Aureliano Buendía, is largely due to the idea of the family's own lack of connection to their past, not just with their mythological roots but also with their multilingual heritage in all its myriad details. Aureliano only comes to understand the history of the family, his own origin, his own identity, when he finally deciphers Melquíades's Sanskrit encoded manuscript. Only at the end of the novel does he come to understand his true last name and his own identity: Babilonia. Only in the end of the novel does the reader begin to grasp the novel's nature as a translation.

The novel begins in an engrossing, narrative fashion. José Arcadio Buendía marches his band into the jungles of the New World to found the new city of Macondo; Colonel Aureliano Buendía leads the Liberals in multiple civil wars against the conservatives; Úrsula Iguarán, the matriarch of the family, holds the clan together despite historical and natural disasters. The reader is immersed in frontier stories, politics, wars, and natural disasters. In addition to the powerful narrative, García Márquez interlaces "magic" throughout the conquest story: a large Spanish galleon appears while José Arcadio is hiking through the jungle; the children of Macondo fly on magic carpets; water boils on a table without any fire; and Remedios the Beauty rises angelically, sheets flapping, from earth. The narrator, generally assumed to be García Márquez, is clearly omnipotent, creating a world out of the elements, and not restricted to the tools that humans (authors) normally use in the construction of a town (novel). Yet the narrator is not García Márquez; it is his fictional construct Melquíades who writes the tale of the House of Buendía in his native language, which is then deciphered and translated into Spanish by Aureliano. Much as García Márquez has said that the entire novel came to him in an instant of time while driving on the highway from Acapulco to Mexico City (where he was working as a translator and as a subtitler of films at the time), so too does the entire history appear in Spanish to Aureliano, the final key unlocking the story being Melquíades's epigraph: "The first of the line is tied to a tree and the last is being eaten by the ants" (1998: 446). Might one claim that the "author" of the story is Melquíades and the "translator" is García Márquez—that is, that the story came to García Márquez from some distant, ur-Latin American source and he is merely translating it into Spanish? At the least, one can claim that, similarly to Borges, García Márquez questions notions of traditional authorship and forms of the traditional novel.

The translational nature of the story is only revealed at the end of the novel, thereby redrawing the entire novel and forcing the reader to rethink earlier identifications and conclusions. García Márquez gives hints of the translational dimension throughout, however. José Arcadio Buendía spends hours, days, even months shut up a small room at the back of the house with his studies and experiments, most of them inspired by the knowledge brought from overseas by his friend and world traveler Melquíades. Yet his experiments—translating the fantastic inventions revealed by the gypsies to practical uses by the colonists—are carried on offstage. José Arcadio, who founded the village and named the streets, is shut up in his room and called "crazy," and readers forget about the patriarch. So too with José Arcadio Segundo, José Arcadio's grandson, who spends most of his time locked up in Melquíades's study poring over the as yet indecipherable parchments. Most of José Arcadio's work is also carried on behind the scenes: it is he who classifies the letters and, by comparing them to a table in an English-language encyclopedia, discovers that the language is Sanskrit. But José Arcadio Segundo's life is not the exciting and dramatic stuff of Colonel Aureliano Buendía's or that of the other powerful men of the story, even though it is he who realizes the lucidity of his grandfather and the insight of the gypsies. He also teaches little Aureliano how to read and write, thereby enabling the story of the history of the family to be told.

Melquíades, however, is the truly ur-multilingual, international figure; he has survived plagues and catastrophes seemingly from everywhere: pellagra in Persia, scurvy in Malaysia, leprosy in Egypt, beriberi in Japan, bubonic plague in Madagascar, and earthquakes in Sicily. He survives the droughts and wars in Latin America as well. He looks ur-Asian in appearance, and his "native" language is Sanskrit. For most of the "rational" members of the Macondo settlers, including Úrsula, he comes to represent the devil, and one cannot help but compare his relation to José Arcadio Buendía to Mephisto's relation to Faust (see the section on Haroldo de Campos in Chapter 4). The mentor for José Arcadio Buendía, and later José Arcadio Segundo, is the gypsy Melquíades, who has extraordinary wisdom and longevity. The most amazing magical event in the book is his return from the dead—the living on in a Derridian sense—of the Buendía story in translation. Some of the inventions the gypsies bring—ice, electric light, magnets—are so startling and magical that when Melquíades returns from the dead, the conditioned reader accepts the resurrection as credible. Most critics suggest that the magic is used to distort lines between the rational and the irrational, fact and fantasy, or myth and reality. In addition, I would suggest that lines between original and translation, between source and target texts, are also being called into question. Is it the Buendías who are living this life and a narrator who is recording it, or is Melquíades telling just another story in his travels and a Buendía is translating it?

Other hints of the translation subcomponent are scattered throughout. There are actually two groups of gypsies in the novel. The first wave is the truly multilingual and international group, full of exciting and original ideas; the second group, whose members come to Macondo later and do not speak Spanish, thus cannot translate their findings to Macondo's New World settlers, thereby frustrating José Arcadio Buendía, who wants to hear tales of their travels and inventions. The children of the Buendía house, Amaranta (daughter of José Arcadio Buendía and Úrsula Iguarán) and Arcadio (son of José Arcadio and Pilar Ternera), are raised not by their parents but by a Guajiro Indian woman named, ironically, Visitación. The children grow up speaking Guajiro, not Spanish. Thus, as with many children of the New World, their entire lives are spent in translation, and pure notions of mother tongue and native language are highly complicated. The children also learn indigenous practices such as drinking lizard broth and eating spider eggs before they learn "proper" culinary habits. José Arcadio, noted for his sexual prowess, also sleeps with a gypsy girl and in the heat of passion releases a string of obscenities, which we are told entered the girl through her ears and "came out of her mouth translated into her language" (García Márquez 1998: 34). This act of translation, corporeal as well as linguistic, results in another disappearance, that of José Arcadio, who runs off with the group of gypsies and is nearly forgotten (deferred) in the narrative of Macondo.

When he reappears some one hundred pages later, José Arcadio has traveled around the world sixty-five times with a crew of sailors "without a country" (1998: 99), and his Spanish is infused with multiple languages and dialects. His tales include being shipwrecked in the Sea of Japan, cannibalizing a fellow sailor who died of sunstroke, and killing a sea dragon in the Gulf of Bengal in whose body was found the remains of a Crusader. His body bears the marks of those international experiences: he is tattooed from head to foot, translation inscribed upon his body. Significantly, he does not sleep in that closed, incestuous Buendía house, but lives in the red light district, making his living by selling his sex. When he incestuously marries his adopted sister Rebeca, the two are banned from the house, and he again is forced to the margin of the narrative. It is his younger brother Aureliano who becomes Colonel Aureliano Buendía, not only the family patriarch but also defender of Macondo in his father's absence. The focus of the narrative shifts to civil wars between Liberals and Conservatives, and the heroic, nearly mythic efforts of the colonel and the resistance, as well as his numerous loves and sons.

Although it is relegated to the margins of the narrative, once one recognizes the translation theme, it is everywhere to be seen. The plague of loss of memory means that everyone in Macondo loses and has to regain their own language; the old man José Arcadio Buendía is thought to be crazy, ranting mindlessly in what is perceived to be an unknown language, which turns out to be Latin, but which no one in the town except the priest can understand. Pietro Crespi, the Italian furniture salesman, translates Petrarchan sonnets for Amaranta. And translation continues in Melquíades's study as the ghost reads to the future generations such as Aureliano, who at this point in the narrative does not understand, but who sets up a counter-line of descendants who will in fact be the ones to carry on the Buendía line after the physical line wears itself out. Thus, the book has a double narrative. The primary one is about heroic conquest and consolidation, of nation formation and patriotism that is written in the history books and memorials; the secondary one, generally pushed out of the household and found only at the margins of the story, contains multiple international interconnections, and concerns the preservation of lost lines and languages found only in cryptic writings and translation. Significantly, at the end of the novel, García Márquez *reverses* the order of the narratives, and the subnarrative of translation becomes the primary leading to the survival of the story and the Buendía line.

García Márquez's story is thus in many ways similar to Borges's. Borges picks ancient narratives such as the tales of Homer, Shahrazad, or Cervantes, written in ur-languages of Greek, Arabic, and Spanish. García Márquez picks a gypsy who writes in Sanscrit, a kind of ur-European, ur-Spanish language. Melquíades becomes a kind of Homeric bard or Shahrazad, weaving a tale with multiple openings and multiple interpretations, one rich enough and all-inclusive enough that it never really ends. The translational nature of the story—its being derivative and original at the same time—is the problem facing not just translators in the Americas but creative writers as well. The narration of lived experiences in the New World is invariably characterized by the use of old, imported European languages that somehow do not fit. Thus, American writers must use translation to smuggle in concepts and characters to refer to all those old Spanish, Italian, Aragonese, British, French, and Portuguese sailors and immigrants who populate their lives, and must use translation to refer to the images of travel and migration, upheaval and revolution, that are more characteristic of culture than anything stable or more permanent like settlements such as Macondo. García Márquez, in his writing Melquíades story, seems to be saying that translation, for all its impurities and shortcomings, is one of the keys to understanding not just Latin America but the whole hemisphere.

Mario Vargas Llosa: *The Storyteller*

In addition to García Márquez, other Latin American writers, such as Mario Vargas Llosa and Julio Cortázar, deal with the topic of translation in major works. In *El hablador* (1987) [*The Storyteller*, 1990], Vargas Llosa focuses on the problems of translation of indigenous tales in Peru, of faithful as against false representation, and the split identity of the Peruvian intellectuals. The novel comprises two stories presented in alternating chapters. The first story involves the search by the narrator (a thinly veiled autobiographical character) for Mascarita (the little masked face), the Machinguenga *hablador* (storyteller) who travels from village to village in the jungles of the Peru telling the stories, histories, and myths of the Machiguenga tribe, a nomadic Amazonian tribe relatively untouched by Western civilization. This search is interspersed with the translated oral tales, comprising everything from creation myths to transformation stories. The *hablador* in the end turns out to be an old friend of the narrator's from college, a man named Saúl Zuratas, who, surprisingly, is not an indigenous native but the son of a Russian/Polish father and a Creole/Jewish mother. Thus, the suffering of the Jewish tribes as they wandered without a homeland is juxtaposed with the wandering Machiguenga tribes. Nevertheless, the stories that the *hablador* tells are presented as authentic translations of oral Machiguenga tales passed on by the *viejos/as* and *abuelos/as*, the wise older men and women of the tribe. The text is focused on questions of translation and appropriation, of how anyone can ever get to know the Other, especially a culture with no connection to the colonizing Spanish or other Western cultures, without altering the very culture one wishes to translate.

The Storyteller opens with the fictional Peruvian narrator (Vargas Llosa) in Florence, Italy, ostensibly to study Dante, Machiavelli, and Renaissance paintings, a translation of the self into old European culture typical of the intelligentsia of Latin America during the period. Vargas Llosa himself left Peru after he completed his degree and lived in Europe for nearly sixteen years. Nevertheless, he felt conflicted about his Latin American identity and remained haunted by his Peruvian roots. In Florence, he comes across an exhibition titled "Natives of the Amazon Forest," in which an Italian photographer had taken a two-week trip to the Amazon region in Peru and describes "without demagoguery or aestheticism" (1990: 4) the daily life of a tribe of Amazonian natives (see the section on Gómez-Peña and Coco Fusco in Chapter 6). Thus, two clichés of translation are introduced from the beginning: first, the European artist/ethnographer traveling to the New World for a very short period of time, "translating" Latin American culture and bringing it to Europe; and second, the equation of photography to translation and its so-called objective nonideological or nonaesthetic representation of the facts. Indeed, the narrator notices that the name of the tribe, the Machiguengas, in a typical appropriative move, was Hispanicized. The exhibition in Italy calls up all sorts of questions for the conflicted narrator, including issues of memory, or, more precisely, false memory, and a complex anxiety caused by his being both a native of the country being represented and a participant in the appropriative process by viewing the photos in a gallery in Europe. When the narrator sees a photograph of his friend the storyteller with the Machiguenga tribe circling around him listening, he wonders how the photograph was possible, given that the tribe keeps such rituals private, not allowing outsiders access, let alone photographing/translating such incidents.

The storyteller Saúl Zuratas is introduced in the second chapter of the novel, although the reader does not yet know Zuratas's "true" identity. At this point in the story, Saúl Zuratas is shown as a talented but frustrated law student in Lima, Peru, where he befriends the narrator. Zuratas is the son of Don Salomón, an immigrant from Central Europe and a successful businessman who has converted from Catholicism to Judaism. Saúl Zuratas's mother is a Creole Indian from Talara, a small town outside of Lima, where the people had little education and could barely read. Thus, the main character is not indigenous at all; rather, he is a hybrid of Polish, Russian, Native American, Spanish, Peruvian, Catholic, and Jewish cultures, symbolic of the hybrid nature of all translation in a postcolonial world. Vargas Llosa erases distinctions between the Old and New Worlds, blending languages and cultures so that "originals" become infused with the past and informed by the future. Yet what is most distinguishing about Saúl Zuratas's identity is not his religious or ethnic background; it is a mark on his body: a large birthmark that covers the entire right half of his face—a wine-colored, feature-distorting mark that covers his lips, nose, ears, and even his hair—which has lent him his nickname Mascarita [Masked Face]. Without going into all the interpretations one might imagine associated with such an image, the connection to the two-faced nature of translation, to the marks of European culture on the body of the Latin American, to both intellectual and physical hybridity as a condition of culture in the postmodern world, and, especially, to the mask as a trope not only for translation but for Latin American identity in general, comes immediately to mind.

The story revolves around the separation of these two friends over the years. One, the narrator/author, successfully completes his literary studies in Lima, goes to Europe, learns European languages, studies Italian Renaissance literature, becomes a successful writer, and eventually returns to Peru as a television producer, producing a show ironically titled "Tower of Babel" (Vargas Llosa 1990: 146). The other, Saúl Zuratas, successfully completes his ethnography degree in Lima, is offered a scholarship to France, but turns it down—the first student ever at the school to turn down a scholarship to Europe—and disappears into the jungle, where he befriends the people of the Machiguenga tribe, a nomadic Peruvian indigenous grouping that has miraculously avoided contact with the Western world. Zuratas not only learns the language and studies their history but also adopts the customs and beliefs of the Machiguengas and begins sharing their existence—in short, identifying his own life with their ways and traditions, going over to the "other" side. The story thus juxtaposes two options for tracing one's identity in Latin American culture: the one path, the road most frequently chosen, involves tracing one's Spanish/European roots, Renaissance art, rational thought, Christian monotheism, urbanization, and all the trappings of Western civilization. Florence, with its dazzling paintings, buildings, fashions, new ideas, and intrigues, embodies this European track. The other path involves studying and learning indigenous cultures and languages, moving to the forest, wearing natural clothing, giving up private property, adopting polytheism, and giving oneself over to the history, mythology, images, and ancestral connections not contaminated by contact with the Europeans. While the narrator (Llosa) has chosen the former path, he is haunted by the latter in the form of the image of the face of Mascarita and the effort made to keep alive the stories, the feelings of community and fraternity, of memory and identity, that many Latin Americans so easily abandon.

Twice in his life the narrator has been to the jungle and has had contact with the Machiguengas: the first when he was just 22 years old, and later when he returned as a television producer. Of course his dealings with the indigenous people must be in translation. Ironically, his interactions are mediated by the only group whose members have managed to learn the Machiguenga language: the Summer Institute for Linguistics, a Protestant Biblical organization, which, under the guise of doing linguistic research, also attempts to convert the indigenous tribes to Christianity. On his first trip, the narrator goes as a guest of a Mexican anthropologist, visiting several different tribes. In the Amazon region, he meets the Schneils, a husband and wife missionary couple and linguists who first tell him about the *hablador*, which they translate for the narrator as a "talker" or "speaker," one who not only brings current news to the nomadic members of the wandering tribe but also speaks of the past, serving as a kind of memory for the diasporic community. While the narrator does not meet any Machiguengas during his first trip, he does hear the stories of the Schneils' first contact with the tribe and receives a transcription/translation of one of their songs, giving him an idea of the sound of the language and the way the words embody a different thought process.

The second trip comes much later in his life when he returns to the region to make a television show for a program called "Tower of Babel." At this point, nearly half of the some 5,000 surviving Machiguengas now live in villages with names such as New Light and New World, showing the "success" of the missionaries' linguistic project. Most tribe members now speak Spanish and attend Bible schools. Thus, the narrator can speak with selected village chiefs and schoolteachers, record dances and songs, and, via translation, inform himself "directly" about Machiguenga life. But certain topics are off limits. He is unable, for example, to get them to talk about the *habladores*, which is a taboo in the Machiguenga culture. Again it is the Schneils who tell him stories about their contact with the *habladores*, and it is here that the narrator learns that one of the storytellers the Schneils have met has a huge birthmark covering the entire side of his face and red hair, none other than the narrator's long-lost friend.

Translation is further problematized in *The Storyteller*: not just any translation will do. As the Schneils and the narrator illustrate, there is no easy access to, nor any unmediated interpretation of, indigenous Peruvian culture. In fact, many of the translations do irreparable harm to the cultures being translated. Two examples serve. The first is the problem that Saúl Zuratas has with his chosen field of study: ethnology. One of the reasons that he refuses the scholarship to France has to do with his doubts regarding the ethics and morals of the profession. Ethnologists, with their tape recorders and interviews, pry into the customs and belief systems of the tribes, introducing foreign ideas and material goods that serve to corrupt and destroy the very beliefs that they are trying to preserve. Zuratas claims that the ethnologists' research is in the same class of activities as those of the rubber tappers, timber cutters, and army recruiters, one that does violence to the local culture by appropriating material and culture, translating in into their own terms and uses, and not giving anything back. Ironically, many of the case studies by the anthropologists and ethnographers are written in Spanish or other European languages and published in North America or Europe. Seldom are they written in any indigenous language, nor are they translated into the native languages so they can be read by the people being studied. Thus, the people being represented have no idea of *how* they are being represented, unless of course they learn the language of the academic investigators, another kind of covert translation imperialism to which many ethnographers seem oblivious.

The second example of problematic translation is that of the missionary/linguistic translators. Here the imperialism is overt: the missionaries attempt to convert the indigenous tribes, have them give up their religious beliefs, their nomadic way of life, and their communal support system in order to adopt the Christian religion, move to villages, and join the capitalist economy. One of the narrator's teachers tells him, "Be careful. Those gringos [of the Institute of Linguistics] will try to buy you" (Vargas Llosa, 1990: 71). The linguists also enjoyed strong ties with the government, including the Ministry of Education and the military. While translating the Bible into Machiguenga, the linguists also work to translate the traditional belief systems out of the indigenous cultures, eradicating one way of life and substituting for it their own.

In a conversation with his friend, Mascarita delivers a fierce diatribe against the Summer Institute of Linguistic "researchers." Zuratas claims:

> Those apostolic linguists of yours are the worst of all. They work their way into the tribes to destroy them from within, just like chiggers. Into

> their spirit, their beliefs, their subconscious.... The others steal their vital space and exploit them.... Your linguists are more refined. They want to kill them in another way.
>
> (Vargas Llosa 1990: 95–96)

When the narrator suggests that they are no different than Dominicans or Spanish missionaries in previous generations, Zuratas claims that while the jungle swallowed up the earlier missionaries, allowing the Machiguengas to slip away and coexist in the Amazon, the linguists, with the economic power and backing of national and international organizations, under the guise of learning aboriginal languages, have been much more successful in implanting their religions, values, and culture. He continues, "What for? To make the Amazonian Indians into good Westerners, good modern men, good capitalists, good Christians.... Not even that. Just to wipe their culture, their gods, their institutions off the map and corrupt even their dreams" (ibid. 97).

In my earlier work in *Contemporary Translation Theories* (Gentzler 1993), I talked about the vested interests of both Bible translation and the so-called linguistically based science of translation (2001: 44–76), raising questions regarding certain fundamental assumptions at the heart of the respective theories. I found Bible translation theories such as those of Eugene Nida clouded by religious presuppositions and missionary goals, and the more scientific, functional approaches based on vague assumptions about supposed innate structures that were more often a reflection of European or North American linguistic theory. In his critique of both ethnography and of Bible translation theories in *The Storyteller* (1990), Vargas Llosa precedes my research by several years, showing how the translation theories of the fictional turn in South America anticipate translation studies research in the decade to follow.

As opposed to the form of translation practiced by the scientists in the form of ethnography, or of the linguists in the form of missionary work, Vargas Llosa posits an alternative form of translation, one that might be called cultural immersion, embodied by Saúl Zuratas giving up his scholarship, going into the jungle, living with and learning the stories of the Machiguengas from the perspective and language of the tribe. This is presented not so much in terms of the story involving the narrator's search for his friend, but instead by the indigenous stories interspersed throughout the novel. While these stories are presented as authentic translations, stories learned by Saúl Zuratas in the jungle from first-hand sources, they are actually fictitious translations, or, in translation studies terms, "pseudo-translations" (Popovič 1976: 20; Toury 1984). While the first several stories about the Machiguengas' wanderings, wars, gods, and sorcerers appear to be authentic, later stories involving stories from Ovid or Jesus Christ reveal their fabricated nature. Nevertheless, the stories take an uncanny form, abandoning Western forms of narration, leaving many cultural terms, names, and places untranslated. The technique retains a degree of authenticity, certainly one of allowing different ideas and perspectives to surface.

Translation scholars such as Lawrence Venuti (1995) would call the techniques used by the storyteller "foreignizing" translation; Antoine Berman (1992) would refer to them as "nonethnocentric" translation. The names of the various gods are left in the original: *Tasurinchi* is a creator, breathing out the animals and the people; *Kientibakori* is the lord of the demos, a crazy god. Place names are left in the original: *Gran Pongo* is a kind of river of heaven where life begins and ends, *Kambarira* is the river of the dead; various indigenous tribes appear: the *Mashcos*, an enemy tribe of the Machiguengas, the *Ashaninkas*, *Piros*, *Amahuacas*, and the *Yaminahuas*. *Viracochas* are clearly white Europeans who track the Machiguenga men down and carry them off to "bleed" trees. Tribal elders have become endowed with spiritual qualities: *seripigari* are good spirits; bad sorcerers include the *machikanari*; *kamagarini* are little devils; a *sopai* is a she-devil. The list of estranging terms goes on, including animals, plants, foods, place names, clothes, and celestial bodies. To follow the stories, the reader must give him- or herself over to a different world with different surroundings, histories, and points of reference.

The style of the narrative of the stories is also different from stories' structures in the West. For one thing, time is conceived differently. First, and most importantly, people are always walking, moving, changing, and adapting, making it difficult to say exactly who or what anyone is. People in Europe are generally identified by their place name (Von Dams, de la Cruz, van der Berg) or by their profession (Smith, Butler, Taylor, Hunter); in Latin America, in cultures that are mobile, with people coming and going with few possessions, one's sense of identity is totally different. Names are temporary, not permanent; what might be a village or a settlement one year might be the jungle the next. A person who is a hunter one year might be a fisherman the next. Proper nouns do not exist in the same way as in Western languages. One might be called "the one just born" one year, "the one who arrives by canoe" at a later time, and "the one whose mother just died" the next year. The calendar is different as well. Time is continually referred to as "that was before" or "that was after." There is no Christ, thus no BCE or AD or Western calendar. Events repeat themselves and go in cycles. Europeans come and go—there are the conquistadores, missionaries, rubber tappers, coffee growers, and Latin American government officials. The Machiguengas move on, slipping away, measuring their nomadic life not by events on earth but rather by movement of the stars and philosophical concepts. Number systems are different as well; while numbers exist for small amounts, such as one, two, or three, larger amounts (five and above) are invariably referred to as "many," giving an ethereal quality to the stories. Most importantly, religion is different; the stories abound with the myths and embellished histories of the exploits of gods and men important to their existence, their periods of happiness and abundance, their periods of war and strife. The Machiguengas' notion of goodness, peace, and prosperity is generally associated with harmony with nature—periods when fish and game are plentiful and the forest is undisturbed—not with the construction of a beautiful building or accumulation of gold and silver.

Thus, the translation strategy involves letting go of certain Western beliefs, terms, and structures and going over to the other side, allowing as many of the sounds, rhythms, and, especially, cultural associations to surface in the translation as possible. Rather than translating a word or term into some Western semiequivalent term that assimilates and explicates, Vargas Llosa, in his fictitious translation, presents a translation model that develops a cultural context within the story to allow fields of association to arise that may allow for understanding or access without assimilation. While one is uncertain how "true" the stories are, the reader suspects that Vargas Llosa has done a quite a lot of research and that many aspects of the stories as well as narrative style are semifictional rather than fictional, just as the fictional narrator's life is presented in a semiautobiographical fashion. I suggest that translation studies scholars have much to learn by reading the fiction of many of the Latin American writers to see how skeptical many people of South America are about translation models as developed in the North, as well as to gain insight into new possible translation strategies that are less exploitative. How does one translate without a certain degree of fictionalization (how does one write an autobiography without fictionalization)? How does one access the Other without giving up one's own language and worldview? If those belonging to a particular culture resist contact with the Western world and refuse to speak about certain aspects of their culture, how then does a Western scholar represent that taboo subject?

Derrida and Benjamin

As Vargas Llosa questions traditional translation theory as a means for accessing and understanding indigenous Amazonian culture, so too has translation theory witnessed a generation of deconstructive scholarship that also questions traditional translation theory and its appropriateness for translation of indigenous and oral cultures. Most of the "theory" underlying such questioning derives from Walter Benjamin's "The Task of the Translator" (1969a) and Jacques Derrida's reading of Benjamin's essay, presented orally in a series of workshops in the 1980s and in written form primarily in "Des tours de Babel" (1985b) and "The Roundtable on Translation" (1985c). Before turning to those essays, I would first like to discuss another Benjamin essay, called "The Storyteller: Reflections on the Works of Nikolai Leskov" (1969b), which immediately follows "The Task of the Translator" in his collection *Illuminations*. In this essay, Benjamin bridges the gap between "The Task of the Translator," in which he discusses the creative potential for translation when it draws upon the plurality of languages rather than some single independent language, and "The Work of Art in the Age of Mechanical Reproduction" (1969c), in which he discusses the difference between a work of art before the era of mass reproduction, when art connected with social actions such as ritual, and the work of art after the invention of lithography, phonography, and photography, in which the aura of earlier art is lost. Reproduction offered by the news media, radio, and television changes the way a culture thinks about and perceives art. While Benjamin finds this liberation emancipating and empowering, he also clearly laments the loss of aura, ritual, magic—in short, the intimacy—of the earlier forms of artistic communication, so clearly lacking in the modern world.

In "The Storyteller," Benjamin discusses the decline of the role of the storyteller in the age of the novel, made possible by the invention of printing. Storytellers' tales derive from their own lived experiences or the experiences told to them by others. In turn, the storyteller makes those experiences part of the lives of the people hearing the stories. Like a translator, the storyteller has traveled afar, has listened to other stories, brings something back across time and distance, and retells the story in the idiom and nuances of the new audience. There is an intimacy, a ritual, a communal experience for those listening. Novelists, on the other hand, work alone, in isolation, then send their texts to the publishers, who print and sell the books to the readers, who never meet the author. Novelists may or may not exchange ideas with other writers, and seldom exchange ideas and experiences with the readers. The exchange is a one-way flow of ideas, for a price, generally from a fairly lonely and isolated figure to an often equally lonely and estranged group of readers.

With the decline of the art of storytelling, Benjamin laments the loss of another form of meaning. Not the unified and decipherable "meaning" of a particular novel, but the access to that pool of oral histories—memories, loves, struggles, traditions, rituals, and fairy tales—passed on from generation to generation that storytellers have at their disposal. The goal of the storyteller is to share those memories and experiences with the audience. Yet each telling changes the story as the storyteller draws upon a variety of psychological ploys to connect with the audience. The precise meaning of any one individual tale is less important then the shared, communal experience (and one can see Benjamin's Marxism creeping in), drawing the audience into that web of experience that networks all of the stories together. One story connects to the next, forming a chain of interwoven tales overlapping and interconnecting. One thinks of Schahrazad, who draws on that pool of stories and histories to derive a new and related story every time any individual story finishes, so that the story never ends. The stories of the storyteller thus have no origin and no end. One also cannot help but think of Borges, whose work predates Benjamin's by over ten years.

As Benjamin in "The Storyteller" allows his readers a glimpse of the web of communal identity, so too does he in "The Task of the Translator" (1969a) discuss translation less in terms of deciphering and reencoding the specific "meaning" of any one individual text than in terms of allowing the reader access to that communal pool of languages that is always evolving from one generation to the next. Benjamin suggests that this constant state of flux or words and sentences (which involves Benjamin's notion of "pure language"), which Benjamin argues is fundamental to the nature of language, invariably remains hidden in individual languages. However, in some forms of translation, aspects of this hidden nature of language—its inherent plurality, the foreignness embedded within any given language—become visible.

Benjamin's essay "The Task of the Translator" (1969a) has been written about by many poststructural and translation scholars (Jacobs 1975; De Man 1986; A. Benjamin 1989; Bannet 1993; Davis 2001; Gentzler 2001). To be brief, the arguments generally are similar. These scholars point frequently to the title of the essay, which in German is "Die Aufgabe des Übersetzers." *Aufgabe* translates idiomatically to "task," "job," or "duty." It derives, however, from the verb *aufgeben*, which means to "give up" or to "give over." Thus, the "Aufgabe" of the translator involves, according to the poststructural readers of Benjamin, a process of giving up the notion of rendering a recoverable, coherent meaning of the text, and instead giving oneself over to this pool of languages and ideas, what Benjamin often refers to as the "kinship of languages" (1969a: 72)—the interrelatedness of languages to each other. Translation thus has an additional aim apart from the mere representation of any one individual text; it also serves the purpose of expressing "the central reciprocal relationship between languages" (ibid.: 72).

Once one rethinks the task of translation less as the reproduction of a text from one language to another and more as an opening to the entire network of evolving and creatively growing pool of languages, one can better see the fascination of Latin American writers for the theme of translation as a reflection of their own cultural evolution. We have seen how Borges calls into question the existence of any original text, instead referring to ambiguous, oral Homeric tales or the never-ending tales of the Arabian Nights as an ephemeral source text; how García Márquez's story invokes a kind of ur-Sanskrit that precedes any individual European or Latin American language in which to tell his story of the Buendía family, who in their patriarchal fashion try to shape and control culture; and how Vargas Llosa's turn to European languages and cultures is haunted by oral tales and histories from his "native" Peru. All of these authors sense the Benjaminian notion of the kinship of languages and call into question notions of ownership, origin, and singular meaning. By foregrounding the theme of translation in the Benjaminian sense, these authors give themselves up to a different notion of authorship and offer alternative notions more connected to translation and storytelling.

The other term in Benjamin's title that poststructural critics play with is *Übersetzen*, which idiomatically is translated as "translation," but which in

German literally implies a process of "carrying over." Critics connect this term to other related terms scattered through Benjamin's essay, including *überleben*, "living on" or in French *survie*, "survival," and *fortleben*, "carrying on" or "carrying forth." Thus, the prefix "trans," in addition to referring to "across," is invoked in a paradigm of associations, including "beyond" and "further" and, significantly, "change" and "renewal." Thus, translation for Benjamin is connected with images of expansion, development, and change. Here the connection to the Spanish explorers deployed in Latin America becomes clear. American identity is caught up in images of exploration, development, expansion, and renewal. In addition, Benjamin's thinking about "trans" in such an exploratory fashion calls to mind images of "wandering," "erring," and "exile." Translation for Benjamin opens into that labyrinth of all languages, their historical interrelatedness, and their development into individual and different languages. From the labyrinths of libraries constructed by Borges, to the complex histories of one displaced family trying to establish a foothold in Macando by García Márquez, to the wandering tribes of the Machinguengas connected only by oral histories of Vargas Llosa, one can see the connection between Latin American translation as a theme of fiction and the translation theory of Benjamin.

Benjamin goes so far as to argue that no translation would be possible if the goal were only "likeness to the original" (1969a: 73). Rather, he suggests that in its afterlife (*fortleben*), which implies a transformation and a renewal of something living, "the original undergoes a change" (ibid.: 73). Not only is a translation not the same as the original but in the process of translation, the translation *changes* the original. The source text in Benjamin's translation theory is not some unified, inviolable original that can be captured and carried across to another culture. Rather, the original also derives from and contributes to this labyrinth of languages and ideas a kind of first draft of an idea that reaches its fulfillment in translation. Translation thus completes the original as a kind of afterlife. Benjamin uses organic metaphors here, talking about the "maturing process" of an original via translation. Translation joins together with the original to form a new organism in a kind of birthing process. The original is conceived of as the seeds or the roots of the organism; the translation as its growth and flowering. Rather than being a sterile equation between two dead languages, translation allows the reader to see the evolutionary process of the original language and the "birth pangs" of the target language (ibid.: 73). The attractiveness of such a concept of birth pangs for Latin American scholars should be clear: in Latin America, not only do the original European languages develop and grow, but also they make apparent the struggles of creating new texts in the target language and forming an independent identity.

The idea that the translation changes the original is sacrilegious to not only traditional (and many contemporary) translation studies scholars but also, more importantly, those European critics and cultural institutions who defend the sanctity of the existing canon—the great books—and the authors who write them. For the fiction writers in the Americas who are struggling with their own identity, trying to incorporate the best of European ideas and writing but nevertheless striving to find their own voice and language to express their own experiences, the idea of adapting rather than adopting the canon has its appeal. Coterminous with the interest by Latin American authors in the theme of translation (see the section on cannibal translation in Chapter 4) was Derrida's seizing upon the ideas of Walter Benjamin and using them to illustrate his deconstructive mode of writing, also meant to challenge the canon and destabilize notions of unified and coherent original texts and theories of art and philosophy (including translation) based on metaphysical ideas.

In "Des tours de Babel" (1985b) and "The Roundtable on Translation" (1985c), Derrida discusses Benjamin's text, giving not what he calls a theoretical reading but a "translation of another text on translation" (1985b: 175). In fact, many of Derrida's texts can be better approached from the perspective of translation rather than critical theory. He picks up on both the expanded field of association generated by the prefix "trans-" and the organic metaphors of Benjamin's text, suggesting that the *Überleben* which the translator endows upon the original is not just a survival, but a "surplus of life" [*un plus de vie*]. The original not only "lives on" in translation but is improved; it lives "more and better, *beyond* the means of its author" (ibid.: 179; italics mine). To express his idea, Derrida invokes the marriage metaphor: just as in marriage two people who are different are joined in an alliance and complete each other, forming a new entity that changes them both as individuals, so too in translation do two languages join together to complete each other, forming a greater language that changes them both (ibid.: 224).

Thus, for Derrida, translation is a creative act, one that transfigures and transforms. Because no translation ever is the same as the original, Derrida actually suggests that we substitute the notion of "transformation" for translation (1981: 20). It is also the vehicle in which difference can be included, and indeed is instrumental to the creative process. Thus, translation is seen as a mode or a form of its own, in many ways similar to creative writing, to fiction. Or, better put, original writing is seen as similar to translation, an idea underscored by the Latin American fiction writers. The fiction of Borges, of García Márquez, of Vargas Llosa, of Cortázar is both translation of the fiction of Europe and North America and at the same time creating something new. Latin American fiction both develops from seeds planted in European forms and languages and extends and enlarges those very forms and languages by adding or adjoining.

The title of the essay "Des tours de Babel" (Derrida 1985b) best illustrates the play of translation that can extend and enlarge language. As Joseph Graham mentions in a "translator's note" to the essay, "*des*" can mean "some," "of the," "from the," or "about the." *Tours* can mean "towers," "tricks," "twists," "turns," or "tropes." Together, the two sound like *détour*, "detour." The title also is very self-referential, calling up fields of associations that Derrida has put into play in other essays, namely his notions of differing and deferring, for which he has coined the neologism *différance*, elaborated in the essay "Différance" from *Margins of Philosophy* (1982a; see Gentzler 2001: 157–167). Thus, the title "Des tours" is polyvalent, drawing upon multiple fields of associations, even referring to forms that have disappeared from contemporary usage. Derrida's point is that any single interpretation (translation) covers up and hides potential meanings that also might inform the text. Derrida's translation strategy (and philosophical project) is not to set (*setzen*) on any one fixed translation or interpretation, but to defer or delay this fixation in order to get beyond one set meaning (*übersetzen*).

In "Des tours de Babel," Derrida refers to the *récit* (the story, the well-known oral history passed down from generation to generation) of the Shem tribe (*shem* means "name"), who wanted not just to construct a tower to reach the heavens but to make a name for themselves, imposing their name and their tongue upon the other tribes of Israel. Derrida reads the story as the Shems trying to force their language upon the world by violence. God destroys this attempt to impose a universal language (which would eliminate the need for translation) by destroying the tower, scattering the tribes, and disallowing the imposition of one language upon the others. While some critics imply that God is condemning humankind to a permanent state of confusion (*Babel* means both "the father" and "confusion"), Derrida instead sees the deconstruction of the tower as a condemnation of hegemonic violence and a liberation of language, a positive affirmation of polyvalence and the free play of different languages mutually interacting. Indeed, in the "Roundtable on Translation," Derrida goes so far as to call God a "deconstructor" (1985c: 102; in the Derridean affirmative sense). He suggests that the interruption of the construction of the Tower of Babel gives a good idea of what deconstruction is: "an unfinished edifice whose half-completed structures are visible, letting one guess at the scaffolding behind them" (ibid.: 102). Deconstruction is thus analogous to dissemination, which Derrida plays with by calling it "dischemination," which calls to mind de-Shemitizing, or detouring or rerouting (the word *chemin* also means "path"), and indirectly connecting with his ideas of differing and deferring.

I suggest that Derrida's "scaffolding" is similar to what the Latin American fiction writers are attempting to expose by their foregrounding the theme of translation. The image of the wandering tribe portrayed by Vargas Llosa, the Machiguenga tribe that haunts the narrator/author of the story, continues to exist behind all the modern constructions of buildings, roads, schools, government palaces in urban areas of Latin America. Saúl Zuratas, who exemplifies not only the native Peruvian American but also the wandering Jew, and even some ur-Celtic, pre-European native, by turning his back on Europe and collecting stories of the wandering natives, attempts to get beyond those reified notions of fiction by going back to his roots. The translations of his stories presented by Vargas Llosa are not meant to capture or fix any one given story as truth, hence their fictional nature; rather, they attempt to open a path to that world of different names, places, times, religions, gods, histories, plants, animals, and wars that have not been recorded, canonized, fixed, or fixated by Western languages and cultures. García Márquez not only portrays the Buendía family as they wander about in the New World looking for a place to settle but, more importantly, lays his novel out as a translation from the Sanskrit, another ur-language predating the hegemony of European languages. The history of the family —about life in the Americas in its polyvalent fashion with its blend of Native American languages, gypsy languages, Spanish, Catalan, Portuguese, English, French, Italian, and Latin as well as the Sanskrit—can only be understood in translation. Borges's short stories also tap into that labyrinth of languages, especially those oral Homeric and Arabian stories that predate the powerful European languages, which often are viewed as colonizing rather than canonical in Latin America. Indeed, Borges's parodying of European fictional and academic forms of writing, of the parceling of knowledge, exposes the hypocrisy and the illusionary quality of the attempts to package and control ideas, and points to *chemins* and paths historically closed off by such forms. In sum, the development of translation as a theme in Latin American fiction is parallel to and mutually interacts with the deconstructive form of writing referred often to by Derrida not as theory, but as translation itself.

The fictional turn and criticism

In the essay "(In)visibilidades na tradução: troca de olhares teóricos e ficcionais" [I(In)visibilities in Translation: Exchanging Theoretical and Fictional Perspectives] (1995–1996a) and in the related article "El ser en 'visible': 'el espejo' en Guimarães Rosa" [Being in "Visible": The Mirror in Guimarães Rosa] (1995–1996b), Brazilian critic Else Vieira discusses how the discourse of fiction has been used as a source for theories about translation, calling this stage the "fictional turn" in translation studies (1995–1996a: 50). She locates her theory in the context of work done by translation scholars Susan Bassnett (1993), Lawrence Venuti (1992a, 1995), and André Lefevere (1992), poststructural theorists such as Foucault (1977), Benjamin (1969a), and Derrida (1985b, c), and Brazilian critics such as Nelson Ascher (1989) and Eneida Maria de Souza (1995). While the theory of the fictional turn is presented only in a sketchy fashion, it turns on an analysis of the trope of mimesis in the work of Brazilian fiction by authors such as Guimarães Rosa. She argues, for example, that the fiction writers anticipate poststructural thought by making subjective thought— difference—visible, even in realistic descriptions. Even in the words of scientific discourse, one can see the convergence of multiple languages.

Fiction narrates experience; fiction represents reality; subjective points of view are invariably expressed. Vieira plays with the image of the "mirror" and the camera lens, both in the fiction and in the criticism, and how they are used as metaphors for realism in fiction and for faithfulness in translation. She asks, how are images reflected? How are different photos of the same thing different? What are the limits such terms impose on literary critics when discussing either fiction or translation? How is the unseen shown in translation? Mirrors and photographs often offer misguided efforts to represent reality. Referring to the work of Borges in fiction and Haroldo de Campos in poetry, Vieira suggests that translation (*tra-duzir*) is better understood as trans-position (*trans-posição*) (1995–1996a: 64). This transposition works in two directions: just as Latin American writers are influenced by and transpose the work of European writers, so too are European writers influenced by and changed by the "translations" by the Latin Americans. The reflections are bidirectional, forming a simultaneous two-way flow of ideas and forms. The exchange of ideas and the cross-fertilization process via translation is necessary for the evolution of ideas and the innovation of new forms of fiction. She too refers to Benjamin and Derrida at the end of "(In)visibilidades na tradução" (1995–1996a), focusing on the organizing metaphors of birth and renewal, of survival and supplementation. Vieira's final image is of a river, similar to the rivers in Guimarães Rosa's fiction, that flow across borders, fertilizing the land for the future growth but also giving new life to the past. So too, she argues, does translation change both the past and the future, revealing and concealing as it participates in the evolution and flow of cultural systems.

Else Vieira's work is indicative of a new wave of Latin American scholars investigating the fictional turn in translation. In the anthology *Translation and Power*, Maria Tymoczko and I have attempted to collect representative essays by Rosemary Arrojo, Adriana Pagano, and Christopher Larkosh to illustrate this movement. In "Writing, Interpreting, and the Power Struggle for the Control of Meaning" (Tymoczko and Gentzler 2002), Brazilian translation studies scholar Rosemary Arrojo looks at metaphors having to do with construction and architecture in stories by Franz Kafka, Jorge Luis Borges, and Dezső Kostolányi. She sees the authors/narrators as builders structuring their texts in an attempt to control the meaning and reception. Yet interpretation and translation inevitably contradict perfect completion, unity, or closure. In "Translation as Testimony: On Official Histories and Subversive Pedagogies in Cortázar" (2002), the Argentine-born Brazilian scholar Adriana Pagano connects the topic of translation to the activity of nation building in Latin America. She analyzes the theme of translation, especially the tension between aesthetic versus ideological choices, in texts by Julio Cortázar, including "Blow-Up" (1967a), *Hopscotch* (1967b), *62: A Model-Kit* (1972), and *A Manual for Manuel* (1978). In "Translating Women: Victoria Ocampo and the Empires of Foreign Fascination," the United States-based Latin Americanist Christopher

Larkosh (2002) looks at the entire corpus of work of Argentine writer, translator, and publisher Victoria Ocampo, including both how her autobiographies, *testimonios*, and translations came to represent the international literary world, and how her publications came to represent Argentine writing as a whole, connecting to translation to the development of Argentine national identity to the world.

Arrojo begins her argument with an analysis of the story "The Burrow" by Franz Kafka (1971). The narrator of the story lives underground and has completed the construction of a burrow, but the passages and openings need to be continually checked; weaknesses are exposed, making the narrator always vulnerable to enemies on the outside. The narrator is thus shown to be less than a master of his own construction, just as no author can ever protect against different interpretations. The Borges story "Death and the Compass" from *Ficciones* (1989b [1944]), analyzed by Arrojo, continues this theme of the attempt to control meaning. As was mentioned earlier, the author figure in this case is the criminal Red Scharlach, who coldly attempts to construct a deadly labyrinth around a detective named Erik Lönnrot, who as the reader/translator figure must not only unravel the clues but also anticipate his adversary's moves. In a typical Borgesian reversal, the criminal becomes the hunter and the detective the hunted, putting the author/interpreter in a dialectical spin. Thus, the criminal Red Scharlach weaves a web to catch the detective. Borges's point, and Arrojo's as well, is that the author/translator as constructor/deconstructor is always caught in a complex interplay, infinitely repeating itself in a vain attempt to construct and control meaning.

Arrojo culminates this argument in the Kosztolányi story "The Kleptomaniac Translator" (Kosztolányi 1996). The main character is named Gallus, who is a talented writer and translator but has a compulsion to steal. He ends up doing more translation work because he cannot get work in his own name, often the translations of trashy texts that editors cannot get more respectable writers to touch. One of these translations is rejected by an editor, and a friend of Gallus decides to find out why. He discovers that the translation, while fluent, artistic, and often better than the original, is missing certain items, such as the jewelry of one female character or certain rugs, safes, watches, suitcases, cash, and silverware. The translator thus has been unable to control his compulsion, criminally tampering with the original, thereby threatening authorial rights and property. What Kosztolányi seems to be arguing, rather like Kafka and Borges, and Derrida, is that this desire to construct an inviolable tower, burrow, or text is fraught with problems; protection from invaders from the outside, from different readings and interpretations, is impossible. Translators, who are often the closest readers of texts, have their own subjective desires (and pathological problems) that directly or indirectly creep into their translations. Fiction writers seem to know this only too well; it is time that translation theory deconstructs some of its own postulates and catches up to the fiction.

Adriana Pagano's work also explores the relationship between fiction, translation, and history, often looking at translation as the site of tension and even of violence—violence through the imposition of words to translate "reality." Thus, according to Pagano, translation cannot be divorced from ideology and powerful cultural institutions involved in the production of culture. Cortázar's "Blow-Up" (1967a), for example, concerns the investigations of Roberto Michel, a French-Chilean living in Paris, who is a full-time translator and part-time amateur photographer. While in the middle of translating a scholarly thesis for a professor from the University of Santiago, he goes to a park, intending to take photos of a conservatory. He happens upon a couple—an older woman and a young boy—who capture his attention. Upon developing and blowing up the photos of the couple, he discovers new items in the scene, including a man in a hat, a newspaper, and a birdlike image, indicating that probably some sort of child abuse was happening or about to happen. Themes blend in Cortázar's fiction; photography is used as a metaphor for translation. Yet, similarly to the limits of the ability of the mirror or the camera lens to record reality pointed out by Vieira above, the role of the translator/photographer is active rather than passive in the participation of events; the boy, for example, runs away when the woman discovers her picture being taken. How the photo/translation is developed, the difficulties of exactly reproducing the original, the displacement of meaning in the process of translation/reproduction, the role of the photographer/translator in the final version of the text, and the violence revealed underlying the idyllic romantic scene are all explored by Cortázar.

In *62: A Model Kit* (Cortázar 1972), the main character is an Argentine translator named Juan, who works for UNICEF in Paris. He makes a mistake when translating a customer's order in a Parisian restaurant. The phrase "Je voudrais un château saignant" ("I'd like a rare steak") becomes "Quisiera un castillo sangriento" ("I'd like a bloody castle"). For those scholars who have taken the fictional turn in translation theory, those "mistakes" are pregnant with ideological and subjective meanings, allowing the unseen to be seen, if no more than the subjective interpretation of the invisible translator to peek through. For Cortázar, the Latin American translator's mind transposes the rare steak into a bloody castle, a king drenched in blood, a European colonizer stained with the blood of the Latin American natives. "Château," an abbreviation for a kind of steak called "Chateaubriand," further calls to mind the French author François-René de Chateaubriand (1768–1848), whose poems were to become the "foundational fictions" for many generations of Latin American intellectuals (Pagano 2002: 84).

Pagano's main focus, however, is on the novel *A Manual for Manuel* (Cortázar 1978), which tells the story of a group of Latin Americans who, while living in Paris, plan to kidnap a Latin American officer linked to repressive paramilitary activities against oppositional groups. During these planning stages, two of the main characters, Patricio and Susan, make a scrapbook for their son Manuel, translating, from French to Spanish, newspaper articles that reflect the tension and violence of the 1970s, including events such as the kidnapping of a West German ambassador in Brazil, the escape of ERP guerrillas from prison in Argentina, and the tension between Argentina and Britain over the Malvinas/Falkland Islands. The ensuing kidnapping is not successful; the police find the kidnappers and imprison them.

Using the translations for the boy, Cortázar questions history, versions, perspectives, facts, and "the truth." The activists, aware that they may be captured or die, want to leave Manuel an alternative to the official history recorded by the journalists and the government. In their translations from French to Spanish, they expand, adding comments on the way the news was reported, letting the boy know how the linguistic choices of the original story also attempt to conceal and censor. In their translations, they decode certain conventions, often presented as facts by the journalists, reading between the lines the political and ideological messages conveyed. In addition to leaving an alternative record, they want to teach their son how to read critically, against the grain. Cortázar seems to be suggesting that translation can be used to rethink national histories and to allow space for alternative versions to coexist within a culture. Translation is likened to a clandestine activity that can be liberating. The violence to culture is done by the original writing that manipulates facts and only partially represents reality. Translation provides a broader perspective and allows openings for repressed and silenced meanings and events to surface. In the case of Latin America, where official versions of events are often used to cover up historical events, such as the massacre of the workers of Macondo by the banana company in *One Hundred Years of Solitude*, translation as difference, as supplementation, as completion, takes on a new meaning, one that does not distort, but allows a more complete picture.

As Pagano connects translation as a mode to critically engage with the established history of a given country, so too does Christopher Larkosh connect translation to the kind of education in foreign languages received by Argentine intellectuals during the nation's late nineteenth- and early twentieth-century history. In "Translating Woman: Victoria Ocampo and the Empires of Foreign Fascination," Larkosh (2002) looks at the life of Victoria Ocampo, whose family life was representative of that of many Argentine intellectuals of the period. They had strong economic and cultural ties with Europe. The nannies and tutors who raised Ocampo taught her French and English; she spent considerable time in Europe, so much so that European cultural life created prejudices for her against her own country. The education, the languages learned, and the translations read ensured perpetuation of European values and ideas. Education was a form of oppression. For Cortázar, the manual for Manuel is offered not only as an alternative history but, according to Pagano, as an alternative form of education for the future. Larkosh shows how Ocampo felt constrained by the languages and cultures of Argentina and Europe, and turned to translation as a means of social and cultural liberation. She was fascinated by those texts beyond the Argentine/European sphere and turned to writers such as the Bengali poet Rabindranath Tagore for inspiration and ideas. Just as women are constrained by the social and political norms of the period, so too are Argentines constrained by European ideas and cultures. Translation for Ocampo becomes another form of cultural intervention, allowing her increased freedom of choice. Thus, translation not only is shown to be a central tool in the construction of Argentine identity in the past, but also becomes an important means by which to critically assess that constructed identity and to offer alternatives. Translation blends together with fiction and theory to offer a new perspective on history, memory, and identity formation. In Argentina's case, Larkosh concludes, the nation is not so much a unified, coherent nation with a fixed Spanish language, rather a Babelian nation with no official language or fixed boundary. The alternative history, the one manifest in translation, is better indicative of the complex intertextual network of languages, texts, and traditions translated and retranslated that transgress boundaries of unified imagery and symbolism (2002: 118)—in sum, the labyrinths suggested by the fictions of Borges.

Just as Borges's fictions inform the theory underlying Larkosh's and Pagano's assessment of the work of Ocampo and Cortázar, so too does Anibal González, who teaches at the University of Texas, Austin, turn to Borges in "Translation and the Novel: *One Hundred Years of Solitude*" (1989). González suggests that Borges is "without a doubt the most important source for García Márquez's literary ideology" (ibid.: 275). Connectng Borges's ideas from "The Homer Versions" (1989c [1932]) and "Pierre Menard" (1989a [1944]) to the ideas of Walter Benjamin and Jacques Derrida, González suggests that translation not only entails a search for and fidelity to origins and originality but also, in the process, reveals its silent accompaniment, the dispersion of meaning and potential confusion. Borges and García Marquez are both suspicious of notions of the sanctity of any one individual text, and instead their fictions are about raising questions about how texts become sacred. Aureliano Babilonia Buendía's task of translating Melquíades's manuscripts about the history of the family/town/nation serves less to reveal its "meaning" than to inscribe the story into the language of kinship, including the kinship taboos and importance of "proper" names (González 1989: 277). The novel is not united in any sense, but actually collapses in translation. Ironically, it can actually never end, for the translator/Spanish narrator Aureliano Buendía is inscribed in the story, imprisoned in a city of "mirrors and mirages" that would be extinguished at the moment Aureliano finished deciphering the manuscript (García Márquez 1998: 458). The translation itself involves a double translation, transcribing the Sanskrit into Spanish and then breaking Melquíades' private code. What is the relationship of a national language to any one individual? Aureliano Babilonia needs to draw on all his resources of languages, encyclopedias, genealogies, linguistics, writing, and translation to decipher the manuscripts. Anibal González not only connects the obvious themes of translation in the novel—Melquíades' manuscripts in Spanish; José Arcadio Buendía's reverting to Latin when tied to the tree; Arcadia and Amaranta speaking Guajiro when young; and José Arcadio's returning from his overseas adventures with his body, including his penis, covered with multilingual tatoos (a phallic Tower of Babel)—but also extends the theme to include translation as migration—the colonel's seventeen sons who are conceived while he is on the march; the gypsies seen as translators wandering across the swamp; José Arcadio and Ursula forced to migrate when José kills Prudencio Aguilar; and, most significantly, translation as dissemination when Aureliano Babilonia and Amaranta Ursula violate the incest taboo. As incest serves to limit and thus define a single kinship system, argues González, so too does translation, in a Benjaminian sense, breach barriers between languages, revealing their interconnectedness often hidden within individual languages. Latin American fiction thus reminds readers of all texts' connections to their own foreign originals and their own translational nature. Those scholars such as Vieira, Arrojo, Pagano, Larkosh, and González, who have taken the fictional turn, see the theme of translation in nearly every text. Translation, in theory, in practice, and in the fiction that narrates Latin American history, inheres in the very constitution of Latin American identity. Reading Latin American fiction from the perspective of translation, I suggest, informs our understanding not only of the nature of translation in the Americas, but also of how our identities have been formed and will continue to be reshaped in the future.

6 Border Writing and the Caribbean

If the borders between languages are in a constant flux, as the scholars of the fictional turn argue, what does that say about the nature of the border? Of distinct and separate nations? Of translation? If the story of the Americas' collective cultural histories can only be told in translation, what does that mean for traditional definitions of translation in monolingual cultures? One of the more recent phenomena in artistic and critical thinking in the Americas derives not from a distinct nation-state—Canada, the United States, Brazil, or the many Spanish-speaking Latin American countries—but from regions on the borders between these nation-states. As those living in such areas record their movements and thoughts, a new body of literature known as border writing is emerging. Genres include visual and performance art, bilingual fiction and poetry, translation, and literary and cultural criticism. Perhaps because the translations often inhere within the texts and do not conform to traditional concepts of translations, new categories arise. Often nontranslation—that is, deliberately leaving a part of the text not translated in order to marginalize the monolingual reader—is emphasized by border writers, thereby undermining definitions of separate and homogeneous cultures. Indeed, the trope of translation and transculturalization has become one of the leading metaphors used to describe border writing, and merits further investigation. In this chapter, I suggest that translation is more than a trope; rather, it is a critical daily process engaging all forms of communication and thought by those whose lives depend upon crossing borders.

Artists writing about borders show how the border, rather than being a distinct and narrow line drawn upon a map between two nations, is more of a growing space that overlaps larger geographical regions. Because of more advanced means of communication and ease of travel—better roads, cars, trains, planes, telephones, and the internet—it is easier than ever to maintain contact in two cultures. Even within single dominant cultures, multiple pockets of subcultures and countercultures exist, and individuals are constantly traversing borders. Definitions of nations and nation-states have served to conceal the fact that border cultures have always existed.

Maps for drawing the nation-states of the Americas, after all, were drawn by the colonizers with little regard for the people living in those spaces. Thus, the indigenous peoples such as the Mayans in Central America or the Quechuas in Peru and Ecuador often found their lands and languages spread over more than one nation-state.

In this chapter, I pay close attention to the islands in the Caribbean, which have shuffled among various imperial European powers multiple times. The lives of the indigenous and creole residents of the islands have continued regardless of the differing imperial languages and laws. Indeed, I suggest that those living on borders or those subgroups within existing nations are more constitutive of so-called national identity than the "national" identity imposed by European colonizing forces. In Chapter 5, we saw how some Latin American writers such as Gabriel García Márquez, Julio Cortázar, and Mario Vargas Llosa began to explore their countries' multilingual and heterogeneous pasts. In this chapter, I focus on writers living on the United States–Mexican border, such as Rolando Hinojosa, Rudolfo Anaya, and Gloria Anzaldúa, as well as performance artists such as Coco Fusco and Guillermo Gómez-Peña. Throughout the chapter I refer to a variety of Caribbean writers, including Trinidadian novelist Sam Selvon, Cuban novelist Alejo Carpentier, Cuban poet Nicolás Guillén, Martinique poet and translator Aimé Césaire, and Cuban essayist and translator Fernando Ortiz. These writers' creative and translation/adaptation work illustrate the multiple ways translation has been used as an artistic tool to create new forms of art and as a subversive tool to resist colonial and neonational definitions of culture and society.

Much ongoing work in critical theory circles also attempts to rethink static definitions of the state and national boundaries, as well as linguistic and cultural unities. Jacques Derrida's work is continually concerned with borders, from his early work "Living On/Border Lines" (1979) to more recent treatments in *The Truth in Painting* (1987b), in which he concerns himself with the concept of the *parregon* or frame that marks the border or a work of art, ostensibly separating the outside work from that which is within the painting, referring by extension to any attempt to draw a border around a philosophical idea or a unified, coherent linguistic text. Perhaps of more interest, however, is the research conducted on smaller regional Caribbean communities by Latin American cultural theorists such as the Cuban essayist Fernando Ortiz, who coined the concept "transculturation" as early as the 1940s, or the Cuban poet and critic Roberto Fernández Retamar, whose concept of "hybrid" cultures, developed in the late 1960s and early 1970s, engendered a new wave of postcolonial scholars writing on hybridity. The concepts have provided an alternative to the multiple theories of acculturation and assimilation predominant in the Americas and have been widely embraced by subsequent Latin American theorists, including, for example, the Uruguayan critic Ángel Rama. This work in the Caribbean and Latin America predated the most widely known theorist of hybridity in translation studies circles, Homi Bhabha, who has even gone so far as to coin the phrase "translational culture" to refer to those hybrid multilingual cultures in which translation becomes a way of life. Other poststructuralist conceptual insights, such as Gayatri Spivak's thinking about translation and subalternity, similarly serve to inform thinking on border writing and translation, although not without creating some uneasiness among Latin American scholars about replacing one kind of political colonialism with a kind of intellectual imperialism.

In border spaces, distinctions between the "original" and "foreign" cultures tend to disappear, for cultures tend to be both simultaneously. Such dissolving of boundaries cannot help but have repercussions for translation theory. If distinctions between original and translation no longer hold, if both cultures tend to be similarly multilingual and multicultural, what then happens to the definition of translation? Such a rethinking of boundaries and languages also cannot help but affect thinking about identity formation, leading at first to a kind of schizophrenic crisis of identity, yet later pointing to new ways of thinking about identities as plural and capable of change. Border writing has developed many tropes to better describe this space —polylingual, heterogeneous, nonsynchronous, fragmented, translational, and transcultural. Rethinking along these lines offers new ideas that not only deconstruct older distinctions based upon binary oppositions—source/target, home/foreign, original/translation, colonial/postcolonial—but offer new categories of thought, consuming and internalizing the above oppositions, not merely taking sides or reversing polarities, but revising and reproducing them in new and highly creative forms of art and writing. One cannot help but think of the anthropophagist translators such as the De Campos brothers mentioned in Chapter 4. Yet these border writers are often cannibalizing two imperializing cultures simultaneously and coming up with new ideas that represent anew as they destabilize.

The results are highly creative. What is it like to think about a nation when one has no home? What is like to think about translation when one has no native language? How is one's identity affected if one's homeland has been dissolved? What do the new hyphenated, compound identity markers such as African-American, Asian-American, or Amer-Indian describe? What do they exclude? Will new markers, maps, and split terms accurately describe the conditions of the nomads, migrants, and exiles caught between borders and national definitions? Can one think about a culture in which there are no centers but only borders? How would such a situation change our definition of translation? Border writers tend to continually invent polyvalent hybrid forms, expropriating elements from both sides to create forms and ideas that are open and inventive. High/low, East/West, North/South, rich/poor, self/other, man/woman become fused until the two are indistinguishable. In many texts, translations appear in contexts where translations are not normally expected. Ironically, mistranslation can reveal more "truth" regarding the source of border culture than a more traditional "accurate" translation. The border writer is often viewed less as a cross-cultural communicator than as a smuggler, and the translator less as a neutral mediator than as an implicated participant in the smuggling process, helping to trespass, steal, reinterpret, remap, and rethink cultural and artistic boundaries. In this chapter, I hope to show how the Americas comprise multiple languages; its peoples speak with multiple voices, and its citizens have multiple identities, which are, consciously or subconsciously, always involved in the process of translation.

La frontera

One of the longest, most visible, and most contested areas in which border writing flourishes is the Mexican–United States border, referred to in Spanish as *la frontera*. The site where the North meets the South, the haves meet the have-nots, English (monolingualism) meets Spanish (bilingualism), the area is further complicated by the fact that large portions of southern California, Nevada, Utah, Colorado, New Mexico, Arizona, and Texas used to belong to Mexico, and were only ceded to the United States after the war between the United States and Mexico (1846–1848). Thus, many Mexicans crossing into the United States in search of jobs find themselves working (often "illegally") on farms that their ancestors used to own, thereby blurring the distinction between homeland and the foreign. Anglo-Texan is still a word used in the southwest United States to describe the descendants of those white "immigrants" who first entered Texas when it was considered part of Mexico. History in the region is characterized by its conflicting versions, a battle that is being waged today. Often, Tex-Mex or Chicano oral histories contradict official written versions, proving a ripe source of information for creative writers emerging from the region.

Rolando Hinojosa, son of a Mexican-American father and an Anglo-Texan mother, is symptomatically representative of a new generation of border writers from the region. He grew up in southern Texas, where Spanish competes with English for dominance, and his father's Mexican ancestors go back to the early 1700s, well before the Mexican–American War. Thus, his family had no sense of being immigrants or foreigners in the region. In his fictional work, including *Estampas del valle y otras obras* (1973), *Klail City y sus alrededores* (1976), *Mi querido Rafa* (1981), *The Valley* (1983), and *Klail City* (1987), Hinojosa constructs the fictional south Texas border town of Klail City in Belken County, located in the Rio Grande River Valley, to represent the contemporary living conditions of the border culture, reminiscent of William Faulker's construction of Yoknapatawpha County as symbolic of post-Civil War southern United States society. Hinojosa documents the fight for survival of the Mexican culture there despite repression by the Anglo-Texans (and selected Mexican-Americans who collude with the whites), drawing especially on oral testimonies and translations as his source material. His work is written in both Spanish and English, with most of the texts originating in Spanish and then being translated—or recreated (*recreaciones*), to use in Hinojosa's words—in English. *Klail City y sus alrededores* (1976) became *Generaciones y semblanzas* (1977), a bilingual edition translated by Rosoura Sánchez, and then *Klail City* (1987) in English, presumably translated by the author, and finally a new version back in Spanish has reappeared under the title *El condado de Belkin: Klail City* (1994). In his some thirteen novels to date, characters get rewritten and further developed, and distinctions between the "original" and the translation/recreation distorted. Hinojoso's written language is often bilingual, with characters often switching codes depending on the subject matter and the participants in the conversations. English phrases appear in the Spanish versions, and Spanish colloquial expressions and proper nouns are scattered through the English (translations). The audience for such texts is presumed to possess at least a degree of bilingualism.

Hinojosa's work resembles a detective novel reminiscent of Jorge Luis Borges's short fictions (see Chapter 5), where the so-called truth of Texas history is contradicted by a variety of different memories and perspectives provided by the original Mexican inhabitants. Hinojosa's work includes many forms of representation: a collage of testimonies, oral memoirs, newspaper reports, legal depositions, and interviews. His narrator, while tracing a history in a narrative form, allows the spoken voices of the original inhabitants to emerge, translating as it were the oral history of the region into the written one, which invariably distrusts and undermines the official, written history of the region. For example, in the story "Sometimes It Just Happens That Way: That's All" from *The Valley* (1983), Hinojosa reports several conflicting testimonies regarding the murder of an Ernesto Tamez by a Baldemar Codero in a southside Klail City bar. Hinojosa records five different versions of the same story, including two newspaper excerpts from the *Klail City Enterprise News* which document the "official" version, namely that a jealous Baldemar Cordero killed Ernesto Tamez because of his advances toward a woman who worked in the bar; two transcripts (with the spelling corrected) of cassette recordings by a "fictional" character, a lawyer named Romeo Hinojosa, first with the defendant Baldemar and second with his sister Marta; and finally, a deposition translated by a certified legal interpreter of the eyewitness account by a Gilberto Castañeda, Cordero's friend and Marta's husband. The oral histories in the characters' own words reveal many complicating factors not part of the official history. The defendant, for example, while admitting to the murder, does not remember actually stabbing the victim because he was too angry or inebriated. The sister's account, which is entirely secondhand, nevertheless reveals much about the defendant's past, including many good qualities, such as his devotion to the family and refraining from fighting in order to stay out of trouble. Castañeda's translated deposition reveals the ridicule suffered by the defendant before the murder. The technique of locating the narrator in the story as a public defender, recording and transcribing cassette tapes of the witnesses' accounts in their own voices, and the translation of an official deposition allow other histories to surface: Mexican-Americans' loyalty to families, conditions of poverty, culture of joking and teasing (*burlándose*), ongoing legal battles, and secret codes of honor. Sometimes the pressure of keeping silent, of repressing such cultural forces, results in sudden outbursts of violence such as those recorded in the *Klail City Enterprise News*. Hinojosa translates the unwritten history into the written and the bilingual culture into English, giving voice to the repressed psychological ideas and values that give cause to the violent outbreaks.

Another *frontera* writer documenting the contemporary United States–Mexican border culture is Rudolfo Anaya, whose work is striking because it reaches back further into history, drawing upon Spanish conquistador and even pre-Columbian cultures and traditions. The border, for Anaya, not only reveals a regional situation, but also suggests possible connections to historical traditions that include both Spanish-American and Native American cultures. Anaya is from east-central New Mexico and has lived, writing and teaching, in Albuquerque for much of his life. His first novel, *Bless Me, Ultima* (1972), reflects the multicultural nature of New Mexico and provides a springboard for contemplation of larger historical and spiritual questions.

Bless Me, Ultima is about the life of a certain Antonio Márez, who struggles to maintain family values as the culture is changing around him. His father was a *vaquero* (cowboy), a free spirit who roamed the *llano* (plains) with other equally independent-minded men until he married and moved into the town of Guadalupe. At 7 years old, Antonio knows very little English. As is the case still today in the Mexican–United States border culture, English is taught in the school, but Spanish is spoken in the home. Since Antonio is the narrator of the story and is only now just learning English, much of the work is already in translation. One of the difficulties in analyzing border writing is that although translation is invariably present, it is not marked as such. As Antonio talks with his friends, sometimes the initial exchanges begin in Spanish and then shift to English, subtly indicating that the dialogue is a translation. At other times we see a blend of the two languages, a kind of Spanglish, with many important terms still in Spanish. But usually conversations take place in English, with Spanish words and phrases thrown in only for colloquial, religious, or familiar expressions. When Antonio's father speaks of *vaquero* culture, or when the priest prays for the sins of the members of his church, the narrator often transcribes their words in English but indicates that the person spoke in Spanish. Thus, much of the novel, which is written in English, is a kind of a *hidden* translation; while not called a translation, the book is in effect a translation from Spanish of the early years of this young boy's life.

The main theme of the book deals with the two different Spanish traditions embodied by the parents and how Ultima bridges that gap. The word *último/a* in Spanish means "the last one," and the wise old woman from the *llano* represents the last in the line of women who have quasi-magical powers of understanding, who have knowledge of the past and present, including the various migration patterns before the arrival of the white Anglo-Americans. Ultima serves as a kind of translator herself, bridging the gap between the peaceful agrarian culture of the mother and the wild independent culture of the plains horsemen. Ultima, for example, understands that the wild salt water of the sea (Márez, the father's family name, means 'sea') and the sweet fresh water of the moon (Luna, the mother's family name, means 'moon') are one and the same: the rain falls, flows in freshwater rivers to the seas, replenishing the ocean. Antonio, who is caught in the middle, arrives at an understanding of his own split identity via the wise old woman.

Yet perhaps more significantly than bridging the gap between different Spanish-American traditions, through Ultima, Anaya translates from the hidden oral and spiritual cultures of the pre-Hispanic cultures that also make up his past. This form of translation in the border cultures is less translation of written texts than it is a form of remembering and historicizing that extends beyond the constraints of language. Reading these historical markers becomes a kind of deciphering of a secret code. In *Bless Me, Ultima*, Anaya reveals a kind of underground culture of people who have access to and can interpret such hidden markers. These characters include not only Ultima but also selected additional characters such as Narciso, a fool and a drunk who nevertheless remains fiercely loyal to Ultima and the Márez clan, and a boy named Cico, whom Anthony meets while fishing and who shows him some of the secrets of the hidden lakes in the region and tells him stories of pre-Hispanic deities. These characters are very careful about whom they invite into their worlds, but Antonio, perhaps because of his close relationship with Ultima, is brought into their hidden circle.

Communication in this sphere takes place not via language but via other semiotic markers such as silence and observation. Ultima and Antonio, for example, gather medicinal herbs and roots in the hills, not talking, but connecting via a kind of nonlinguistic form of translation to another world, not Spanish or English, not Christian or secular, but one shared with other traditions—with the Aztecs, the Mayas, and even the Moors from back in the Middle Ages of Spain. In "The Politics of Translation," Gayatri Spivak talks about a kind of translation that is passed on with its marks of *un*translatability (1992: 193–194; see Chapter 7). Ultima's story is untranslatable, but is nevertheless communicated by reading the traces, marks, and memories that are covered up by the dominant languages. Derrida refers to these traces (*Spuren*) as simultaneously present and not present, for they cannot be explained in the dominant conceptual categories. People in the town of Guadalupe turn to Ultima for help when Western medicine and the Catholic religion fail to cure people from illnesses and then watch in awe as her pre-Hispanic medicines cure the afflicted. Some members of the town nevertheless whisper about her being a *bruja* (witch) and talk about her blasphemous ways, for her actions cannot be understood in terms of Catholic conceptions. Antonio himself begins to question Christian precepts when he sees the success of Ultima in helping others in need. In another example, Antonio's friend Cico shows Antonio how the land is actually surrounded by waters composed of hidden rivers and lakes, just as the Hispanic cities and towns are surrounded and supported by indigenous cultures, with the implication that without the support of the pre-Hispanic cultures, the new cities and towns might sink and disappear. Other markers are less visible, ranging from the medicinal roots below the earth's surface, to contradictions in blessings given by priests, mixed pre-Hispanic traditions in religious ceremonies, feuds among families, games children play, the farmers' almost spiritual feel for the earth, the scents in the wind, and even the different shapes and patterns seen in the stars.

The entire book *Bless Me, Ultima* might best be characterized as an attempt to translate this Other culture by reading its strange marks and traces. One of the most frequent adjectives in the book is the term "strange": the "strange brotherhood" of Cico, Samuel, and Antonio (Anaya 1972: 108), the "strange power" of the water, the "strange music" of the winds, cliffs, and water (ibid.: 108–109), the "strange cries" of the birds (ibid.: 97), and the "strange premonitions" of the fool and drunk Narciso (ibid.: 119). To read these hidden markers, Anaya uses a variety of innovative techniques: novel, autobiography, dream sequences, magical realism, and, especially, written, oral, and intersemiotic translation. The border, thus, in this case is not just the geographic Rio Grande river valley region between the United States and Mexico, but also that between pre-Hispanic and Hispanic cultures. Antonio, the main autobiographical character, by learning the techniques of Ultima to decipher and translate this hidden language, not only comes to a better understanding of his own identity but also discovers a means to preserve such knowledge via his own writing and translating in the future. The book performs thus a kind of double translation. As Ultima (and Antonio's parents, for that matter) do not speak English, the book translates their ideas and conversations from Spanish to English. In addition, through Ultima, other old people, and a few selected younger people such as Narciso, Anaya translates from pre-Hispanic cultures and beliefs to the present. The book holds an uncanny resonance for Chicano as well as North American audiences; the book is in its twentieth edition and is read in high schools and colleges throughout the nation. Its translation component, however, often invisible to mainstream culture, including most critics, is only just now being realized.

The new *mestizo/a*

Perhaps the writer most frequently associated with *la frontera* is Gloria Anzaldúa. In works such as *This Bridge Called My Back: Writings by*

Radical Women of Color, coedited with Cherríe Moraga (Moraga and Anzaldúa 1981), and *Borderlands/La frontera: The New Mestiza* (Anzaldúa 1987), Anzaldúa not only talks about experiences on the Texas–Mexico border but also brings a lesbian woman of color's perspective to the equation. Her work has been influential in redefining feminism, cultural studies, ethnic studies, queer theory, and postcolonial studies, but translation studies scholars have been slow to engage with her thinking. This is surprising, for Anzaldúa herself is a translator, translating her own work from English to Spanish, and translation and mediation is one of the primary themes throughout her work.

Anzaldúa brings a poet's sensibility to the subject matter of the border, and her writings are particularly poignant. Her most famous book, *Borderlands/La frontera* (1987), is divided into two parts. The first contains a series of essays discussing the contemporary cultural scene and its history on the border; the second contains six sections of bilingual poetry devoted to different peoples of color and to historical figures and relics that continue to have meaning in the region. She talks about the border as being a "vague and undetermined place," often in a state of "transition" (ibid.: 3), where one is both "at home" and "a stranger" (ibid.: 194). She describes those living on the border not only as black, white, Hispanic, or *mestiza*, but also as "the squint-eyed, the perverse, the queer, the troublesome, the mongrel, the mulatto, the half-breed, the half dead" (ibid.: 3). The whites living in the area invariably define the inhabitants of the border as transgressors and aliens, and they pass laws prohibiting the transgressors/trespassers, legally documented or not, from entering many places and institutions. The tension is continually manifest, and the threats of incarceration, violence, and death are palpable. For a woman on the border, the dangers are even greater, with the threats of physical and sexual abuse coming from men of all colors and persuasions.

The use of violence often serves to intimidate into silence those who cross the border. In writing, Anzaldúa attempts to articulate this silence, giving voice both to the rebellious feelings of those living on the border and to the more dominant forces that repress those urges, causing the border-dwellers to quietly acquiesce, obey, and accept the conditions of intimidation. In order to avoid conflict, border inhabitants suppress their own customs and values, dressing, talking, and acting differently in order to conform to the dominant culture. In short, they suppress their own identity in order to avoid being sent back to the other side or punished on the North American side. For Anzaldúa and other women of color, the problem is not just an either/or situation—the difference between the United States and Mexican cultures—but also the culture of men from both sides who value subservient women. Women are expected to be humble and selfless, devote themselves to the family, and work to preserve domestic hierarchies, which include the grandparents and the parents, as well as societal hierarchies in which men are dominant in the community, state, and national levels.

Women, Anzaldúa argues, are near the bottom of the hierarchy, one step above the "deviants," for which often the Chicano, Mexican, and many Indian cultures have even less tolerance than North American. Anzaldúa's status as a lesbian woman makes her feel even more unacceptable: faulty, damaged, fearful, and isolated. She talks of women shivering in their cells in enclosed cities, fearing the discrimination and violence, shutting down their senses and beliefs. She does not feel safe in her own culture, and white culture is doubly intimidating. The intimidation, she suggests, blocks and immobilizes women, preventing them from full engagement. The border thus being described by Anzaldúa is not just the border between the United States and Mexico, but, more importantly, the border between a state where someone else is in control, where one is felt to be a victim of circumstances, in hiding and invisible, and the state where one feels strong and in control, able to shape culture, visibly participating in the organization of events. The analogy to translation should be obvious. The author is always the one in control, shaping the text; the translator is always being controlled, subservient to the dominant order, faceless and voiceless.

Anzaldúa writes about border culture in two senses, the first being the very physical sense of the geographical area of the Rio Grande on the gulf coast of the Mexico–Texas border, and the second being the spiritual sense of religious and mythical figures who have come to represent Chicano/a peoples of the *frontera*. When Anzaldúa talks of the border peoples, she means not just a culture caught between two languages, but a culture that is always translating among several languages. In *Borderlands/La frontera*, she describes some of those languages spoken by the Chicanos/as: standard English, working-class English, standard Spanish, Mexican Spanish, north Mexican Spanish dialect, Chicano Spanish, Tex-Mex, and *Pachuco* [a language of rebellion against both standard Spanish and standard English containing all sorts of neologisms and insider codes comprising mostly slang words from both English and Spanish] (1987: 55–56). Chicano Spanglish thus makes multiple references in every utterance, communicating not only overtly in terms of linguistic semantic reference, but also clandestinely, via a kind of secret code to those who can read between the lines, who also know the seven or eight varieties of languages invoked when spoken. The word "Chicano/a" itself, a slang derivative of Me*xicano/a*, used to be a derogatory term, but its meaning now connotes a great deal of pride. Chicano Spanglish is a tool used not just to communicate or to translate between cultures but also to *create* an identity for those in between. Those on the border often do not identify with either standard Castilian Spanish or standard American English. Their culture is complex and heterogeneous, and Chicano Spanglish is increasingly viewed as a language in its own right, one that speaks to realities and values of the peoples living on the borders.

Chicano Spanish is developing in a culture of extreme prejudices; purists on both sides consider Chicano Spanish an "inferior" Spanish. Chicanos/as

Border Writing and the Caribbean   153

often feel uncomfortable even speaking Spanish to other people of Central and South America because of this inferiority complex. This low estimation of the language has translated into a low estimation of themselves. A double prejudice is operative in this situation, for to switch to English implies selling out to the *gringos*, the North Americans. While ethnic studies scholars are slow to think in terms of language minorities, they are even slower to think in terms of border culture minorities. Yet as Anzaldúa and other border writers know, ethnic identity is closely related to the language one speaks. Increasingly, border writers who write in Chicano Spanish are feeling comfortable writing as they speak, without "correcting" their Spanish or English, switching codes frequently without explaining or translating, accommodating neither the native English nor the native Spanish speakers, but forcing them to confront the multilingual space of the border.

In terms of translation theory, border writing thus attempts to communicate across cultures, to be sure, but in a mode that translates and does not translate simultaneously. Concepts such as faithfulness to the source language need not apply; the faithfulness of the border writer is to that creative nonlanguage that is yet to be described, one that is in constant flux and evolution. Adequacy to the target culture does not apply, either; target culture languages often prove hopelessly inadequate, thus bringing the target culture closer to the border culture rather than the other way around. Bilingual passages are sometimes translated but more frequently than not are left untranslated, explained only by context and culture rather than by linguistic means. Border writing also contains many hidden codes, secret meanings only available to those who speak Chicano. The struggle to translate or not to translate is equated with the struggle to identify with the Other culture—in this case, a defined culture such as Spanish, English, Mexican, American, Latin American, Hispanic, or even Mexican-American —or to identify with that nonarticulated *mestizo/a* culture, one which affirms a mixed cultural heritage, including, but not limited to, Mesoamerican, Spanish, Mexican, English, and North American and *all* the languages associated with them.

Translation/nontranslation is thus used not just as a trope to describe the physical situation in which border nations find themselves in the present; it also invokes a spiritual dimension that bridges contemporary culture to the past. In *Borderlands/La frontera*, Anzaldúa writes:

> *La gente Chicana tiene tres madres* [Chicano people have three mothers]. All three are mediators: *Guadalupe*, the virgin mother who has not abandoned us, *la Chingada* (*Malinche*), the raped mother whom we have abandoned, and *la Llorona*, the mother who seeks her lost children and is a combination of the other two.
>
> (1987: 30)

Guadalupe is, of course, the virgin mother who appeared miraculously to Juan Diego, a poor Indian in Tepeyác, and is perhaps the most powerful cultural image in Mexico. While she represents the Virgin Mary, mother of Christ, in the religion of the conquistadores, she also represents Coatlalopeuh, a descendant of the fertility and Earth goddess Coatlicue, in the religion of the Mesoamericans. In fact, the Spanish word "Guadalupe" might be seen as a kind of a poor phonetic translation of the Nahuatl word "Coatlalopeuh." While the Roman Catholic Church considers Guadalupe to be the mother of God, in Mexico and Texas, for those living in the area, via a kind of surreptitious translation she is also still very much connected to the Earth mother of Mesoamerican culture: the serpent goddess (*coatl* means "serpent"), goddess of the animals. Guadalupe is thus a hybrid figure, blending Old World and New World religions and beliefs, but, more importantly, she has taken upon herself the psychological and physical devastation wrought upon both men and women by the conquerors and colonizers. She, in sum, is a symbol of secret rebellion against the colonizing white men, offering a way to subversively preserve, via translation, traces of indigenous cultures and beliefs by means of the creation of a border figure, half Spanish, half indigenous, whose full meaning can only be realized in translation.

If the Virgin Guadalupe is the most revered cultural icon by both men and women in Indian, Mexican, and *frontera* culture, another hybrid–border–translational figure follows closely behind. She is, of course, La Malinche, also translated as Malintzin, or Malinali in more Native American versions, or Doña Marina in the more Hispanicized versions, who was Cortéz's translator and interpreter during the conquest of Mexico. According to the story in Bernal Díaz del Castillo's chronicles, she was offered to Cortéz by Moctezuma (also known as Motecuhzoma, depending upon the transliteration) as a slave, but because of her language skills—she knew both Nahuatl, the language of the Aztecs, and coastal Mayan, her native language, and also, according to legend, learned Spanish in just two weeks— she was quickly elevated to translator. She was also supposedly beautiful and just as quickly became Cortéz's mistress. For many Mexicans, she is viewed as a traitor—through her Cortéz discovered the real power, location, weapons, and strategies of the Aztecs. In popular culture, thus, the oft-used pejorative word *Malinchista* is heard on the streets, referring to a traitor, a coward (a woman, a "pussy"), or, even more often, *Chingada*, the "fucked one," referring to Malinche's betraying her race by sleeping with Cortéz. But in more recent thinking, the status of La Malinche is rising. Minimally, she is thought of less as a traitor than as a victim, a person who was sold into slavery not once, but twice—first by her Mayan father to the Aztec Moctezuma and later by Moctezuma to the Spanish conquistador Cortéz. Her role as Cortéz's mistress is viewed less as a voluntary action and more as a coerced behavior, a kind of rape. Her facility with language shows her high degree of intelligence, and more recent scholars feel that Malinche actually helped persuade the Indians not to resist in situations when their arms were inferior, and the Spanish not to arbitrarily kill indigenous peoples when they did not represent a threat. In other words, without Malinche's "translations/interpretations," the fidelity of which is suspect, the massacre would have been much worse. Because she was able to smuggle in via translation certain delaying and evasive tactics, smoothing over belligerent rhetoric, many lives were saved. So, too, in many historical situations, interpreters and translators, because of their ability to negotiate through translations—that is, to find neutral and/or ambiguous concepts, or, on occasion, to manipulate terms that they know would be interpreted very differently in a different cultural context—have been able to prevent bloodshed. The Indian–Mexican–*frontera* culture may be the most visible culture that has a translator as its heroine, the founder of its *mestizo/a* (of mixed heritage) race.

The third figure who is viewed as part of the spiritual trilogy of Anzaldúa's description of borderland peoples is a kind of a hybrid of the two above hybrid figures. La Llorona [weeping woman] represents a strange combination of the Virgin Guadalupe and the whore Malinche. La Llorona is heard crying for her lost children, usually at night, in dark alleyways in urban areas, in and around temples, or in dark secluded river valleys in rural areas. She is both spiritual-mythical (Guadalupe–Earth Mother) and physical (Malinche–Raped Mother), or a blend of the two—indigenous mother crying for her lost children, the original peoples of Mesoamerica who have been either taken from her by the Spanish or sacrificed by warlike indigenous peoples such as the Aztecs. She often is not mentioned often in the tales of Mesoamerica; sometimes just believing in her would be grounds for expulsion and even death. She appears, for example, in Rodolfo Anaya's *Bless Me, Ultima*; Antonio hears her weeping in one of the hidden river gorges. But few of the people of the village believe in her or acknowledge that they hear her cries for fear of ostracization, persecution, or worse. This hybrid mythological figure bridges the gap between the mother and children, between the past and the present, between Anglo/Spanish and Mesoamerican cultures and, especially, between the physical realm and the spiritual. As all Mexicans and *frontera* peoples are *mestizos/as*, bastard children of an enslaved and raped indigenous mother and a white European father, the hybrid trilogy Guadalupe–Malinche–La Llorona, referred to both pejoratively and reverentially, is in sum a translational figure, bridging cultures of the present and of the past.

The new *mestizo/a* refers to a contradictory figure that is not part of any one defined and unified culture but one defined by translation and transition. While this figure is located at the border, the borders do not hold. The Mexican–United States border is increasingly being fortified to keep the undesirable people and ideas out of North America. But the border peoples have found ingenious ways to get around and escape such rigid frontiers. Some of them include moving as coyotes at night to slip people through and around the fences and walls; others include using translation as a kind of surreptitious activity to slip ideas across the borders and to even subvert the ideas held so rigidly in religious and political circles. Thus, the new *mestizo/a* is fashioned as a flexible, heterogeneous, creative person who is able to think and write in a new mode and in a new language. Reminiscent of Amerindian shape-shifters, the *mestiza/o* can shift out of conventional thinking and traditional Western analytical reasoning to discover new modes of thought and conceptualization (Anzaldúa 1987: 79). Anzaldúa talks about the new *mestiza* (Anzaldúa invariably writes "*mestiza*," implying the mixed-race, lesbian woman figure) embracing the contradictions of her cultural heritage, learning to be an Indian in Mexican culture and a Mexican in Anglo culture. She has a plural personality, always juggling cultures (ibid.: 79). Pejorative terms become relative terms: whores become gods, and gods become whores, depending upon the cultural perspective. The suffering endured in one culture becomes power in another, used to break down cultural and institutional edifices. Indeed, the work of the border writer is to use this double knowledge to try to break down not just the physical fences dividing peoples and the language differences impeding communication but also the rigid, closed conceptual categories. Anzaldúa's work thus attempts to link both the social and the linguistic divisions of the Texas–Mexican border and Latin and Anglo-America historically and spiritually to the pre-Hispanic cultures from which they have been separated.

The second half of *Borderlands/La frontera* contains six sections of English, Spanish and bilingual/multilingual poems written by Anzaldúa. There are poems about the men who cross the borders: the *mojados* [wetbacks] looking for work, the farm workers sweating in the sun, and even the few Mexican rancheros who, despite the discrimination, have been able to eke out a living on small farms. But most of the poems are about actual women: mothers, grandmothers, sisters, and relatives who do the cooking, laundry, cleaning, and fieldwork. Other poems are dedicated to friends and fellow women writers. Finally, some poems reflect Anzaldúa's concern for the spiritual dimensions and refer metaphorically to women deities and women figures in pre-Hispanic and Hispanic culture. Excerpts of songs to figures such as La Llorona are inserted before poems. There is a poem about cervicide (breaking of the neck; historically, the killing of a deer) in which a Mexican family who are keeping a pet deer have to kill the deer before the border patrol finds it (keeping wild game as pets is prohibited). The killing of the fawn is metaphorically connected to the sacrifice of young women to the conquerors or to the gods.

Translation operates in a variety of manners in Anzaldúa's poems. Only a couple of poems are directly translated in a traditional sense by the author. For example, the poem "Mar de repollos," dedicated to all those who have worked in the fields, is translated as "A Sea of Cabbages" (1987: 130–133) and is "faithful" to the Spanish "source" text; another example of traditional translation is the final poem of the collection "No se raje, chicanita," dedicated to her daughter Missy Anzaldúa and literally translated by the author as "Don't Give In, *Chicanita*" (1987: 200–203). With the exception of an inversion of a line here and the addition of the occasional phrase there, usually for syntactic clarity rather than explanation, and the occasional Spanish word left in the original ("*Chicanita*"), the translations are faithful and traditional. Yet even traditional translation is deceptive when carried out by the author, for it raises the question inherent in all self-translation: what is the "source" text and what is the "target" text? The first self-translation, because of its language and imagery—the hard work, bending, pain, heat, sun, and suffering—has the feel of being written first in Spanish: for example, the leading and unifying metaphor—*Mar* in the title of the poem—conjures up not just the endless fields appearing like a sea but also a feeling invoked by the Spanish verb *marear* or its past participle *mareado*, which literally translates as "seasickness." Its translation into English as "dizzyness" loses the visual, spatial, and physical nauseous feeling of the Spanish. The final poem "Don't Give In, *Chicanita*," while dedicated to her daughter (*m'ijita*), seems more directed at the next generation of *La Raza* (literally "The Race"; generally referring to the Chicano/a race), with hopes for improved future relations with the monolingual English audience, thus blurring the difference between "original" and "translation."

In the bilingual/multilingual poems, however, the translations are more complex. Some have certain Spanish phrases and cultural references footnoted, especially the earlier poems. Yet nontranslation plays an even more active role, for not all the poems are explicated. Sometimes some of the semantic information is parsed out and passed on to the English reader, invariably rewritten in a different context rather than a direct translation. Equally often, the Spanish passages of the bilingual poems are not translated, forcing Anglo readers to perform the translation themselves or to miss much of the meaning of the poems. Minimally, the English reader is left unaware that the poems originate from a bilingual culture with a very different historical and mythological background. As one reads the book as a whole, however, the combination of the prose with the poems and with the selected footnotes and rewritings allows many of the initially estranging lexical and mythical Spanish and Nahuatl references to take a life of their own. Surreptitiously, Anzaldúa builds a cultural space combining Spanish and English, the United States of Mexico and America, men and women, past and present, to which the non-Spanish speaker gains access. The technique allows Anzaldúa's creativity to shine as she weaves a rich multilingual tapestry that takes on a life of its own. Ironically, the border region becomes boundless, a *frontera sin fronteras* (1987: 195).

The New World Border

If Anzaldúa has opened the border up for its creative possibilities, Guillermo Gómez-Peña has exploded the border to begin thinking less of how the border is a region for minorities and outcasts and instead a location that has become boundless, spilling over everywhere. In *The New World Border*

(1996), he argues that monolingual, homogeneous cultures will become (or are now) the minority. Otherness, hybridity, changing borders, fragmentation, multiculturality is the new norm—the new world (b)order. As with Anzaldúa, deliberate nontranslation figures prominently in Gómez-Peña's work. However, in addition, Gómez-Peña adds a new category, deliberate mistranslation, as an aesthetic and political strategy of misleading and parodying the monolingual members of the audience. This strategy of antitranslation, denying access to the original, makes the monolingual audience member feel insecure and bereft of their normal power. Deliberate nontranslation becomes a tool which Gómez-Peña uses to *reverse* the relations of power. In Hinojosa's, Anaya's, and Anzaldúa's cases, the Anglo-Texans held the power. In Gómez-Peña's writing, the power of translation is held by the Chicano audience.

For Gómez-Peña, the existence of a standard English, standard Spanish, or a lingua franca is highly suspect. For him, there are only hybrid forms of language—Spanglish, Gringoñol, colloquial French, and shifting indigenous languages—which he uses strategically to exclude traditional Western readers unwilling to do the work needed to read their way into the plays. In *The New World Border* (1996) and, more importantly in his performance art and performative texts, the Mexican-born Gómez-Peña, who now leads a nomadic international life of continuous border crossings, invokes any number of real and imagined border cultures that separate the North and South. While his early work initially focused on the Tijuana–California border culture, he has evolved into an intercultural, transnational, and, figuratively, intergalactic traveller, operating between old genres such as the printed word in prose, poetry, and theater and new ones such as the electronic word in pop music, performance art, and the Internet. Above all, he is viewed as an experimental artist, linguist, and translator, mapping out new territories for artistic exploration and cross-cultural communication.

The first performance text in *The New World Border* is "Freefalling toward a Borderless Future," which gives the reader an idea of Gómez-Peña's innovative ideas about translation, identity, and the Americas. In the stage directions, he writes that the voice is to be performed with a delayed effect and with "live simultaneous translation into French, Gringoñol, or Esperanto" (1996: 1). Translation, thus, is something that occurs not *after* an original but simultaneously with it. For Gómez-Peña, translation is always present, happening continuously in the increasingly polyvalent languages. Translators cease to be a minority, and creative writers or translators have multiple languages and discourses as a raw material with which to work. Indeed, the definition of the artist is very much tied to the definition of the translator. The artist operates as a kind of politically engaged cross-cultural translator or, in Gómez-Peña's words, an "intercultural translator, or political trickster," one who smuggles in ideas, an "intellectual *coyote*" (1996: 12). The very terms Gómez-Peña uses to discuss the role of artists are ones traditionally reserved for translators; he writes that their job is to "trespass, bridge, interconnect, reinterpret, remap, and redefine; to find the outer limits of [their] culture and cross them" (1996: 12). Thus, artists, like many translators, continues Gómez-Peña, always speak from more than one perspective about more than one reality.

Gómez-Peña's ideas about identity move along parallel lines. Monocultures, linguae francae, fixed national identities, and sacred cultural traditions lose importance. His conception of a borderless future includes hybrids both real and imagined: "cholo-punks, pachuco krishnas, Irish concheros, butoh rappers, cyber-Aztecs, Gringofarians, Hopi rockers" (1996: 1). Borders are constantly being traversed, from South to North, East to West, and vice versa. Borders include not just geographical borders but also musical, religious, gender, generational, and genre borders. Rather than seeing this as a problem, Gómez-Peña sees it as a *solution* to problems of cultural prejudice, fears, and discrimination. In the next piece, "The Free Trade Art Agreement/ *El tratado de libre cultura*," Gómez-Peña talks about his own migratory, nomadic status, traveling from city to city and country to country, connecting less with people from specific countries than with other border peoples who share his ideas. "Home" is neither "here" nor "there," but someplace "in between" (1996: 5). The border, thus, travels with him, and he discovers new borders and hybrid identities wherever he goes.

Gómez-Peña's definition of the Americas undergoes a similar transformation. The continent is no longer described by any traditional maps separating Canada from the United States, Brazil, Hispanic Latin America, and the Caribbean; instead, these areas are viewed as amalgamations of multiple different peoples living in multiracial and multilingual urban areas as well as micronational rural areas that do and do not belong to larger geopolitical nation-states. Many of these areas are constantly in contact and contest with outside influences, predominantly of European and North American origin. Loyalty is less to any larger geopolitical state and more to other micronationals and regional groups. Peoples, ideas, and languages thus intersect less across direct borders and more across larger cultural boundaries: Gómez-Peña suggests that people from Quebec may be closer to Latin Americans than to those in the United States, or that the peoples of Indian nations of Canada are closer to indigenous communities in Latin America than to the Spanish or Anglo peoples who govern them. North/South, East/West become outdated abstractions; the Third World, for example, is ever-present in many North American cities. In the New World Border, there are no centers; hybridity, *mestizaje*, is the dominant culture, and definitions of identity shift accordingly. In sum, the Americas are envisioned as a continent without borders, or, in other words, as a huge border zone no longer defined by race, ethnicity, language, or geographically defined nation-states. Thus translation is heavily tied to Gómez-Peña's conceptions of identity not just at the borders but in the Americas in general.

Yet the most innovative idea for translation studies emerging from Gómez-Peña's intercultural work is his deliberate use of mistranslation as a tool to reverse the power relations between the monolingual and multilingual cultures. In the central performance piece of the collection, "The New World Border: Prophecies for the End of the Century," the languages in which the text is written include Spanish, French, English, Spanglish, Chicano, Franglé, several made-up computer languages, a pseudo-Nahuatl, Neanderthal grumblings, and other assorted dialects and accents. In the introduction to the piece, Gómez-Peña writes that the "simultaneous translations" were "purposely incorrect" in order to "force the audience to experience the cultural vertigo of living in a multilingual/multiracial society" (1996: 21). In the play, the United States–Mexico border disappears, Spanglish becomes the official language, the hybrid state is a political entity, and the social hierarchy overturned, with whites now viewed as a minority. The play is about a radio broadcast narrated by a disk jockey and an anchorman. Their voices, however, are not monolingual, reliable, and identifiable; rather, they switch languages, discourses, and registers easily and frequently, from English to Chicano, to French, to English with a French accent, to Spanish with a Chicano accent, and to English with a Texan accent. The register varies from academic discourse to working-class Chicano. Electronic voices interrupt: computer voices, prerecorded voices, musical voices, as well as rock and roll songs comprise significant parts of the broadcast. Translation is meant to be ongoing continuously, but it is equally unreliable, and on many occasions withheld. The minority culture in the performance text (and often in the audience, sometimes purposely seated in the poorest seats) are the so-called "waspanos, waspitos, wasperos, or waspbacks" (ibid.: 34). Their rights are constantly being violated, and there is no one to defend them. So, too, do the radio broadcasters offend them. Gómez-Peña (GP below) and his performance partner Roberto Sifuentes (RS below) write/broadcast/perform:

> GP: Estoy perdido . . .
> RS (interrupting): Translation please!
> GP: . . . al norte de un sur inexistente. Me captas cavernícola, ¿mexplico?
> RS: Translation please!
>
> *GP makes Neanderthal sounds.*
>
> RS (angry): Translation please!!
> GP: Okay, okay. Lección de español número cinco for advanced English speakers . . .¿Falsa democracia?
> RS: Translation please!
>
> (Gómez-Peña 1996: 34–35)

The passage continues in a similar vein, with Gómez-Peña speaking in his multilingual punning fashion, simultaneously making fun of and discriminating against the monolingual whites in the audience, and Roberto Sifuentes begging for translation, but getting only mistranslation or gibberish in return. The passage ends with Gómez-Peña didactically saying, with typical irreverence, "Los norteamericanos que no aprendieron a hablar español sufrieron una marginación total . . se les consideraba retrasados mentales" [Those North Americans who did not learn to speak Spanish suffer complete marginalization . . . they were considered mentally retarded] (1996: 36). The play and its power is best understood by bilingual audience members who can supply the translations; the monolingual audience member—Spanish, Chicano, or English—is excluded.

As this exclusion is part of the performance art, nontranslation and mistranslation are built into the piece. But what happens if the piece is performed in Mexico or another Spanish-speaking country? Or to a solely Chicano-speaking audience? In an interview with Cuban-born writer and artist Coco Fusco, a frequent performance partner and collaborator, published in the volume *English Is Broken Here* (Fusco 1995), Gómez-Peña talks about the translation problem for border artists who perform in different countries with different languages and cultural contexts. If he performs in Mexico, then in order to preserve a sense of linguistic exclusion or otherness, 75 percent of the play would need to be in Spanish, the rest in English; but in an English setting, the reverse would be true, ensuring that many in the audience would not fully understand (ibid.: 151). In a Chicano context, the exclusion part gets even trickier, with Gómez-Peña carefully rewriting in order to exploit the portions and registers of both English and Spanish that Chicanos do not speak. Thus, the "original" text is always undergoing a process of retranslation before each performance, depending upon the cultural context in which the piece is performed, begging again questions of "original" and "translation." For Gómez-Peña, the Chicano hybrid language has an indefinable shape, one that is bilingual but not fully bilingual, which he then exploits by nontranslation and mistranslation to introduce his alienation effects.

The strategy of reversing power relations in "The New World Border" is related to and an extension of the strategy of reverse anthropology presented in Gómez-Peña's most famous performance piece, codeveloped with Coco Fusco, called at times "The Guatinaui World Tour" and, in specific locations, "Two Undiscovered Amerindians Visit [the name of the city in question]." Postperformance analysis is difficult because there is no text to the piece; the authors/performers Fusco and Gómez-Peña are silent, pretending they do not speak the language of the place of the performance. They are dressed in pseudo-Amerindian clothes and spend three days in a cage equipped with "authentic" artifacts from the (fictional) Guatinaui culture. The performers are accompanied by two "guards," who are there ostensibly to protect them but who answer questions, and fake museum workers/anthropologists who hand-feed the performers and walk them to the bathroom on leashes. Fake museum plates describe their costumes and their physical characteristics, and a map of Mexico with "Guatinaui Island" prominently displayed in the Gulf of Mexico between the Yucatán peninsula and Veracruz. The descriptions of the Amerindians and the Guatinaui tribe are so "scientifically" written, with descriptions of the history of the tribe, the genealogy, the physical, facial, and motor characteristics, right down to how often they initiate sexual intercourse, that the plates are reminiscent of Borges's false genealogies. In the cage, Gómez-Peña and Fusco perform "authentic" rituals, including hybridized activities: they dance, chant, write on laptop computers, listen to Latin American rock music, and watch home videos of their "native" land. The piece was performed all over the world, from Colombo Plaza in Madrid as part of the 1992 quincentennial celebration of Madrid as the capital of European culture, to London's Covent Garden, the Smithsonian Institution in Washington, the Field Museum in Chicago, the Whitney Museum in New York, the Australia Museum in Sydney, and the Fundación Banco Patricios in Buenos Aires. While statistics on the number of people visiting the performance/exhibition are inexact, over 120,000 attended in Washington, DC alone.

As with "The New World Border," Gómez-Peña and Fusco intended their representation to be understood by about three-quarters of the audience; only those very isolated and provincial audience members would be deceived. The performance nature of the piece was meant to be understood ironically, not literally, and the markers were very clear: Gómez-Peña was dressed as a kind of Aztec wrestler; Fusco as an Indian straight from the old US television show *Gilligan's Island*. Fusco's "authentic" dances were transparently inauthentic (Gómez-Peña 1996: 97–8). Gómez-Peña assumed that if whites were not necessarily bilingual, they would certainly be bicultural enough to read the parody. Nevertheless, to the surprise of the performers, audiences all over the world predominantly read the performances as accurate and reacted accordingly. As in any performance art, the audience's response is part of the piece, and since each performance is ephemeral, much of the "meaning" of the piece has necessarily been lost. The best-recorded history of the audience's reactions comes from Coco Fusco's essay "The Other History of Intercultural Performance" in *English Is Broken Here* (1995), in which she talks about how audience members revealed their hidden colonist agendas and their dormant racist beliefs.

The artists clearly underestimated the power of the genre in Europe and North America of displaying Mesoamerican, African, Asian, or Eskimo "specimens" as cultural artifacts—everything from the first Arawak brought back by Columbus to Spain in the fifteenth century to Ishi, the last "Stone Age Indian," on display at the Museum of the University of California in the twentieth century. In addition, North Americans and Europeans hold a deep belief in the authenticity of the displays in museums. Fusco tells us that more than 50 percent of the people visiting the exhibition/performance thought that it was "real" (1995: 50). The white audience members, thinking that they could not be understood, frequently made abusive verbal racial and sexual remarks; others wanted the Amerindians to perform humiliating or sexual acts and would pay extra money to feed them a banana or see their genitals. Many asked the guards questions about the Amerindians' sexual behavior. Those who believed in the authenticity of the exhibit invariably felt it appropriate for the humans to be caged merely because they were different. Others rationalized the appropriateness of the cage, suggesting that the Indians might hurt themselves or others if set free. On the other hand, those people of color who believed that the performance was real tended to express discomfort because of their identification with the situation. Cross-racial identification among whites was less frequent, although some whites who had been in prison could identify with the actors. According to Fusco, one Native American cried, as did one museum guard. One Pueblo elder actually thought the performance was more "real" than any other display on Native Indians in the Smithsonian. Shockingly, no Latino, Native American, North American, or European ever criticized the cage environment or the costumes as "inauthentic." No one from the United States (though two Mexicans did) ever questioned the authenticity of the map accompanying the exhibit.

With regard to those who were aware that the piece was performance and not "real," reactions varied widely. Some took advantage of the general mood to collude with other white racist responses. One middle-class white man, accompanied by his "elegantly dressed wife," paid extra to be photographed feeding Fusco a banana (1995: 50). To be sure, while many people attending the exhibit "Two Undiscovered Amerindians" voiced a moral outrage at human beings displayed in a cage, it was generally expressed in paternalistic terms to the guards rather than to the performers or museum officials, and these audience members calmed down quickly enough, soon becoming comfortable with the scenario. Those who became aware that they were viewing a performance more often than not expressed outrage at the museum for displaying such misinformation. Yet even those who could read the performance markers of the piece expressed their racist beliefs in other fashions. Many assumed that Gómez-Peña and Fusco were merely performers, who, because of their color, could not possibly be the creative "authors." Even leftist reviews wrote patronizing articles about the exhibit, referring to the performers by their first names. Some working in the museums who knew about the piece's tour were particularly disturbed, for the reality of the piece struck very close to home; the fact that Gómez-Peña and Fusco were deliberately lying and misrepresenting Amerindian culture revealed only too well related lies and misrepresentations exhibited at the respective museums. Pressure increased on museum officials to expose the fiction (and thereby "protect" their other exhibits, less transparently fabricated). In fact, for those who knew that the piece was a performance, the primary outrage was about the "immoral" act of duping the audiences, not the museum's participation in a long tradition of misrepresentation and colonization for profit. Thus, the focus of the postperformance criticism, from conservative art critics to progressive journalists and even museum curators, shifted the emphasis away from the racism exposed by the audience reaction (part of the art) and more toward the ethics of the artists.

As accuracy and faithfulness are part of the ethics of representations of Third World culture in the great museums in the United States and Europe, so too are accuracy and truthfulness the ethics of translations of Third World culture into Western languages. Gómez-Peña and Fusco seem to be questioning both. One characteristic of translation in the Americas, beginning with Borges (see Chapter 5), is that this ethic is being called into question. One main problem facing translation studies (and ethnography and anthropology as well) is the theoretical problem of representation. When using translation to represent the Other, how does one not distort that being represented by the language and the belief system of the target culture? In the United States and Europe, how does one put an artifact or a person on display without objectifying, humiliating, sexualizing, or committing other abuses to that object? The biggest theoretical as well as practical problem facing translation studies is that threat of the very impenetrability of languages and the closed nature of cultural conceptions. Translators (or anthropologists, or museum curators) can never be totally neutral; their worldview and cultural traditions invariably distort that which they are trying to impartially represent. Some museum officials realized this contradiction only too clearly during the "Guatinaui World Tour"; the implications for translators and translation studies scholars may prove equally disturbing.

Just as museum curators and anthropologists do not want to be accused of misrepresenting the cultures they purport to represent, so too do translators not want to be accused of mistranslating the texts they purport to be faithfully reproducing. As the world grows more globally interconnected, however, the balance of power may be seen as shifting to those who have multilingual translational and intercultural skills. Because the identity of border-crossers invariably has been the product of the ongoing clash between and among cultures, those operating in border cultures, or, as Mary Louise Pratt puts it, "the contact zone" (1992: 6), are perhaps *most* aware of how translation figures in the exercise of power. This knowledge, which in the past has led only to fear, mistrust, and often silence, might in the future, if articulated, lead to the exposing of certain racist beliefs held by the differing cultures and, in the end, to more open and inclusive notions of the self and identity in any number of the cultures of the Americas. Translations do not necessarily "fail" if they are unfaithful; in fact, the "truth" that mistranslations on occasion expose may in some ways be more revealing than those uncritically transparent translations currently found in museum exhibits and literary anthologies. Translation in the Americas necessarily includes questions of power, of resistance, of ethics, of representation, and, in a cultural studies sense, the construction of meaning, and in this book I argue for expanding the realm of translation studies to address such questions. Translation is fundamental to all border writers' identities, for Mexicans, *mestizos/as*, and border-crossers are all in some ways children of America's first translator of the conquest era: *hijos de Malinche*.

The Caribbean continuum

Border artists are not necessarily doing something all that "new"; border writing originated in the oldest colonies of the Americas, those in the Caribbean islands. Beginning with the "original" Amerindian peoples—the Arawaks and the Caribs—who were all but exterminated by European colonizers, continuing first through African slaves and next through Indian and Chinese indentured servants brought in to work on the sugar plantations, then to the competing European powers' periods of proprietorship, and most recently to the United States' economic and military intervention and interference, if any region of the world is characterized by border clashes with international powers, it is that of the Caribbean. Languages are constantly in flux in the region, "native" language is almost an oxymoron, and translational identity is a given.

Colonization, while initiated via military invasion, was primarily carried out in the school systems and in the indigenous, black, and immigrant communities of the colonies, with European languages being the norm and Amerindian, African, East Indian, and Asian languages being marginalized or even eradicated. The further one advanced through the schools and social institutions, the more Europeanized one's writing and speaking became. For those who wanted to get ahead, the primary means was to learn the language of the colonizer and to translate oneself, linguistically and culturally, into that language. Yet as with any translation, markers from the "original" languages remained, and thus the new language became known as "creole language"—a *mestizaje*, hybrid language. The term "creole" in English (probably initially translated from *crioulo* in Portuguese, derived from *criar*, "to raise up," or "to bring up") is problematic, with complex histories, variable meanings, and ideological overtones: the terms *créole* in French, *criollo* in Spanish, *kreyòl* in Haitian all have different frames of reference. The Spanish term initially was used to refer to anyone born of *Spanish* parents. In other cultures in the Americas, it more broadly referred to anyone born in the Americas, as distinguished from someone born in the "home" European country (accordingly, *all* nonindigenous Americans are Creoles). Later the term was modified, especially in many French *créole* cultures, to refer to someone born of mixed blood, of European and non-European (read black) ancestry. Over time, a creole language implied a language that would reflect both European and native languages and cultures, and a language that was in a constant state of flux. Today, several creole languages are stable and have been standardized, such as *Kreyòl ayisyen*, or Haitian Kreyol. However defined, I suggest that those markers used by linguists to describe creole languages, including indigenous lexical items and syntactical structures, various borrowings and interferences, repetition, and any number of neologisms and ambiguous terms, are well known to translation studies scholars, who use similar terms to describe translations, particularly "errors" in translation.

In order to better analyze Caribbean languages without resorting to models describing dialects, linguistics of the 1970s, such as Derek Bickerton (1975), proposed the "creole continuum," sometimes referred to as the "post-creole continuum," to look at deeper grammatical structures, lexical items, and phonetic variables. The linguistic tool measured the degree of "Europeanness" of language spoken in the respective colonies. The closer one is to the standard English, French, Spanish, Dutch, or whatever the "official" language of the country or colony is, the further along the continuum one finds oneself, and the more power for self-advancement a speaker accumulates. The linguistic tool reflects the cultural prejudices regarding "standard" European languages and the so-called substandard or "broken" creole languages spoken by Caribbean inhabitants. The more "interference" from the multiple non-European languages spoken and non-official European standard, the less far along the continuum one finds oneself. The process valued, thus, is the process of *de*creolization, of modifying one's speech in the direction of the European standard, of cleansing one's language of multilingual influences, of, in short, giving up one's native language and identity for that of the colonizer. Native creole speakers, however, often maintained a degree of multilingual dexterity in oral culture, demonstrating a virtuosity undetected by the non-Creole colonizer, changing registers and dialects along the continuum depending on whom one was speaking with and why. Many Creoles could write in standard English or French, but would prefer a performative creole in their oral interactions. Because of this continuum, this constant degree of flux, linguists have had trouble describing a fixed creole language; indeed, in contrast to European languages, the very definition of creole implies a nonfixed, variant system. While Haitian scholars have in recent years standardized their *Kreyòl*, teach it in the schools, and use it in business and government transactions, many Caribbean countries still use the fixed standard European language as their "official" language and the variant creoles in their oral dealings, finding their daily lives in a state of constant translation.

Creative writers in the Caribbean were the first to exploit this multilingual/translational nature of their culture. The Trinidadian writer Sam Selvon, for example, author of works such as *A Brighter Sun* (1952), *The Lonely Londoners* (1956), and *Moses Ascending* (1975), is generally considered the first writer to exploit the Trinidadian creole oral language and use it in the written form. Trinidad serves as a good example of the complexity of describing a creole culture, for its language history is filled with all its border clashes from all directions. From the European and North American sides, it was first colonized by the Spanish, contested for a short time by the Portuguese, then settled by the French, later established as a colony by the British, economically exploited by the United States, finally gaining independence in 1962. From the non-European direction, the indigenous Amerindians were largely exterminated; African slaves were imported, and a large number of East Indians, mostly Hindi-speaking, with some Chinese, indentured and brought in to work the sugar fields. Trinibarianese, the English-based Trinidadian Creole, thus contains lexical and syntactic markers of a half-dozen non-European as well as major non-English European languages. A French-based creole is still spoken in some rural areas as well. However, the official language of the country is English. If ever there was a fount for border writing to emerge, it is Trinidad, which perhaps explains why there are so many fine contemporary Trinidadian writers, including Sam Selvon, V.S. Naipaul, Lakshmi Persaud, Derek Walcott, and Earl Lovelace.

As early as 1952, Selvon published *A Brighter Sun*, the first such novel to include Creole characters and to record their oral interactions. The story concerns a West Indian worker named Tiger, who was brought up in a traditional Hindi village in the sugarcane area but who then moves to a multicultural region near the capital, Port of Spain. His movement from rural to urban parallels his movement along the creole continuum, from a "low" creole to a "middle" one. His advancement along the social hierarchy is mirrored by his language acquisition. Selvon is well known for his ability to move easily and well among the variety of dialects and languages spoken along the spectrum: for example, the creole Tiger speaks with his wife, the result of an arranged marriage, is different than the one he speaks with his North American bosses. Switching codes, translating back and forth, becomes a characteristic of life in Caribbean culture; cultural capital is tied to linguistic fluency and translation.

Selvon also uses the variations along the creole scale to subvert standard English as the "official" language and the language of power, and the English novel as the standard literary form and the genre of power. His punning in creole, the virtuosity of his ability to charm, cajole, and intertwine registers and dialects of English, undermines standard English and opens the language up for new possibilities. The introduction of new terms transcribed or translated from Hindi, African, and Amerindian enriches the English language. Interference creates neologisms pregnant with new meanings. New audiences are reached via such writing, and audience identification with the new form of writing spreads its popularity. A genre that was reserved for the elite in the Caribbean (and the rest of the world) now was more accessible for more middle-class individuals.

As with all border writing, as outlined above, in creole texts distinctions between the original and the translation are reduced; the original, now in its hybrid form, is, in so many ways, already in translation. I suggest that border writing, with its translational component, is not something new and fashionable that has come to the Americas recently via a new academic interest in Latin American studies, gender studies, and performance art. Rather, it is fundamentally constitutive of American writing, present since the Europeans arrived in the earliest of colonies, those of the Caribbean. As exemplified by Selvon's creative writing from the 1950s, the realization that translation is constitutive of the daily lives of its inhabitants, fundamental to their sense of identity, is particularly clear in Caribbean cultures, yet also discernible transnationally across the borders of the nation-states of the Americas.

Deconstruction and borders

Border writers are well aware of the concept of deconstruction, and in fact many of them use it as a concept with which to describe their art. Gloria Anzaldúa, for example, talks about putting history through a sieve and winnowing out all lies, making a "conscious rupture with all oppressive traditions" (1987: 82). She continues by saying that the new *mestiza* "reinterprets history and, using new symbols, she shapes new myths. She adopts new perspectives toward the darkskinned, women and queers. . . . She surrenders all notions of safety, of the familiar. Deconstruct, construct" (ibid.: 82). Border writers accomplish this destructuring not by bringing in new ideas from the outside but by using means that are inherent in the culture but have been erased or covered up by the dominant majority, bringing the *à traduire* to the fore. Taking the language of the oppressor, border writers rewrite from within, elevating those myths, ideas, and voices that have historically been silenced. Using translation in a polyvalent fashion, they add meanings and resonances to the familiar terms, showing their arbitrary and constructed nature. In many ways, translation is the tool *par excellence* to dislodge and displace from within, to allow new meanings and possibilities to surface. It should come as no surprise, then, that Derrida writes frequently about translation and borders, using similar techniques and strategies in his philosophical project.

One of Derrida's earliest and most famous works on translation is also about border writing. Called "Living On/Border Lines" (1979), the piece is actually a double text: the first part, "Living On," is Derrida's foray into deconstruction and literary criticism in which he "interprets" several texts, including Shelley's unfinished poem "The Triumph of Life," written in 1822 just before he drowned (does it "live on" after Shelley died?), and Maurice Blanchot's *La Folie du jour* [*The Madness of the Day*, 1981) and *L'arrêt de mort* [*Death Sentence*, 1978] in light of his concept of difference, a mode of interpretation that delays, defers, and displaces from within (see Gentzler 2001: 157–161). Although Derrida talks frequently of translation in the first part of the dual essay, presented as an upper half of the pages of the text, of more interest to translation theorists has been his accompanying essay, "Border Lines," which runs across the border at the bottom of each page like an extended footnote. Because Derrida is writing in French in an essay that will be translated and appear in English as part of his contribution to the Yale School of Deconstruction, whose members include Harold Bloom, Paul de Man, Geoffrey Hartman, and J. Hillis Miller, he is much concerned about how his words and ideas will be translated. His text "Border Lines" creates a new genre, a translator's note written before the translation, wondering how a translator will translate a certain concept, or hoping that a translator will take into consideration some of his earlier writings about a particular idea before translating a certain passage about that idea. The note is written in a deliberately fragmented style, not only as a means to economize on space but also because Derrida feels that all writing is fragmentary, presenting only bits and pieces of ideas and not larger concepts.

The partial text "Border Lines" raises the questions of the nature of translation and the nature of borders. Borders discussed in the literary critical article above (although Derrida would not agree that he is doing literary criticism, which implies a positive/negative binary) concern borderlines between life and death (in one of Blanchot's stories, the main character "lives on" years after a doctor told her she would die); the edge between the sea and land (Shelley's "Triumph of Life" was written at sea, and he ending up drowning, as did his first wife), and between fantasy and reality (many of Blanchot's stories deal with drowning, and Blanchot's characters frequently are described in states of dreaming and madness). In addition, the border between where one of the dual texts leaves off and the other begins—how does Shelley's text inform Blanchot's, and vice versa?—becomes increasingly blurred. How do creative writers "translate" ideas from other authors? How does literary criticism "translate" authors' ideas? How does the translation of those texts inform our interpretation of the originals? Derrida's double essay thus is most concerned with blurring boundaries or expanding boundaries until the texts, ideas, and languages merge.

In "Border Lines," Derrida makes his famous statement regarding translation and the continuation, the survival of any one author's ideas via translation or rewriting:

> A text lives only if it lives *on* [*sur-vit*], and it lives *on* only if it is *at once* translatable *and* untranslatable.... Totally translatable, it disappears as a text, as writing, as a body of language [*langue*]. Totally untranslatable, even within what is believed to be one language, it dies immediately. Thus triumphant translation is neither the life nor the death of the text, only or already its living *on*, its life after life, its life after death.
> (Derrida 1979: 102–103; italics and brackets in the original)

We can see that the same terms with which Derrida discusses translation are the ones used to discuss the literary texts in the accompanying essay

—triumphing over life, overcoming death, and living on. Indeed, for Derrida the two are interchangeable, which is why the essays are juxtaposed accordingly. Derrida's literary criticism is a form of translation study. In addition, the terms with which he discusses Shelley's and Blanchot's literary texts and speculates on translation are the same ones he uses to describe his "theory" of deconstruction. "Marks," "traces," "writing," and "grams," too, neither live nor die, but live on, although often under the erasure of the dominant discourse. Thus, for Derrida, all writing and literary interpretations are intertwined with translation and border writing. The marks and traces of the subdominant, nonstandard border languages, indeed those marks that determine creole, hybrid writing, echo Derrida's deconstruction.

In his fears and hopes for translation as revealed in "Border Lines," Derrida also reveals much about the nature of his writing in his "native" language, French, which is anything but monolingual. Derrida frequently refers to Nietzsche and Freud in his essay, sometimes quoting them in French and sometimes in German. German informs all of Derrida's ideas—many argue that "deconstruction" originated in or is minimally derived from Heidegger's ideas of *destruktion*. The very terminology of "Border Lines," of translation as survival or living on, derives from Walter Benjamin's essay "Die Aufgabe des Übersetzers," 1955 ["The Task of the Translator," 1969a]. *Über-setzen* (trans-late), *Über-tragen* (trans-fer), *fort-leben* (*sur-vit*; live-on), *nach-leben* (after-life) are all Benjaminian terms, and Derrida was giving seminars entitled "Die Aufgabe des Übersetzers" in Paris in the mid-1970s. Derrida reads Shelley in English, of course, but he interprets him in French. He also discusses Greek etymologies for many of his philosophical terms, and he hopes his translators will at least consult Greek compendiums before translating certain terms. In addition, he refers to biblical passages, citing both Greek and Latin sources and their French translations—the first border being crossed being the creation of the world (from what?); "In the beginning," from Genesis, is translated by Chouraqui as "*Entête* [In-head] Elohim created heaven and earth" (Derrida 1979: 93). Many of the legal terms Derrida uses are articulated in French but derive from Latin, as he talks frequently about laws, political economies, and university systems. Perhaps most importantly, because he knows that he is writing for future translation into English, many of his multilingual references in his note are meant to be guideposts for some future English translator, so that Derrida's ideas, too, live on in translation. The text "Border Lines" is thus written not only at the border below "Living On," but also in that gray in-between space between French and a future English. Borders blur between the original and the translation (is it French or English?), and both the original and the translation are informed minimally by Hebrew, Greek, Latin, German, French, and English. And as we saw in Chapter 2, given the fact that Derrida was Algerian by birth, there are probably parts of at least one dialect of French as well as traces of North African languages.

Thus, for Derrida and for border writers, there is no such thing as a standard monolingual individual language. His language, like all languages, are always already multilingual, polyvalent, overlapping, culturally bound, and mutually informing each other. One of the main points of the marginal text "Border Lines" is Derrida's entry into translation studies: one borderline he wishes to distinguish is that between translation studies governed by classical models of translation—one that assumes national languages and a kind of universality achievable through the translatability of that language into other national languages—and a translation studies that challenges and destructures such notions—one that embraces multilingual reference, polysemia, and dissemination (1979: 92ff.). Just as Shelley's "Triumph" is unfinished, so too are translations invariably unfinished, especially those that attempt to preserve double meanings and *double entendres*, which generally describes all of Derrida's writings and most literary texts. Playing with Blanchot's *L'Arrêt de mort*, Derrida talks about the impossibility of ever stopping (*arrêter*) or fixing unlimited semiosis, of ever closing the boundaries of any single text or concept. While Derrida admits that his participation in this literary criticism exercise in English and at Yale is only possible through translation, this translation will not be from one national language to another or from one institution or department to another; rather, it takes a circuitous route, from everything that informs and haunts Derrida's writing, to everything that informs and haunts Shelley's and Blanchot's language and writing. As Gómez-Peña takes border writing from the local to the continental or intercontinental, so too does Derrida take literary criticism from the monolingual to the comparative, multilingual, polyvalent, and creative. One primary border being addressed with "Border Lines," and the reason Derrida published the essay in translation and at Yale, is the difference between literary criticism (critical) and deconstructive literary criticism (creative). Derrida is very much in favor of deconstructing the pedagogical institutions and departments that teach, support, and perpetuate the national languages. These institutions, he feels, at Yale or wherever, are actually responsible for impeding translation studies and border writing, for they cannot bear any form of writing or translation that concerns, changes, and challenges concepts of nationalism (ibid.: 94).

Translation and Calibanization

In the late 1960s and early 1970s, two literary texts appeared in the Caribbean that changed the landscape of literary and social studies, and translation played a critical role in both. The first was the publication of a loosely based translation/adaptation of Shakespeare's *The Tempest* titled *Une tempête: Adaptation de "La Tempête" de Shakespeare pour un théâtre nègre* (1969) by the Martinican poet and playwright Aimé Césaire. The second, and perhaps more relevant to this discussion of translation and the Americas, is the essay "Caliban: Notes toward a Discussion of Culture in

Our America" (1971) by the Cuban critic Roberto Fernández Retamar, which has been reproduced in *Caliban and Other Essays* (Retamar 1989).

Césaire's translation came at the height of the period in which he was developing his concept of Négritude, a movement led by Francophone black writers such as the Senegalese poet and president Léopold Senghor, praising the thought, ideas, and writings of black intellectuals around the world. Black worldviews, experiences, and languages are viewed positively, and social and moral domination by whites are questioned. In Césaire's work, the characters are the same as Shakespeare's, with just a couple of changes. Ariel is depicted as a mulatto slave, Caliban as a black Caribbean slave; and Prospero is a slave owner. Ariel is depicted as a wavering (Latin American) intellectual, sympathetic to the ideas and ethics of Prospero; Caliban, on the other hand, is much more of a revolutionary; his worldview is incompatible with Prospero's. Césaire also introduces a new character, the Yoruban god Eshu, and the play ends with the two antagonists, Prospero and Caliban, colonizer and the colonized, remaining on the island, haunted by spirits, in a state of perpetual war.

In terms of its social and political power, and its contribution to fields such as postcolonial studies, one cannot overestimate its importance. Caliban, though enslaved, is not depicted as an ignorant savage—deformed, brutish, and lusting after Miranda—but instead very much as Prospero's equal, intellectually and spiritually. Caliban's name is based upon the Carib Indians of the Caribbean, noted for their fierce resistance to the European explorers. The first word he speaks is "Uhuru," a Kiswahili word meaning freedom, connecting Caliban both to his African indigenous roots and to the East African independence movements of the 1960s. Caliban sings the names of African deities such as Shango, a Yoruba god of thunder, but here no doubt a reference to syncretic faiths such as Santería, popular throughout the Caribbean, and Quetzal, a colorful bird native to Central America, and believed in Mayan culture to be a god. In many ways, Caliban, which is Shakespeare's anagram for "cannibal," has been cannibalized by Césaire in a similar fashion to De Campos's cannibalization of Goethe's *Faust*: a classic of Western literature is read and rewritten from the perspective of the Americas. The result is the construction of a powerful metaphor for translation, or, perhaps better said, mistranslation and resistance.

The second text on Caliban, Retamar's essay, traces the complex and varied treatment of the Caliban figure historically, whose representation as positive icon of Latin American identity and independence comes rather late. The term "Canibals" first appears as a proper noun in Columbus's journal of November 23, 1492: "They [the Arawak Indians] said that this land was very extensive and that in it were people who had one eye in the forehead, and others whom they called 'Canibals'" (Columbus 1968: 68–69; quoted in Cheyfitz 1997: 41). The European word "cannibal," with its man-eating and savage connotations, is thus a kind of mistranslation of the term referring to the Carib (mispronounced Canib) Indians, one of the Indian tribes encountered by the Spanish upon arriving in the New World. Retamar suggests that the mistranslation occurs because Columbus was searching for the Orient and the *Gran Can* (Great Khan), and thus was predisposed to hearing the "n" sound. One must wonder who is performing the translations and how this European worldview is inscribed upon the indigenous peoples encountered. This savage image of the colonized, of course, provides justification for the violence perpetuated against them in the subsequent years, not just for the Carib Indians but for all Native American peoples. This process of (mis)translation/manipulation, as I try to show in this text, becomes a kind of internalized ideology that becomes part of the psyche of the Native Americans. Retamar writes, "That we ourselves may have one time believed in this version only proves to what extent we are infected with the ideology of the enemy" (1989: 7). Retamar's retranslation of the term, tracing the evolution of the reception of the Caliban figure and its ideological overtones, is one method of resisting neocolonial (read post-postcolonial) representations that continue to repress peoples today.

Surprisingly, the semantic wandering of the Caliban character first is taken to refer not to indigenous Americans but to *Europeans*. Retamar discusses the work of the French writer Ernest Renan, who in *Caliban, suite de La Tempête* (1878) portrays Caliban as the incarnation of the (evil) democratic forces in France, which the French bourgeoisie needed to beat down. The Calibans of this foreign race were only good for work as serfs: agricultural or industrial laborers. Only the elite intellectuals, such as Prospero, were fit for government. At the turn of the twentieth century, Latin Americans such as the Franco-Argentine writer Paul Groussac viewed Caliban as a Yankee industrialist, one whom the cultured and sophisticated European Latin Americans rejected. The Uruguayan writer José Enrique Rodó, author of *Ariel*, published in 1900, identified Latin America more with the Ariel character, who came to represent the best of civilization, than with Caliban.

Against these historical precedents, Retamar argues that Caliban best represents the Latin American condition. Referring to *mestizo* inhabitants of the islands where Caliban lived, Retamar argues:

> Prospero invaded the islands, killed our ancestors, enslaved Caliban, and taught him his language to make himself understood. What else can Caliban do but use that same language—today he has no other—to curse him? . . . I know of no other metaphor more expressive of our cultural condition.
>
> (1989: 14)

After naming other heroes of Latin American culture, from Túpac Amaru and Toussaint-Louverture through Fidel Castro and Che Guevara, he concludes, "what is our history, what is our culture, if not the history and culture of Caliban?" (ibid.: 14). By reclaiming the mistranslation of Caliban, reversing the social values associated with the character, emphasizing his African origins, taking pride in his history, and admiring his act of rebellion, Retamar suggests that all Latin Americans need to rethink their position *vis-à-vis* the European colonizers and rewrite their history from the other side. It will be hard, for much of the data of and languages for opposition have been lost. Retamar is well aware that even the term "Caliban" is not entirely indigenous, having undergone a long period of European construction and elaboration. Yet this is true for almost all language in Latin America; as I mentioned in the Introduction, the very name Latin America is already a translation (there were no Romans in South America). So too is the name and metaphor Caliban laden with white racial presuppositions. The adoption with pride of such a prejudicial term, similar to the Latinos in North America adopting the pejorative Chicano, performs a kind of back-translation: the use of the term in the Other's hands exposes the racial contempt of those who first used the term.

Translation studies criticism and border writing

In Canada, a handful of scholars are becoming increasingly interested in border writing and Caribbean writing. In "Creole . . . English: West Indian Writing as Translation," (1997), Joanne Akai from the University of Montreal connects the "original" creative writing of two Trinidadian writers, Sam Selvon and V.S. Naipaul, and two Guyanan writers, Arnold Itwaru and Cyril Dabydeen, to translation. Selvon, Itwaru, and Dabydeen, not unsurprisingly, have spent long periods of time living in Canada, and Naipaul emigrated to England, making them border-crossers in their own right. Akai quotes Susan Bassnett and André Lefevere from the general editor's preface to Lawrence Venuti's *The Translator's Invisibility*, in which they suggest that every translation is a "rewriting" from an "original" text, and that all rewritings reflect a certain ideology and poetics, which in turn "manipulate" literature to function in the target culture in a certain way (Bassnett and Lefevere, 1995: vii). Akai suggests that West Indian writers are translating or rewriting their "original" oral creole languages into a written literary English. In fact, this direction of crossing borders, at least in terms of written, literary translation, is the only one available to them. Yet rather than merely capitulating to the colonizer and the colonizer's language, Caribbean writers, because they are self-translating, find ways to manipulate the ideology and poetics of the English to allow them to introduce creole sounds, cultural traits, and previously invisible histories. Since translation always involves making choices at the lexical level —whether to transcribe a foreign term by borrowing a source culture term, translating it into a concept in the target culture, or transcribing and adding explanatory material in terms of paraphrasing, footnoting, or adding a glossary—these choices give West Indian writers a range of strategies for their translation and creative writing. Akai provides an inventory of techniques West Indian writers use in their translations and creative writing, including phonetic spellings, hybridized neologisms, exaggeration, repetition, non-English intensifiers, and onomatopoeic devices. Akai's examples document the plethora of code switching, fusion, punning, and polyphonic overtones going on in West Indian writing; one cannot help but see the creative possibilities for such a new multilingual/translational genre. Akai's essay shows that West Indian writing/translation is more than a theoretical idea; it is a concrete translational practice, one that cannot help but change West Indian writing, but also, in turn, change the nature of literature in English cultures. Borders are crossed; distinctions between English and Creole dissipate; and the difference between translation and original writing blurs. In terms of identity formation, these writers are translating themselves and their own experiences into English. Their identities and the identities of the peoples represented in their texts correspondingly change or are transcultured. Akai suggests that in terms of identity, the "original" is not accessible in written form; only the translation is (1997: 191). However, rather than leave the job of translation of their "own" cultures to outsiders (the English), West Indian writers have taken on the responsibility of translating their own culture, and thereby can better control (or manipulate, in Bassnett and Lefevere's words) the poetics as well as the sociohistorical content.

The best example of translation scholarship coming out of the Caribbean border cultures of the Americas has been the work of the Cuban Gustavo Pérez Firmat, author of *The Cuban Condition: Translation and Identity in Modern Cuban Literature* (1989). Pérez Firmat studies writers of the first half of the twentieth century, the period just after Cuba gained independence from Spain and after several interventions by the United States. Focusing on the work by writers such as the sociologist Fernando Ortiz, the poet Nicolás Guillén, and the novelist Carlos Loveira, Pérez Firmat argues that during this period Cuban identity came into being, determined more by the forces of translation than by any other genre. He argues that because of Cuba's language, history, and geographic location, Cuban artists, as do many Caribbean writers, enjoy what he calls a "translation sensibility" (ibid.: 4). Always on the border, always in some ways transient, Cuban writers are accustomed to looking outward toward foreign literary models, a condition lending itself well to translational activity. However, the use of foreign models is not a passive, derivative activity during this period; in contrast, Pérez Firmat argues, Cuban writers are open to the creative possibilities inherent in translation, using translation as a powerful instrument in the development of a national style and a Cuban literary vernacular. Translation in the traditional European sense is a timid genre, showing one's dependence upon European literary forms and ideas; translation in the Cuban Caribbean sense is a resistant genre, showing one's independence from European forms and leading to new and highly original styles. Pérez Firmat writes that "Cuban style *is* translational style" (ibid.: 4; emphasis in the original).

The early twentieth century was also the time when the Cuban literary vernacular emerged from the stranglehold of the Spanish mother tongue, a project much related to translation. Cuban writers inherited a language, a linguistic grammar, and a variety of literary forms and resources, which they then combined with elements from other linguistic and literary traditions to author their own hybrid, creole vernacular. Several important dictionaries were published during this period, including Constantino Suárez's *Diccionario de voces cubanos* (1921) or Ortiz's own *Catauro de cubanismos* (1985 [1923]), articulating the blend of the formal Spanish language with the multicultural everyday speech of Cubans. In a similar vein, in *History of the Voice: The Development of Nation Language in Anglophone Caribbean Poetry* (1984), the West Indian poet and critic Edward Kamau Brathwaite discusses a similar development in the former English colonies such as Jamaica, Trinidad, and Barbados, "nation language" referring in this case to the Anglo-creole version of standard English spoken in the Anglophone Caribbean. One of Pérez Firmat's main concepts in *The Cuban Condition* is what he refers to as "critical criollism" (1989: 9), which refers not so much to the creole vernacular as described in the lexicons as to the subtle nuances of language in the creative writing and translations in which Caribbean writers manipulate the foreign language in a deliberate fashion to underscore indigenous terms and themes and to distance themselves from the European source. Pérez Firmat suggests that such works have a "double edge": not only do they record regionalisms of spoken Cuban Spanish, but they also reveal an independent stance in which their very usage displaces and replaces the inherited language and forms. Pérez Firmat writes:

> The result is an interesting tug-of-words between insular usage and peninsular precedent. Recognizing that the search for a literary vernacular can be furthered only by recasting, refashioning, adapting—in short, by translating—exogenous models, critical criollists shade local color with foreign hues.
>
> (1989: 9)

In a chapter titled "Mr. Cuba," Pérez Firmat turns to the most famous Cuban writer of the period, Fernando Ortiz, to illustrate his claims. Ortiz, in essays such as "Del fenómeno social de la 'transculturación' y de su importancia en Cuba" [On the social phenomenon of transculturation and its importance in Cuba], is well known for his coinage of the term *transculturación* to describe Cuban culture (Ortiz 1940; trans. 1973; Pérez Firmat 1989: 20), a concept of increasing relevance to translation studies, especially to those scholars who have taken the cultural turn. In Ortiz's mind, transculturation is a translation from the Caribbean perspective of the concept "acculturation" so much desired by the colonizing powers. In terms of translation theory, one way to think about the Caribbean perspective is that the very term used to refer to translation is itself a translation. The theory, thus, is articulated less in a logical, European, descriptive fashion and more via a creative discursive practice, one that takes Western terminology and refashions it, recontextualizing it from the perspective of the creole border culture. These refashionings lend the language, whether it is prose, poetry, fiction, description, or translation, its nuanced edge: critical criollism.

From the Caribbean perspective, "acculturation" is an inaccurate, one-sided description of that complex activity of living and adapting to foreign powers controlling the economic and social institutions in the region. Acculturation implies that the indigenous and immigrant populations assume the culture of the dominant power, be it Britain, France, Spain, the Netherlands, or the United States, all of which have vested interests in the Caribbean. Those that live in such a border region, however, know that the term falls short of describing the complex, two-way, or even three- or four-way, flow of culture, language, and ideas in the region. Pérez Firmat suggests that the cultural contact actually has three phases: deculturation, the shredding of elements of the original culture; acculturation, the acquisition of elements from the new culture; and neoculturation, a merging of the original and the new (1989: 21). In the case of Cuba, deculturation would refer to the black population being torn from its African roots, acculturation would involve the imposition and acquisition of the Spanish and/or Anglo-American white culture, and neoculturation would involve the synthesis of the African with the European-American culture. For the indigenous Amerindian populations or the immigrant West Indian populations, the process is similar. Translation thus ceases to be a marginal activity, and becomes an ongoing, permanent activity fundamental to the lives and the identities of the vast majority of Caribbean citizens. I suggest that this psychosocial condition in the Caribbean of always being involved in multiple processes of translation can give scholars insight into the nature of translation and identity formation in the Americas and perhaps in other cultures worldwide as well.

When discussing the importance of the concept of transculturation with regard to Cuba specifically, Ortiz goes on to suggest that the process is incomplete, that Cuba is yet to reach the stage of neoculturation. He talks in terms of Cuba being in a permanent state of uprootedness and constant fluidity, of how everything is felt to be foreign, provisional, and therefore mutable (Ortiz 1940: 133; Pérez Firmat 1989: 23). The concept of fluidity and change, rather than concepts of fixity and permanence, characterizes Ortiz's discussion of Cuba, and Pérez Firmat is quick to point out the number of terms with the prefix *tras-* or *trans-* in his prose, including *trascendentes, transmigraciones, transitoriedad, transmutación, transplantación, transmigrar, transición,* and *traspasar*. One cannot help but be reminded of the inventive terms coined by Haroldo and Augusto de Campos in Brazil to refer to the Brazilian translational condition. Pérez Firmat (1989: 23) correctly points out that while Ortiz often uses "transculturation" to refer to a synthesis of cultures (Ortiz 1940: 130), the term more accurately invokes notions of fermentation and turmoil that a culture experiences before synthesis (1989: 23). The word thus denotes processes of translation, passage, transition, and change, calling into question any fixed notion of a stabile culture or text. Here the concepts Derrida uses to refer to border writing and deconstruction might prove helpful. The peoples of Cuba and the Caribbean find themselves in a permanent state of deferral, delay, and displacement. That which lives on and survives is not a monolingual individual language but a multilingual, polyvalent language always in a state of change. Translation and transculturation challenge and destructure notions of separate and fixed national languages as well as definitions of translations brokering between the two. As translations are invariably unfinished, so too are cultures and individual identities equally unfinished. Caribbean writing, with its double or multiple discourses, well illustrates this form of unlimited semiosis.

Most of Pérez Firmat's *The Cuban Condition* is devoted to a series of case studies supporting his thesis of critical criollism. The case studies include Fernando Ortiz's free translation (with commentary) from Spanish to Spanish of Benito Pérez Galdós's *El caballero encantado* (1977 [1909]); in which Ortiz flaunts his unfaithfulness by commenting on, rearranging, and supplementing the original in an attempt to free Cuban Spanish from Castilian Spanish. Another work discussed is Carlos Loveira's picaresque novel *Juan Criollo* (1927), which is analyzed in terms of its autobiographical features. The narrator has a split Spanish/Cuban identity, recording and transfiguring his Cuban oral memories in a Spanish written form. Luis Felipe Rodríguez's criollist novel *Ciénaga* (1937) is discussed in a quasi-naturalistic fashion. The narrator, while seeking a base in Cuban natural, historical, and political foundations, instead discovers a kind of bottomless quagmire, a groundless island, a swamp that engulfs all attempts to describe or translate it. Pérez Firmat also discusses Alejo Carpentier's famous novel *Los pasos perdidos* (1985), whose bilingual Spanish/English narrator blends many languages—Spanish, French, German, and English—in his mind, to the point that the "original" voice becomes blurred and invisible translations predominate, calling into question which language constitutes his identity. In one of the most convincing examples, Pérez Firmat discusses the work of one of the most famous Cuban poets, Nicolás Guillén, author of a dozen books of poetry, including *Motivos de son* (1930). While Guillén is best known for his vernacular, "mulatto" poetry, some calling him Cuba's "Black Orpheus" (Depestre 1974: 121; Pérez Firmat 1989: 68), Guillén's transculturation of the sonnet, mainstay of Western poetic forms, is of more interest to Pérez Firmat's focus on translation. While the rhyme and meter of Guillén's sonnets remain much the same as in Petrarchan models, the characters and content are mixed and transfigured: courtly modes of behavior are transformed into colonial Cuban relations; white angelic lady figures become dark subversive mulatto ones. Once one figure is transformed, the poetry cannot help but be read in terms of a cascading series of radical inversions: assumptions about race, class, religion, ethics, nature, and natural/courtly behavior all are called into question. Significantly, even the meter of the poem—the sound—changes; one cannot help but hear the tone and cadence of African voices in Guillén's poetry, making the *son* Cuba's own sonnet, a sound identifiable to all Cubans. Pérez Firmat goes so far as to suggest that the Cuban *son* and the Italian sonnet are distant relatives (1989: 75).

In sum, writers in border and Caribbean cultures use translation as one of the primary tools in their search for their own voice and identity. It could not be otherwise, given their location in an always shifting rather than stable culture. As the language of the original is confused, so too must the language of translation be unstable; translations cannot help but be unfaithful. As Caribbean sources, sounds, and rhythms are often seen as older than the source texts from which the Cuban tradition derives, definitions of the direction of the intercontinental flow of translations arise. Pérez Firmat suggests that the attempt to establish a foundation of Cuban creolist literature was always a precarious enterprise, given the paradoxical nature of the simultaneously native and foreign language, a nation without nationhood, and a people without an identity (1989: 157). With such a lack of an indigenous language or tradition, the foundation cannot help but be translational, always speaking in another's words. Indeed, as the ever-changing nature of the floating, fluid islands indicates, so too, in a Derridean fashion, might all translational phenomena in the Americas be seen as groundless, the original disappearing into a paradigm of an endless signifying chain of translations of translations, language disappearing into language, ideas disappearing into ideas. Yet as I hope to show in the last chapter, the tracing of this chain of signification, and its ideological and psychological implications, becomes one method of dealing with the language oppression so common throughout the Americas. Translation studies scholars are particularly well suited for such a task.

7 Conclusion
New Directions

This study opened with a discussion of monolingualism versus multilingualism in the United States, traced the role of translation within feminist and theater groups in Canada, discussed the centrality of translation in new theoretical concepts such as cannibalism in Brazil, looked at new locations for translation theory in the fiction of Latin America, and concluded with the ideas of acculturation versus transculturation as developed by Caribbean scholars. With such new theoretical constructs entering the discourse of translation studies, issues of identity must be part of the discussion. Transcultural implies cultural change. I suggest that in the new global age, with increasingly faster electronic means of communication, new forms of transportation, and increased access to alternative media sites, the processes of hybridization will only increase. Michael Cronin's *Translation and Identity* (2006) speaks directly toward this point. Susan Bassnett and André Lefevere, when proposing the cultural turn in translation, suggested that scholars look at both the poetics and the ideology of translation, which led to over a decade of strong investigations into issues of translation, power, and politics. Cronin suggests that the analysis of identity should now be the focal point of the field: "If previously ideology had been the principal way of structuring political communication, identity has now taken over" (2006: 1). The previous chapter, on the Caribbean islands' evolution, with different peoples and cultures continuously intersecting and crossing borders, provides an excellent arena for this study of translation and identity in the Americas. Rather than viewing such conflicts in political terms, conservative or progressive, my goal has been to recognize the positive aspects of such resilience and point to new openings for continuation and strategies for survival. Translation, whether in an overt or covert fashion, is ingrained in the very psyche of the individuals who live in the Americas. I suggest that the next turn in translation studies should be a social-psychological one, expanding a functional approach to include social effects and individual affecs.

If one accepts broadening the definition of the field to include social and psychological aspects, one question that arises concerns the difficulty of access to translational formative sites. This is particularly true if the translational data have been lost or covered up by other, more dominant language histories. In "The Politics of Translation" (1993 [1992]), Gayatri

Spivak discusses the near impossibility of translating from a lost African language in Toni Morrison's novel *Beloved* (1987). Spivak, of course, is well known for her translations of Jacques Derrida from French (Derrida 1997) and Mahasweta Devi from Bengali (Devi 1995), and is especially well known for her work as a postcolonial critic, including her work on tribal groups in India. But she does not have an extensive body of literary criticism on American literature. She uses the Morrison example to illustrate how translation studies in a narrow sense might have broader applications. Spivak focuses on a conversation between Sethe, the mother, and her daughter Beloved, in which Sethe remembers her mother's friend and fellow slave Nan. Morrison writes, "What Nan told her she had forgotten, along with the language she told it in. The same language her ma'am spoke, and which would never come back. But the message—that was—and had been there all along" (1987: 62, quoted by Spivak 1993: 195). Here the lost language, the slave language, is, impossibly, remembered and, equally impossibly, is translated and passed on to the daughter. How is this done? Sethe picks up her daughter and takes her behind the smokehouse, where she opens her dress and points out a scar on her ribcage. The mark is a brand, a circle with a cross in it, which was inscribed on her body by the slaveholder. The message is clear. The brand is reclaimed by the mother, and passed on to the daughter, via Sethe slapping Beloved hard and leaving her own mark. Morrison coins a term for this form of translation, which she calls "rememory," perhaps a useful term for translation studies. Spivak talks about the event as caught in the web of translatability and untranslatability, a Derridean life and death of translation (see the section "Deconstruction and borders" in Chapter 6). Spivak writes, "[H]ere the author represents with violence a certain birth-in-death, a death-in-birth of a story that is not to translate or pass on. . . . And yet it is passed on, with the mark of untranslatability on it" (1993: 195). The story, the memory, is translated into a semiotic sign system that extends beyond language, a scarring upon the body, which conveys the suffering endured by Sethe, Nan, and the other slaves of her generation. The "rememory" provides a kind of identification, a sense of one's roots and one's past, and offers a kind of healing, recreating history despite the massive oppression, and creating possibilities for a new inscription for the future.

In "The Politics of Translation," Spivak also draws upon the work of Guyanese writer Wilson Harris, author of *The Guyana Quartet* (1985). Spivak writes that Harris "hails the (re)birth of the native imagination as not merely trans-lation but the trans-substantiation of the species" (1993: 196). Spivak is calling for the translator to deal both with the overtly expressed text *and* with the covert markers, including those of silence, the body, and rhetoric. Spivak quotes Harris:

> The Caribbean bone flute, made of human bone, is a seed in the soul of the Caribbean. . . . Consuming our bias and prejudices in ourselves we

can let the bone flute help us open ourselves rather than read it the other way—as a metonymic devouring of a bit of flesh.

(Harris 1990, quoted by Spivak 1993: 196)

Here Harris connects the musical instrument with cannibalism, recalling Chapter 4 of this book, reclaiming the metaphor and allowing it to unleash a freer and more open Caribbean imagination. Again, Harris resorts to a nonlinguistic semiotic system, that of music. One cannot help but think of jazz, especially Morrison's novel of that name, as well as the riffing, rhetorical qualities of *Beloved*, which serve to inexplicably express the inexpressible. Even a lost language need not remain totally untranslatable. As Anibal González used translation studies techniques to read the translational markers in *One Hundred Years of Solitude*, so too could one use translation studies methods as a means to unpack the translation markers, rhythms, and gaps within Morrison's texts. Although the fictional turn in translation studies, discussed in Chapter 5, is in its infant state, one area for future collaboration will be between translation studies scholars and ethnic minority American writers such as Morrison.

In "Translation, Poststructuralism, and Power" (Gentzler 2002), I briefly discussed Spivak's "Can the Subaltern Speak?" (1988) and its connection to translation studies. Her question, which pertains to this study, is whether or not it is possible for the subaltern to speak in light of generations of intellectuals—historians, ethnographers, and, yes, translators—reporting what the minority populations say, as if any of the discourses of history, journalism, anthropology, politics were transparent. Her answer, while not encouraging, is not altogether fruitless. She suggests that access to the "subaltern consciousness" might be gained not through what has been said or written, but through gaps in, silences in, and contradictions of those texts and translations. She goes on to suggest that a form of Marxism, as articulated by Pierre Macherey's formula for measuring silences (Macherey 1978: 87) or Terry Eagleton's reading against the grain (Eagleton 1986), and a form of poststructuralism, such as Michel Foucault's use of countermemory or Derrida's deconstruction, may provide tools for unpacking such hidden meanings. The attempt is less one of uncovering a "true" or "essential" subaltern consciousness and more of one of coming to an understanding of the effects of processes of colonization and language oppression in specific cultural conditions. In an interview with Ellen Rooney in *Outside in the Teaching Machine*, Spivak says:

> Reading the work of Subaltern Studies from within but against the grain, I would suggest that elements in their text would warrant a reading of the project to retrieve the subaltern consciousness as an attempt to *undo a massive historiographic metalepsis* and "situate" the effect of the subject as subaltern.
>
> (1993: 286; italics mine)

Translation is deeply implicated within this construction of a massive historiographic metalepsis, a Greek rhetorical device that generally refers to the substitution of one figure of speech for another, equally figurative form, as in a metaphor for a metaphor, or metonym for a metonym. When Spivak uses the term, she is invariably suggesting that an "effect" is substituted for a "cause," as in the view of the subject as a universally superior being (effect) being substituted for the cause (usually some sort of racial/gender/economic discrimination). She uses the construction of such "subject-effects" in her work on history, gender, and race, but it could equally apply to linguistic minorities, language, and translation. Spivak argues that the subaltern (slave/indigenous/immigrant) assimilates to the dominant culture or belief system and begins to accept, socially and mentally, the often unified and philosophical explanation for the condition, thereby reifying the ideological construct or effect and losing sight of the complex causes, which often are multiple and conflicting. I suggest that translation studies scholars in the Americas are increasingly viewing translation less as a rhetorical form aimed at accessing some unified original essence than as a discursive practice that reveals multiple signs of the heterogeneous and polyvalent nature of the construction of culture. Studying translations can help reveal those processes of language and culture assimilation at work.

This study also suggests that the costs of such language and cultural assimilation have been traumatizing for many of the minority peoples of the Americas. While the trauma may not be readily apparent, once one begins to read the cultural map against the grain, it is everywhere to be seen: Native Americans' histories and codices confiscated and burned; slaves who have been separated from their families to prevent them from speaking their native languages, or, worse yet, their tongues cut out for not speaking English; young Cajun girls not allowed to speak French at school and being detained, beaten, and raped for not conforming; young Latino men in the United States profiled, arrested, and jailed for speaking Spanish; Jewish immigrants confined to ghettos in urban areas; not to mention the Arab-American detainees being denied due process and equal rights as I write. In the Americas, both North and South, language rights are consistently denied in many realms of social and political life—at the hospitals, schools, businesses, voting booths, banks, and social services—invariably in contradiction to the very definitions of equality and liberty that define citizenship. Nontranslation is itself a translation policy, one with domestic repercussions.

Here I turn to the psychoanalytical theories of Jean Laplanche, especially his coinage of the term *à traduire* to refer to the unconscious. In his "Temporalité et traduction," for example, Laplanche writes, "le 'à traduire' primordial, nous le nommons: l'inconscient" [the "*à traduire*," we name it: the unconscious] (1989a: 29), translating something primordially unformed into language. I find it ironic that he uses translation terminology to describe individual repression and trauma in a way similar to the way that I am suggesting using translation concepts to unpack cultural crises and suffering.

There are differences, to be sure, for Laplanche, like Freud, uses translation in the sense of the translation of dreams into language, or, as is more often the case, the failure of translation in the child's inability to understand the sexual communication of the caresses by the adult (or understanding them very well, but repressing them for reasons of self-preservation). But perhaps the connection is not without coincidence. For most Freudian and Lacanian therapists, there is a close connection between the formation of identity, or consciousness, and the acquisition of language. There is also the suggestion that with a psychoanalytic reworking of an event, through the process of transference, an alternative translation is possible, one that is less repressive and more therapeutic. In the face of decades of repression and avoidance, such translation is no easy task. That is the work of the therapist: to help break down the defenses, the ideological rationalizations, in order to allow that which has not yet been incorporated into the symbolic order to resurface. In terms of the larger culture as a whole, Spivak calls this work the undoing of the massive historiographic metalepsis; at the individual level, Laplanche refers to it as a form of "de-translation." He writes, "In so far as the analytic method can be understood by the analogy with the process of translation, interpretation in terms of the past (infantile, archaic) is not a translation but a de-translation, a dismantling, a reversal of the translation" (1992: 170). Such references to "de-translation" and "dismantling" help explain my frequent reliance on Derrida and deconstruction to help better explain the nature of translation in the Americas in the chapters above.

Laplanche's use of the term "primordial" is potentially disturbing, as if he is describing some sort of pre-ontological essence. Whatever one's view on the existence of the unconsciousness may be, humans *do* have pasts, memories, associations, some of which are personally troubling and are repressed, others of which may be culturally unacceptable and censored. In *The Political Unconscious*, Fredric Jameson has written, "History is what hurts" (1981: 102). Such memories are not primordial but based on sociocultural experiences with others. In *Bless Me, Ultima*, when Rudolfo Anaya translates from oral and spiritual pre-Hispanic beliefs, these memories and associations, however unacceptable or repressed, are still part of his identity, no matter how much the Anglo-American culture of the present might wish them not to be. The form of translation I discuss in this study is less translation of written texts than a form of remembering and re-historicizing that extends beyond the constraints of any single language. Reading these historical markers is like deciphering a secret code, and the tools of psychoanalysis—interpreting dreams, reading slips of the tongue, jokes, angry outbursts, and contradictions—may prove helpful. New terminology, such as Morrison's concept of "rememory" or Spivak's concept of "metalepsis," may also inform such psychologically oriented translation investigations.

By focusing on the social-psychological aspects of translation, scholars can both come to a better understanding of individuals within the domestic cultures of the Americas and begin to understand translational concerns in a larger, global context. In *The Poetics of Imperialism: Translation and Colonization from* The Tempest *to* Tarzan (1997), Eric Cheyfitz addresses the international repercussions of translation in two chapters: "Tarzan and the Apes: U.S. Foreign Policy in the Twentieth Century" and "The Foreign Policy of Metaphor." Cheyfitz establishes an argument for what perhaps in history and the political sciences may seem trivial: that the translational policies from the Jamestown settlement in 1607 through to the present involve a consistent Anglo-American foreign policy that includes translation and rhetoric. The analysis of social conflict resulting in the use of military force, so prominent in historical studies, has been consistently rationalized in terms of idealized beliefs that European culture was higher, more advanced and civilized. The Eurocentric assumption was that the Native Americans (blacks, immigrants) would want to assimilate and conform, to seamlessly translate themselves into the Anglo-American culture. A domestic policy of nontranslation in the public sphere forced minorities to translate themselves into the dominant language and cultural system. Yet while the coerced indigenous peoples and minorities could not match the colonizers' military might, many resisted (and continue to resist) in terms of their language, both oral and written. The seamless translation has not gone as smoothly as anticipated.

In light of the traumatic effects of September 11, 2001, such a view of the social-psychological effects of an international policy of translation could not be more relevant. In *The Translation Zone: A New Comparative Literature* (2006), Emily Apter draws attention to the urgent social and political need for a more open translational policy. Nowhere was the failure of the monolingual policy of the United States more exposed than by its military and foreign policy failures in the Middle East; nowhere was the need for increased translation, understanding, and international cooperation across linguistic, cultural, political, and religious borders more apparent. Apter, significantly, focuses upon mistranslation and all the breakdowns that occurred in diplomatic, military, and domestic circles in the Afghan and Iraqi wars. She quotes, for example, Carl von Clausewitz as saying, "War is a mere continuation of policy by other means" (Clausewitz 1982: 119), to which Apter adds, "War is the continuation of extreme mistranslation or disagreement by other means" (2006: 16). Apter kept a running log of all the translational errors, breakdowns, and omissions leading up to and during the war in Iraq, illustrating translational failures at training sites, in the field, by intelligence agencies, in the prisons, with the media, and internally within their own offices. She concludes that translation, or in this case mistranslation, is a "concrete particular of the art of war, crucial to its strategy and tactics, part and parcel of the way in which images and bodies are read, and constitutive of *matériel*" (ibid.: 15).

I would extend Apter's claim that translation is constitutive of military culture to argue that translation is constitutive of civilian culture as well. One could argue that during the twentieth century the foreign policy of North America was turned in on itself and became a form of domestic policy. The fears and suspicions of the Other from within, the attempts to quarantine the foreign Other on reservations and in ghettos, prisons, and asylums, the overt vigilante enforcement of a monolingual language policy, led to repression, psychological trauma, and social conflict. Yet those who have not given up their languages, cultures, and worldviews, those who have refused to translate themselves into the dominant discourse, those who attempt to translate their own languages and ideas into the dominant culture, are increasingly coming to the fore. Minority groups within the Americas, from Canada to the United States, Latin America, Brazil, and the Caribbean, are increasingly using translation, perhaps *more* than any other genre, to forge their own identities. In Chapter 6 I discussed Pérez Firmat's argument that because of Cuba's alternative language, history, and location, Cuban writers possess a "translation sensibility" (Pérez Firmat 1989: 4). However, the use of translation is not a passive, secondary activity; nor need it be traumatic and anxiety producing; rather it can be seen as a proactive, liberating (therapeutic) activity, open to innovative possibilities. Translation in the traditional sense has been a fairly timid genre, showing one's dependence upon canonical literary forms and ideas; translation in the American sense is a bold genre, one at the very center of artistic movements and cultural generation, often showing one's independence from standard forms and leading to new and highly original styles and ideas.

In translation studies discourse, the psychoanalytic aspect of translational activity has not been entirely ignored. In Canada in particular, there have been investigations, such as those published in a special issue of *Meta* (1982), edited by François Peraldi, or *TTR* (1998), edited by Ginette Michaud. Michaud correctly points out that studies of psychoanalysis and translation tend to be grouped under certain rubrics, such as the translation of psychoanalytical texts, translation within psychoanalytical discourse, the inter-language of psychoanalysis, or psychoanalytic readings of literary texts (Michaud 1998: 10), and do not discuss larger theoretical concerns. The problem of translation within psychoanalysis has invariably been one of the central problems, and the theoretical complexity of "translating" from an unconscious nondiscourse into any language or symbolic system is fraught with difficulties, to the point where some critics suggest that it cannot be studied scientifically at all. Andrew Benjamin, a philosopher from the Monash University in Australia, has written on translation, philosophy, and psychoanalysis, focusing on translations from Freud with a larger view of raising philosophical questions of origin and being. In "Translating Origins: Psychoanalysis and Philosophy," collected in Lawrence Venuti's anthology *Rethinking Translation* (1992), Andrew Benjamin discusses this problem by considering Freud's letters to Wilhelm Flisss, in particular the one dated December 6, 1896, in which Freud writes, "Die Versagung der Übersetzung, das ist das, was klinisch 'Verdrängung' heist" [The failure of translation, that is what is clinically called "repression"] (Freud 1985: 208, quoted by Benjamin 1992: 19). Benjamin goes on to explore this idea, suggesting that a failure of translation is already a translation, thus positing the presence of an already present translation and calling into question any philosophy that posits a concept of origin, truth, or preontological being. Such a belief is much in line with the thinking of Derrida, who also posits similar questions of philosophical truth or original essence. For Derrida, there is no pure meaning or truth behind any text; rather, every text is already a translation of a translation of a translation in a continually receding *mis en abîme*. What does exist for Derrida—hence my reference to *Living On/Border Lines* above—is a form of living on (*überleben*) that he finds present in translation and serves as his starting point for thinking about language, life, and identity. As he argues in "Des tours de Babel" (1985b), Derrida holds that translations reaffirm, complement, and supplement the original, enacting survival (*fortleben*; *survivre*). Translation ensures the process of regeneration and rebirth, the means by which languages grow and by which individuals come to terms with their personal narratives and complex identities (ibid.: 191; see also Gentzler 2002: 163–164). To put it in the framework of Laplanche's psychoanalytical approach, the largely unconscious realm called the *à traduire*, if articulated, might help us better understand some of the reasons for past cultural trauma and open avenues for new translations, those that reaffirm fundamental values such as cultural diversity, linguistic independence, and individual creativity. For translation studies scholars, investigations of such sociopsychological openings via translation present a whole new world of possibilities.

Bibliography

Akai, Joanne (1997) "Creole . . . English: West Indian Writing as Translation," *TTR* 10 (1): 165–193.
Alonzo, Anne-Marie (1986) "Rituel," *Tessera* 57: 47–49; trans. Susanne de Lotbinière-Harwood (1986) "Ritual," *Tessera* 57: 50–52.
Álvarez, Román, and M. Carmen-África Vidal (eds.) (1996) *Translation Power Subversion*, Clevedon, UK: Multilingual Matters.
Anaya, Rudolfo (1972) *Bless Me, Ultima*, Berkeley: Quinto Sol.
Andrade, Joachim Pedro de (dir.) (1969) *Macunaíma*, N.P.
Andrade, Joachim Pedro de (dir.) (1982) *O homem do Pau-Brasil*, N.P.
Andrade, Mário de (1928) *Macunaíma: O herói sem nenhum caráter*, Florianópolis: Editora da UFSC.
Andrade, Mário de (1980) *Paulicéia Desvairada. Poesias completas*, 2 vols., São Paulo: Livraria Martins Editora, I: 13–32.
Andrade, Oswald de (1924) "Manifesto da poesia Pau-Brasil," *Correio da Manhã* (18 March); trans. Stella M. de Sá Rego (1986) "Manifesto of Pau-Brasil Poetry," *Latin American Literary Review* 14 (27) (January–June): 184–187.
Andrade, Oswald de (1928) "Manifesto Antropófago," *Revista de Antropofagia* 1 (May): 1; trans. Leslie Bary "Oswald de Andrade's 'Cannibalist Manifesto,'" *Latin American Literary Review* 19 (38) (July–December, 1991): 35–47.
Anzaldúa, Gloria (1987) *Borderlands/La frontera: The New Mestiza*, San Francisco: Spinsters/Aunt Lute.
Anzaldúa, Gloria (2000) *Interviews/Entrevistas*, ed. AnaLouise Keating, London: Routledge.
Apter, Emily (2006) *The Translation Zone: A New Comparative Literature*, Princeton, NJ: Princeton University Press.
Arrojo, Rosemary (1986) "Paulo Vizioili e Nelson Ascher discutem John Donne: A que são fiéis tradutores e críticos de tradução?" *Tradução e Communicação* 9 (São Paulo): 133–142.
Arrojo, Rosemary (1995) "Jorge Luis Borges's Labyrinths and João Guimarães Rosa's 'Sertão': Images of Reality as Text," dissertation, Johns Hopkins University.
Arrojo, Rosemary (2002) "Writing, Interpreting, and the Power Struggle for the Control of Meaning: Scenes from Kafka, Borges, and Kosztolányi," in Maria Tymoczko and Edwin Gentzler (eds.) *Translation and Power*, Amherst: University of Massachusetts Press, 63–79.
Ascher, Nelson (1989) "O texto e sua sombra: Teses sobre a teoria da intradução

[The Text and Its Shadow: Theses on a Theory of Intra-translation], *34 Letras* (Rio de Janeiro) 3 (March): 142–157.
Athayde, Tristão de (1966) *Estudos Literários*, Rio de Janeiro: Aguilar, 914–927.
Bailyn, Bernard (ed.) (1965) *Pamphlets of the American Revolution, 1750–1776*, Cambridge, MA: Belknap Press of Harvard University Press.
Bannet, Eve Tavor (1993) "The Scene of Translation: After Jakobson, Benjamin, de Man, and Derrida," *New Literary History* 24 (3) (Summer): 577–595.
Bary, Leslie (trans.) (1991) "Oswald de Andrade's 'Cannibalist Manifesto,'" *Latin American Literary Review* 19 (38) (July–December): 35–47.
Bassnett, Susan (1992) "Writing in No Man's Land: Questions of Gender and Translation," in Malcolm Coulthard (ed.) *Studies in Translation, Ilha do Desterro* 28: 63–73.
Bassnett, Susan (1993) *Comparative Literature: A Critical Introduction*, Oxford: Blackwell.
Bassnett, Susan, and André Lefevere (eds.) (1990) *Translation, History and Culture*, London: Pinter.
Bassnett, Susan, and André Lefevere (1995) "General Editor's Preface" to Lawrence Venuti, *Translator's Invisibility*, London: Routledge, vii–viii.
Bassnett, Susan, and André Lefevere (1998) *Constructing Cultures: Essays on Literary Translation*, Clevedon, UK: Multilingual Matters.
Bassnett, Susan, and Harish Trevedi (eds.) (1999) *Post-colonial Translation: Theory and Practice*, London: Routledge.
Bellei, Sérgio Luiz Prado (1998) "Brazilian Anthropophagy Revisited," in Francis Barker, Peter Hulme, and Margaret Iverson (eds.) *Cannibalism and the Colonial World*, Cambridge: Cambridge University Press, 87–109.
Benjamin, Andrew (1989) *Translation and the Nature of Philosophy: A New Theory of Words*, London: Routledge.
Benjamin, Andrew (1992) "Translating Origins: Psychoanalysis and Philosophy," in Lawrence Venuti (ed.) *Rethinking Translation: Discourse, Subjectivity, Ideology*, London: Routledge.
Benjamin, Walter (1955) "Die Aufgabe des Übersetzers," in *Illuminationen*, Frankfurt: Suhrkamp; trans. Harry Zohn (1969a) "The Task of the Translator," in *Illuminations*, New York: Schocken Books, 69–82.
Benjamin, Walter (1969b) "The Storyteller: Reflections on the Works of Nikolai Leskov," trans. Harry Zohn, in *Illuminations*, New York: Schocken Books, 83–110.
Benjamin, Walter (1969c) "The Work of Art in the Age of Mechanical Reproduction," trans. Harry Zohn, in *Illuminations*, New York: Schocken Books, 217–252.
Bereziartu, Xabier Mendiguren (2002) "Shakespeare's Plays in Basque," *Senez* 24, available at http://www.eizie.org/eu/Argitalpenak/senez/20021001/Mendi2 (accessed 20 July 2005).
Berman, Antoine (1992) *The Experience of the Foreign: Culture and Translation in Romantic Germany*, trans. S. Heyvaert, Albany: State University of New York Press.
Bersianik, Louky (1987) *Les Terribles Vivantes/Firewords*, Canadian National Film Board/Studio D Film, dir. Dorothy Hénaut.
Bhabha, Homi K. (1994) *The Location of Culture*, London: Routledge.

Bickerton, Derek (1975) *Dynamics of a Creole Continuum*, Cambridge: Cambridge University Press.
Blanchot, Maurice (1978) *Death Sentence*, trans. Lydia Davis, Barrytown, NY: Station Hill Press.
Blanchot, Maurice (1981) *The Madness of the Day*, transl. Lydia Davis, Barrytown, NY: Station Hill Press.
Blumgarten, Solomon [pseudonym Yehoyesh] (trans.) (1922–1927) *Tanakh* [The Torah], No surviving copy.
Blumgarten, Solomon [pseudonym Yehoyesh] (trans.) (1910) *Dos Lied fun Hiavat'a*. New York: Yehoash Verlag.
Bly, Robert (1980) *Talking all Morning*, Ann Arbor: University of Michigan Press.
Borges, Jorge Luis (1926) "Sobre las dos maneras de traducir" [On the Two Ways of Translating], in *La Prensa* (August 1).
Borges, Jorge Luis (1962) *Labyrinths: Selected Stories and Other Writings*, ed. and trans. Donald Yates and James Irby, New York: New Directions.
Borges, Jorge Luis (1989a [1944]) "Pierre Menard, autor del Quijote," *Ficciones*, in *Obras Completas 1923–1949*, Barcelona: Emecé Editores, 444–450; trans. Andrew Hurley (1998a) "Pierre Menard, Author of the *Quixote*," in *Collected Fictions*, New York: Viking, 88–95.
Borges, Jorge Luis (1989b [1944]) "La muerte y la brújula," *Ficciones*, in *Obras Completas 1923–1949*, Barcelona: Emecé Editores, 499–507; trans. Andrew Hurley (1998b) "Death and the Compass," in *Collected Fictions*, New York: Viking, 147–156.
Borges, Jorge Luis (1989c [1932]) "Las versiones homéricas," *Discusión* (1932), in *Obras Completas 1923–1949*, Barcelona: Emecé Editores, 239–243; trans. Eliot Weinberger (1999a) "The Homeric Versions," in Eliot Weinberger (ed.) *Selected Non-fictions*, New York: Viking, 69–74.
Borges, Jorge Luis (1989d [1936]) "Los traductores de las 1001 noches," *Historia de la Eternidad*, in *Obras Completas 1923–1949*, Barcelona: Emecé Editores, 397–413; trans. Andrew Hurley (1981) "The Translators of the *1001 Nights*," in Emir Rodríguez Monegal and Alastair Reid (eds.) *Borges: A Reader*, New York: Dutton, 73–86.
Borges, Jorge Luis (1989e [1932]) "El escritor argentino y la tradición," *Discusión*, in *Obras Completas 1923–1949*, Barcelona: Emecé Editores, 267–274; trans. Esther Allen (1999b) "The Argentine Writer and Tradition," in Eliot Weinberger (ed.) *Selected Non-fictions*, New York: Viking, 420–427.
Borges, Jorge Luis (1989f [1949]) "Emma Zunz," *El Aleph*, in *Obras Completas 1923–1949*, Barcelona: Emecé Editores, 564–569; trans. Andrew Hurley (1998e) "Emma Zunz," in *Collected Fictions*, New York: Viking, 215–219.
Borges, Jorge Luis (1989g [1949]) "La busca de Averroes," *El Aleph*, in *Obras Completas 1923–1949*, Barcelona: Emecé Editores, 564–569; trans. Andrew Hurley (1998f) "Averroës' Search," in *Collected Fictions*, New York: Viking, 235–241.
Borges, Jorge Luis (1998c) "The Library of Babel," trans. Andrew Hurley, in *Collected Fictions*, New York: Viking, 112–118.
Borges, Jorge Luis (1998d) "The Garden of Forking Paths," trans. Andrew Hurley, in *Collected Fictions*, New York: Viking, 119–128.
Bradford, William (1962 [*ca.* 1650]) *Of Plymouth Plantation*, New York: Capricorn.

Brathwaite, Edward Kamau (1984) *History of the Voice: The Development of Nation Language in Anglophone Caribbean Poetry*, London: New Beacon.
Brisset, Annie (1990) *Sociocritique de la traduction: Théâtre et altérité au Québec (1968–1988)*, Montreal: Les éditions du Préambules; trans. Rosalind Gill and Roger Gannon (1996) *A Sociocritique of Translation: Theatre and Alterity in Quebec 1968–1988*, Toronto: University of Toronto Press.
Brossard, Nicole (1982) *Picture theory*, Montreal: éditions Nouvelle-Optique; trans. Barbara Godard (1991) *Picture Theory*, Montreal: Guernica.
Brossard, Nicole (1983) *These Our Mothers, or, The Disintegrating Chapter*, trans. Barbara Goddard, Toronto: Coach House Press.
Brossard, Nicole (1985) *La Lettre aérienne*, Montreal: L'Hexagone.
Brossard, Nicole (1987a) *Le Désert mauve*, Montreal: L'Hexagone; trans. Susanne de Lotbinière-Harwood (1990) *Mauve Desert*, Toronto: Coach House.
Brossard, Nicole (1987b) *Sous la langue/Under Tongue*, trans. Susanne de Lotbinière-Harwood, Montreal: L'Essentielle.
Brossard, Nicole, and Daphne Marlatt (1986) *Characters/Jeu de letters*, Montreal: La Nouvelle Barre du Jour.
Burke, Edmund (2001 [1790]) *Reflections on the Revolution in France*, Stanford, CA: Stanford University Press.
Cabrera Infante, Guillermo (1967) *Tres tristes tigres*, Barcelona: Seix Barral; trans. Donald Gardner and Suzanne Jill Levine in collaboration with the author (1971) *Three Trapped Tigers*, New York: Harper and Row.
Cabrera Infante, Guillermo (1974) "Exorcising a Sty(le)," trans. Suzanne Jill Levine, *Review* (New York), 61–62.
Cabrera Infante, Guillermo (1976) "'Los Idus de Marzo', según Plutacro . . . y según Shakespeare, y según Mankiewicz, y según el limpiabotas Chicho Charol," *Exorcismos de esti(l)o*, Barcelona: Seix Barral.
Cabrera Infante, Guillermo (1979) *La Habana para un infante defunto*, Barcelona: Seix Barral; trans. Suzanne Jill Levine in collaboration with the author (1984) *Infante's Inferno*, New York: Harper and Row.
Cahan, Abraham (1993 [1917]) *The Rise of David Levinsky*, New York: Penguin.
Campos, Augusto de (1978a) *Verso, reverso e controverso*, São Paulo: Editora Perspectiva.
Campos, Augusto de (1978b) 'Revistas re-vistas: os antropófagos," *Poesia, antipoesia, antropofagia*, São Paulo: Cortez e Morães, 107–124.
Campos, Augusto de (1985) "Póstudo," *Folha de São Paulo* (January 27).
Campos, Augusto de, Décio Pignatari, and Haroldo de Campos (1975) *Teoria da poesia concreta: Textos críticos e manifestos 1950–60*, São Paulo: Livraria Duas Cidades.
Campos, Haroldo de (1967) *Oswald de Andrade – Trechos escolhidos*, Rio de Janeiro: Agir.
Campos, Haroldo de (1973) *Morphologia do Macunaíma*, São Paulo: Editora Perspectiva.
Campos, Haroldo de (1976) *A operação do texto*, São Paulo: Editora Perspectiva.
Campos, Haroldo de (1981) *Deus e o Diabo no Fausto de Goethe*, São Paulo: Perspectiva.
Campos, Haroldo de (1986) "The Rule of Anthropophagy: Europe under the Sign of Devoration," trans. María Tai Wolff, *Latin American Literary Review* 14 (27) (January–June): 48–60.

Campos, Haroldo de (1987) "Transblanco: Reflexión sobre la transcreación de "Blanco" de Octavio Paz, con una digresión sobre la teoría de la traducción del poeta mexicano," trans. Carlos Pelligrino, in Jacques Derrida, Emir Rodríguez Monegal, Haroldo de Campos, J. Hillis Miller, and Geoffrey Hartman *Diseminario: La desconstrucción, otro descubrimiento de América*, Montevideo: XYZ Comunicaciones, 147–156.

Campos, Haroldo de (1989) "Da tradução à transficcionalidade," *34 Letras* 3 (March): 82–95.

Campos, Haroldo de (1992) "Da tradução como criação e como crítica," *Metalinguagem e outras metas: Ensaios de teoria e crítica literária*, 4th rev. edn., São Paulo: Editora Perspectiva.

Candido, Antonio (1977) *Vários escritos*, São Paulo: Duas Cidades.

Carpentier, Alejo (1985) *Los pasos perdidos*, Madrid: Cátedra.

Cartier, Jacques (1556) *Delle navigationi et viaggi*, trans. Giovanni Battista Ramusio, Venice: Guinti.

Cartier, Jacques (1580) *A Short and Brief Narration of the Two Navigations and Discoveries to the Northwest Parts called Newe Fravnce*, first translated out of French into Italian by Gio. Babt. Ramutius and now turned into English by Iohn Florio, London: H. Bynneman.

Cather, Willa (1988 [1913]) *O Pioneers!* Boston: Houghton Mifflin.

Cather, Willa (1999 [1918]) *My Ántonia*, New York: Penguin.

Causse, Michèle (1988) "L'Interloquée," *Trivia* 13 (Winter): 79–90.

Césaire, Aimé (1969) *Une tempête: Adaptation de "La Tempête" de Shakespeare pour un théâtre nègre*, Paris: éditions du Seuil.

Chamberlain, Lori (1992) "Gender and the Metaphorics of Translation," in Lawrence Venuti (ed.) *Rethinking Translation: Discourse, Subjectivity, Ideology*, London: Routledge, 57–74.

Champlain, Samuel de (1632) *Les Voyages de la Nouvelle France occidentale, dicte Canada, faits par le sieur de Champlain*, Paris: Louis Sevestre.

Champlain, Samuel de (1994 [1613]) *Voyages*, Paris: Imprimerie nationale.

Chekhov, Anton (1983) *Oncle Vania*, trans. Michel Tremblay and Kim Yaroshevskaya, Montreal: Leméac.

Cheyfitz, Eric (1997) *The Poetics of Imperialism: Translation and Colonization from The Tempest to Tarzan*, exp. edn., Philadelphia: University of Philadelphia Press.

Chopin, Kate (1994 [1899]) *The Awakening*, New York: Norton.

Cixous, Hélène (1975) "Le Rire de la Méduse," *L'Arc* 61: 39–54; trans. Keith Cohen and Paula Cohen (1976) "The Laugh of Medusa," *Signs* 1 (Summer): 875–899.

Cixous, Hélène, and Catherine Clément (1975) *Le Jeune Née*, Paris: Union Générale d'éditions.

Cixous, Hélène, and Catherine Clément (1986) *The Newly Born Woman*, trans. Betsy Wing, Minneapolis: University of Minnesota Press.

Clausewitz, Carl von (1982) *On War*, trans. J.J. Graham, London: Penguin.

Columbus, Christopher (1968) *The Journal of Christopher Columbus (1492–93)*, trans. Cecil Jane, London: Anthony Blond.

Corrêa, José Celso Martinez (1937) *O rei da vela*, N.P.

Cortázar, Julio (1967a) "Blow-Up," trans. Paul Blackburn, *End of the Game and Other Stories* (later retitled *Blow-Up and Other Stories*), New York: Pantheon, 114–131.

Cortázar, Julio (1967b) *Hopscotch*, trans. Gregory Rabassa, New York: Signet.

Cortázar, Julio (1969) *Cronopios and Famas*, trans. Paul Blackburn, New York: Pantheon.
Cortázar, Julio (1972) *62: A Model-Kit*, trans. Gregory Rabassa, New York: Pantheon.
Cortázar, Julio (1978) *A Manual for Manuel*, trans. Gregory Rabassa, New York: Pantheon.
Cowan, Robert Ernest (1919) *A Bibliography of the Spanish Press of California 1833-1845*, Cambridge, MA: Harvard University Press.
Cronin, Michael (2006) *Translation and Identity*, London: Routledge.
Crystal, David (1992) *An Encyclopedic Dictionary of Language and Languages*, Oxford: Blackwell.
Davis, Kathleen (2001) *Deconstruction and Translation*, Manchester: St. Jerome.
DeCamp, David (1971) "Towards a Generative Analysis of a Post-creole Speech Continuum," in Dell Hymes (ed.) *Pidginization and Creolization of Languages*, Cambridge: Cambridge University Press, 349-370.
Déclaration des droits de l'homme et du citoyen, La (1988 [1789]), ed. Stéphane Rials. Paris: Hachette.
Declaration of Independence and the Constitution of the United States of America (1995) Washington, DC: National Defense University Press.
Delisle, Jean (1987) *La Traduction au Canada/Translation in Canada, 1534-1984*, Ottawa: Les Presses de l'Université d'Ottawa.
Delisle, Jean, and Judith Woodsworth (eds.) (1995) *Translators through History*, Amsterdam: John Benjamins.
DeMenil, Alexander Nicolas (1904) *The Literature of the Louisiana Territory*, St. Louis: The St. Louis News Co.
Depestre, René (1974) "Orfeo negro," in Nancy Morejón (ed.) *Recopilación de textos sobre Nicolás Guillén*, Havana: Casa de las Américas, 121-125.
Derrida, Jacques (1979) "Living On/Border Lines," trans. James Hulbert, in Harold Bloom, Paul de Man, Jacques Derrida, Geoffrey Hartman, and J. Hillis Miller, *Deconstruction and Criticism*, New York: Seabury Press, 75-176.
Derrida, Jacques (1981) *Positions*, trans. Alan Bass, Chicago: University of Chicago Press.
Derrida, Jacques (1982a) "Différance," trans. Alan Bass, *Margins of Philosophy*, Chicago: University of Chicago Press, 1-28.
Derrida, Jacques (1982b) *L'Oreille de l'autre*, Montreal: VLB Éditeur; trans. Peggy Kamuf (1985a) *The Ear of the Other: Texts and Discussions with Jacques Derrida*, ed. Christie McDonald, Lincoln: University of Nebraska Press.
Derrida, Jacques (1985b) "Des tours de Babel," in Joseph Graham (ed.) *Difference and Translation*, Ithaca, NY: Cornell University Press, 165-248.
Derrida, Jacques (1985c) "The Roundtable on Translation," trans. Peggy Kamuf, in Christie McDonald (ed.) *The Ear of the Other: Texts and Discussions with Jacques Derrida*, Lincoln: University of Nebraska Press, 92-161.
Derrida, Jacques (1987a) "Nacionalidad y nacionalismo filisófico," trans. Marie-Christine Peyrrone, in Jacques Derrida, Emir Rodríguez Monegal, Haroldo de Campos, J. Hillis Miller, and Geoffrey Hartman, *Diseminario: La desconstrucción, otro descubrimiento de América*, Montevideo: XYZ Comunicaciones, 27-47.
Derrida, Jacques (1987b) *The Truth in Painting*, trans. Geoffrey Bennington and Ian McLeod, Chicago: University of Chicago Press.

Derrida, Jacques (1996) *Le Monolinguisme de l'autre: ou la prothèse d'origine*, Paris: éditions Galilée; trans. Patrick Mensah (1998) *Monolingualism of the Other; or The Prosthesis of Origin*, Stanford, CA: Stanford University Press.
Derrida, Jacques (1997) *Of Grammatology*, trans. Gayatri Chakravorty Spivak, Baltimore: Johns Hopkins Press.
Derrida, Jacques, Emir Rodríguez Monegal, Haroldo de Campos, J. Hillis Miller, and Geoffrey Hartman (1987) *Diseminario: La desconstrucción, otro descubrimiento de América*, Montevideo: XYZ Comunicaciones.
Devi, Mahasweta (1995) *Imaginary Maps: Three Stories*, trans. Gayatri Chakravorty Spivak, London: Routledge.
Dimock, Wai Chee (2006) *Through Other Continents: American Literature across Deep Time*, Princeton, NJ: Princeton University Press.
Dingwaney, Anuradha, and Carol Maier (eds.) (1995) *Between Languages and Cultures: Translating Cross-cultural Texts*, Pittsburgh: University of Pittsburgh Press.
Donck, Adriaen van der (1849 [1650]) *Vertoogh van Nieu-Neder-land: The Representation of New Netherlands*, trans. Henry C. Murphy, New York: New York Historical Society, 2nd ser., vol. 2, pt. 8: 251–338.
Donck, Adriaen van der (1968 [1655]) *Beschryvinge van Nieuw Nederlant*, Syracuse, NY: Syracuse University Press.
Dos Santos, Nelson Pereira (dir.) (1971) *Como era gostoso o meu francês* [How Tasty Was My Little Frenchman].
Driedger, Leo (1996) *Multi-ethnic Canada: Identities and Inequalities*, Oxford: Oxford University Press.
Du Bartas, Guillaume de Salluste (1578) *La Sepmaine; ou, Création du monde*; trans. Joshua Sylvester (1979 [1605]) *The Divine Weeks and Works*, New York: Oxford.
Eagleton, Terry (1986) *Against the Grain: Essays 1975–85*, London: Verso.
Edwards, Jonathan (2003 [1741]) "Sinners in the Hands of an Angry God," in Harry S. Stout and Nathan O. Hatch (eds.) *Sermons and Discourses 1739–1742*, New Haven, CT: Yale University Press.
Eliot, John (1654) *A Catechism in the Massachusetts Indian Languages*, N.P.
Eliot, John (trans.) (1663) *Mamusse wunneetupanatamwe Up-Biblum God naneeswe Nukkone Testament kah wonk Wusku Testament / ne quoshkinnumuk nashpe Wuttinneumoh Christ noh asoowesit* [The Holy Bible], Cambridge, MA: Samuel Green and Marmaduke Johnson.
Elliot, Emory (ed.) (1988) *Columbia Literary History of the United States*, New York: Columbia University Press.
Elyot, Thomas (1883 [1531]) *The Boke Named The Gouvernour*, ed. Henry Herbert Stephen Croft, 2 vols., London: Kegan Paul.
Emerson, Ralph Waldo (1836) *Nature*, Boston: J. Munroe.
Emerson, Ralph Waldo (1901 [1837]) *The American Scholar*, New York: Laurentian Press.
Emerson, Ralph Waldo (1940 [1841]) "Self-reliance," in Brooks Atkinson (ed.) *The Complete Essays and Other Writings of Ralph Waldo Emerson*, New York: The Modern Library, 145–152.
Erdrich, Louise (1984) *Love Medicine*, New York: Holt, Rinehart, and Winston.
Even-Zohar, Itamar (1990) *Polysystem Studies, Poetics Today* 11 (1) (Spring).

Fichte, Johann Gottlieb (1979 [1808]) *Addresses to the German Nation*, trans. R.F. Jones, Westport, CT: Greenwood Press.
Firmat, Gustavo Pérez (1989) *The Cuban Condition: Translation and Identity in Modern Cuban Literature*, Cambridge: Cambridge University Press.
Fletcher, John, and Martin Stanton (1992) *Jean Laplanche: Seduction, Translation and the Drives*, trans. Martin Stanton, London: Institute of Contemporary Arts.
Foucault, Michel (1977) *Language, Counter-memory, Practice*, trans. Donald F. Bouchard and Sherry Simon, Ithaca, NY: Cornell University Press.
Freud, Sigmund (1985) *The Complete Letters of Sigmund Freud to Wilhelm Fliess 1887–1904*, ed. and trans. Jeffrey M. Masson, Cambridge, MA: Harvard University Press.
Fusco, Coco (1995) *English Is Broken Here: Notes on Cultural Fusion in the Americas*, New York: The New Press.
Galdós, Benito Pérez (1977 [1909]) *El caballero encantado*, Madrid: Cátedra.
García Márquez, Gabriel (1998) *One Hundred Years of Solitude*, trans. Gregory Rabassa, New York: Harper Perennial Classics.
Garreau, Louis-Armand (2003 [1849]) *Louisiana*, Shreveport: éditions Tintamarre.
Gayarré, Charles Etienne Arthur (1854) *History of Louisiana: The French Domination*, 2 vols., New York: Redfield; (1854) *History of Louisiana: The Spanish Domination*, New York: Redfield; (1866) *History of Louisiana: The American Domination*, New York: William J. Widdleton.
Gehring, Charles T. (1978) *A Guide to Dutch Manuscripts Relating to New Netherlands*, Albany: SUNY Press.
Gehring, Charles T. (1981) *Delaware Papers: Dutch Period, 1648–1664*, New York Historical Manuscripts Series, Baltimore: Genealogical Publishing Co.
Gehring, Charles T. (trans. and ed.) (1995) *Council Minutes, 1655–56*, New Netherlands Document Series. Syracuse: Syracuse University Press.
Gehring, Charles T. (trans. and ed.) (2000) *Correspondence, 1647–1653*, New Netherlands Document Series: Syracuse: Syracuse University Press.
Gentzler, Edwin (1996) "Translation, Counter-culture and the Fifties," in Román Álvarez and M. Carmen África Vidal (eds.) *Translation, Power, Subversion*. Clevedon, UK: Multilingual Matters, 116–137.
Gentzler, Edwin (2000) "Translating Metaphor: Beyond the Western Tradition," in Marilyn Gaddis Rose (ed.) *Beyond the Western Tradition*, Translation Perspectives XI, Binghamton: State University of New York
Gentzler, Edwin (2002) "Translation, Poststructuralism, and Power," in Maria Tymoczko and Edwin Gentzler (eds.) *Translation and Power*, Amherst: University of Massachusetts Press.
Gentzler, Edwin (1993) *Contemporary Translation Theories*, London: Routledge; reissued (2001) *Contemporary Translation Theories*, rev. 2nd edn, Clevedon, UK: Multilingual Matters.
Gentzler, Edwin, and Maria Tymoczko (2002) "Introduction," in Maria Tymoczko and Edwin Gentzler (eds.) *Translation and Power*, Amherst: University of Massachusetts Press, xi–xxviii.
Germain, Jean-Claude (1983) *A Canadian Play/Une Plaie canadienne*, Montreal: VLB.
Godard, Barbara (1989) "Theorizing Feminist Discourse/Translation," *Tessera* 6 (Spring): 42–53; reprinted in Susan Bassnett and André Lefevere (eds.) (1990) *Translation, History, and Culture*, London: Pinter, 87–96.

Godard, Barbara (1995) "A Translator's Journal," in Sherry Simon (ed.) *Culture in Transit: Translating the Literature of Quebec*, Montreal: Véhicule Press, 69–82.

Goethe, Johann Wolfgang von (1872 [1819]) *West-östlicher Divan*, Berlin: G. Hempel.

Goethe, Johann Wolfgang von (1998 [1836]) *Conversations of Goethe with Johann Peter Eckermann*, trans. John Oxenford, New York: D.

Gómez-Peña, Guillermo (1996) *The New World Border*, San Francisco: City Lights.

Gómez-Peña, Guillermo, and Coco Fusco (1992–93) "The Guatinaui World Tour," Performance piece, unpublished.

González, Anibal (1989) "Translation and the Novel: *One Hundred Years of Solitude*," in Harold Bloom (ed.) *Modern Critical Views: Gabriel García Márquez*, New York: Chelsea House, 271–282.

Grismer, Raymond Leonard (1939) *A Reference Index to 12,000 Spanish American Authors*, New York: Wilson.

Gruesz, Kirsten Silva (2005) *Ambassadors of Culture: The Transamerican Origins of Latino Writing*, Princeton, NJ: Princeton University Press.

Guillén, Nicolás (1930) *Motivos de son*; reprinted (1974) in *Obra poética 1920–1972*, Havana: Editorial de Arte y Literatura.

Hamilton, Alexander, James Madison, and John Jay (1970 [1787–1788]) *The Federalist; or The New Constitution*, London: J.M. Dent.

Hamilton, Alexander, James Madison, and John Jay (1999 [1787–1788]) *The Federalist Papers*, ed. Clinton Rossiter. New York: Mentor.

Haraszti, Zoltán (ed.) (1956 [1640]) *The Bay Psalm Book: A Facsimile Reprint of the First Edition of 1640*, facsimile edn., Chicago: University of Chicago Press.

Harris, Wilson (1985) *The Guyana Quartet*, London: Faber.

Harris, Wilson (1990) "Cross-cultural Crisis: Imagery, Language, and the Intuitive Imagination," Commonwealth Lectures: University of Cambridge, Lecture 2 (October 31).

Henripin, Jacques (1993) "Population Trends and Policies in Quebec," in Alain-G. Gagnon (ed.) *Quebec: State and Society*, 2nd ed., Scarborough, Ont.: Nelson Canada.

Herrmann, Claudine (1976) *Les Voleuses de langue*, Paris: Éditions des Femmes; trans. Nancy Kline (1989) *The Tongue Snatchers*, Lincoln: University of Nebraska Press.

Hinojosa, Rolando (1973) *Estampas del valle y otras obras*, Berkeley: Quinto Sol.

Hinojosa, Rolando (1976) *Klail City y sus alrededores*, Havana: Casa de las Américas.

Hinojosa, Rolando (1977) *Generaciones y semblanzas*, Berkeley: Justa.

Hinojosa, Rolando (1981) *Mi querido Rafa*, Houston: Arte Público.

Hinojosa, Rolando (1983) *The Valley*, Tempe: Bilingual Press.

Hinojosa, Rolando (1987) *Klail City*, Houston: Arte Público.

Hinojosa, Rolando (1994) *El condado de Belken: Klail City*, Tempe: Bilingual Press.

Hobbes, Thomas (trans.) (1843 [1629]) *The History of the Grecian War, Written by Thucydides*, in William Molesworth (ed.) *The English Works of Thomas Hobbes of Malmesbury*, vol. 8–9, London: John Bohn.

Hobsbawm, Eric J. (1962) *The Age of Revolution 1789–1842*, London: Abacus.

Holmes, James (1988) "On Matching and Making Maps: From a Translator's Notebook," *Translated! Papers on Literary Translation and Translation Studies*, Amsterdam: Rodopi, 53–64.

Holmes, James S., José Lambert, and Raymond van den Broeck (eds.) (1978) *Literature and Translation: New Perspectives in Literary Studies*, Leuven, Belgium: Acco.
Irigaray, Luce (1977) *Ce sexe qui n'en est pas un*, Paris: éditions de Minuit; trans. Catherine Porter and Carolyn Burke (1985) *This Sex Which Is Not One*, Ithaca, NY: Cornell University Press.
Irigaray, Luce (1990) *Je, tu, nous*, Paris: Éditions Grasset et Fasquelle; trans. Alison Martin (1993) *Je, tu, nous*, London: Routledge.
Jacobs, Carol (1975) "The Monstrosity of Translation," *Modern Language Notes* 90 (6) (December): 775–766.
James, Henry (1968 [1907]) *The American Scene*, Bloomington: Indiana University Press.
Jameson, Fredric (1981) *The Political Unconscious: Narrative as a Socially Symbolic Act*, Ithaca, NY: Cornell University Press.
Johnson, Barbara (1985) "Taking Fidelity Philosophically," in Joseph F. Graham (ed.) *Difference and Translation*, Ithaca, NY: Cornell University Press.
Johnson, Randal (1987) "Tupy or Not Tupy: Cannibalism and Nationalism in Contemporary Brazilian Literature," in John King (ed.) *Modern Latin American Fiction*, London: Faber and Faber, 41–59.
Johnson, Randal (ed.) (1993) *Tropical Paths: Essays on Modern Brazilian Literature*, New York: Garland.
Johnson, Randal, and Robert Stam (eds.) (1995) *Brazilian Cinema*, exp. ed. New York: Columbia University Press.
Jouve, Nicole Ward (1991) "To fly/to steal: No more? Translating French Feminism into English," *White Woman Speaks with Forked Tongue: Criticism as Autobiography*, London: Routledge.
Kafka, Franz (1971) "The Burrow," trans. Willa and Edwin Muir, in Nahum N. Glatzer (ed.) *The Complete Stories*, New York: Schocken Books, 325–359.
Kenner, Hugh (1954) Introduction to Ezra Pound's *Translations*, New York: New Directions.
Khatibi, Abdelkebir (1971) *La Mémoire tatouée*, Paris: Denoël.
Khatabi, Abdelkebir (1981) Preface to Marc Gontard, *La Violence du texte*, Paris: L'Harmattan.
Khatibi, Abdelkebir (1985) *Du bilinguisme*, Paris: Denoël.
Khatibi, Abdelkebir (1990) *Amour bilingue*, trans. Richard Howard, Minneapolis: University of Minnesota Press.
Kline, Nancy (1989) "Introduction" to Claudine Herrmann, *The Tongue Snatchers*, trans. Nancy Kline, Lincoln: University of Nebraska Press, vii–xxx.
Kosztolányi, Dezsö (1996) "O tradutor cleptomaníaco" [The Kleptomaniac Translator] in *O tradutor cleptomaníaco e outras histórias de Kornél Esti*, trans. Ladislao Szabo, Rio de Janeiro: Editora 34, 7–11.
Krupat, Arnold (1996) *The Turn to the Native: Studies in Criticism and Culture*, Lincoln: University of Nebraska Press.
Lafrentz, Ferdinand W. (1881/1882) *Nordische Klänge: Plattdütsche Riemels*, Chicago: L.W. Neele.
Lamy, Suzanne (1979) *d'elles*, Montreal: L'Hexagone.
Landry, Rodrigue, and Réal Allard (1996) "French in South Louisiana: Towards Language Loss," *Journal of Multilingual and Multicultural Development* 17 (6): 442–68.

Laplanche, Jean (1989a) "Temporalité et traduction: Pour une remise au travail de la philosophie du temps," *Psychanalyse à l'université* 53 (January): 17–35; trans. Terry Thomas (1989b) "Temporality and Translation," *Stanford Literary Review* (Fall): 241–259.

Laplanche, Jean Laplanche, Jean (1989c) *New Foundations for Psychoanalysis*, trans. David Macey, Oxford: Basil Blackwell.

Laplanche, Jean (1992) "Psychoanalysis, Time and Translation," trans. Martin Stanton, in John Fletcher and Martin Stanton (eds.) *Jean Laplanche: Seduction, Translation, and Drive*, London: Institute of Contemporary Arts.

Laplanche, Jean (1999) *Essays on Otherness*, trans. Luke Thurston, Leslie Hill, and Philip Slotkin, London: Routledge.

Larkosh, Christopher (1996) "Limits of the Translatable Foreign: Fictions of Translation, Migration, and Sexuality in Twentieth-Century Argentine Literature," Dissertation, University of California at Berkeley.

Larkosh, Christopher (2002) "Translating Woman: Victoria Ocampo and the Empires of Foreign Fascination," in Maria Tymoczko and Edwin Gentzler (eds.) *Translation and Power*, Amherst: University of Massachusetts Press, 99–121.

Latham, Earl (ed.) (1976) *The Declaration of Independence and The Constitution*, Lexington, MA: Heath.

Lauter, Paul (ed.) (2002) *The Heath Anthology of American Literature*, 4th edn., Boston: Houghton Mifflin.

Lecercle, Jean-Jacques (1990) *The Violence of Language*, London: Routledge.

Lefevere, André (1992) *Translation, Rewriting, and the Manipulation of Literary Fame*, London: Routledge.

Levine, Suzanne Jill (1991) *The Subversive Scribe: Translating Latin American Fiction*, St. Paul: Graywolf Press.

Lianeri, Alexandra (2002) "Translation and the Establishment of Liberal Democracy in Nineteenth-Century England: Constructing the Political as an Interpretive Act," in Maria Tymoczko and Edwin Gentzler (eds.) *Translation and Power*, Amherst: University of Massachusetts Press, 1–24.

Longfellow, Henry Wadsworth (1910) "Song of Hiawatha," trans. Solomon Blumgarten, *Dos Lied fun Hiavat'a*, New York: Yehoash Verlag.

Lotbinière-Harwood, Susanne de (1991) *Re-belle et infidèl: La traduction comme pratique de réécriture au feminin/The Body Bilingual: Translation as a Rewriting in the Feminine*, Montreal: Les éditions du Remue-ménage/Toronto: Women's Press.

Lotbinière-Harwood, Susanne de (1995) "Geo-graphies of Why," in Sherry Simon (ed.) *Culture in Transit: Translating the Literature of Quebec*, Montreal: Véhicule Press.

Loveira, Carlos (1927) *Juan Criollo*, Havana: Editorial Cultural.

Lukács, Georg (1971) *The Theory of the Novel*, trans. Anna Bostock, Cambridge, MA: MIT Press.

McGuirk, Bernard (1997) "Z/Z: On *Midrash* and *écriture féminine* in Jorge Luis Borges' 'Emma Zunz,'" *Symptoms, Risks and Strategies of Post-Structural Criticism*, London: Routledge, 185–206.

Macherey, Pierre (1978) *A Theory of Literature Production*, trans. Geoffrey Wall, London: Routledge.

Maier, Carol (1995) "Toward a Theoretical Practice for Cross-cultural Translation," in Anuradha Dingwaney and Carol Maier (eds.) *Between Languages and*

Cultures: Translation and Cross-cultural Texts, Pittsburgh: University of Pittsburgh Press, 21–38.

Man, Paul de (1986) "'Conclusions': Walter Benjamin's 'The Task of the Translator,'" *The Resistance to Theory*, Minneapolis: University of Minnesota Press, 73–105.

Martin, Helen Reimensnyder (1904) *Tille, a Mennonite Maid*, New York: The Century Co.

Marx, Karl, and Friedrich Engels (1947 [1845]) *The German Ideology*, trans. R. Pascal. New York: International Books.

Mehrez, Samia (1992) "Translation and the Postcolonial Experience: The Francophone North African Text," in Lawrence Venuti (ed.) *Rethinking Translation: Discourse, Subjectivity, Ideology*, London: Routledge, 120–138.

Michaud, Ginette (ed.) (1998) *Psychanalyse et traduction: Voies de traverse/ Psychoanalysis and Translation: Passages Between and Beyond*, TTR 11.2.

Miron, Gaston (1970) *L'Homme rapaillé*, Montreal: Presses de l'Université de Montréal.

Möllhausen, Heinrich Balduin (1858) *Tagebuch einer Reise vom Mississippi nach den Küsten der Südsee*; trans. Percy Sinnett, *Diary of a Journey from the Mississippi to the Coasts of the Pacific with a United States Government Expedition*, London: Longman, Brown, Green, Longman, and Roberts.

Möllhausen, Heinrich Balduin (1861a) *Der Halbindianer*, Leipzig: Hermann Costenoble.

Möllhausen, Heinrich Balduin (1861b) *Der Flüchtling*, Leipzig: Hermann Costenoble.

Moraga, Cherríe, and Gloria Anzaldúa (eds.) (1983) *This Bridge Called my Back: Writings by Radical Women of Color*, 2nd edn., New York: Kitchen Table.

Morgan, Edmund Sears (ed.) (1964) *The Founding of Massachusetts*, Indianapolis: Bobbs-Merrill.

Morrison, Toni (1987) *Beloved*, New York: Plume Books.

Münter, Carl (1879) *Nu sünd wie in Amerika: En plattdütsch Riemels*, Cincinatti: Köhler.

Myers, Albert Cook (ed.) (1967 [1912]) *Narratives of Early Pennsylvania, West New Jersey, and Delaware, 1630–1707*, New York: Barnes and Noble.

Neate, Wilson (1904) "Unwelcome Remainders, Welcome Reminders: Ethnicity within National Identity," *MELUS* 19 (2) (Summer): 17–34.

Neihardt, John G. (1961 [1932]) *Black Elk Speaks*, Lincoln: University of Nebraska Press.

Nies, Konrad, and Herman Rosenthal (1888/1890) *Deutsch-amerikanische Dichtung*, Reference Guide 20, The German Society of Pennsylvania, Washington, DC: German Historical Institute.

Nietzsche, Friedrich Wilhelm (1968 [1908]) *Ecce Homo*, trans. Walter Kaufmann, in Walter Kaufman (ed.) *The Basic Writings of Nietzsche*, New York: The Modern Library, 657–800.

Niranjana, Tejaswini (1992) *Siting Translation: History, Post-structuralism, and the Colonial Context*, Berkeley: University of California Press.

Nunes, Benedito (1984) "Anthropophagisme et surréalisme," in *Surréalisme périphérique*, Montreal: Université de Montréal, 159–179.

O'Connell, Barry (1993) Foreword to Brian Swann, *Song of the Sky*, Amherst: University of Massachusetts Press.

Ortiz, Fernando (1940) "Del fenómeno social de la 'transculturación' y de su importancia en Cuba," *Revista Bimestre Cubano* 46: 273–78.
Ortiz, Fernando (1985 [1923]) *Catauro de cubanismos*, Havana: Editorial de Ciencias Sociales.
Otis, James (1764) *The Rights of the British Colonies Asserted and Proved*, Boston: Edes and Gill.
Ovid (1690) *Metamorphoses*, trans. George Sandys, 8th edn., London: Brewster.
Pagano, Adriana S. (2002) "Translation as Testimony: On Official Histories and Subversive Pedagogies in Cortázar," in Maria Tymoczko and Edwin Gentzler (eds.) *Translation and Power*, 80–98.
Paine, Thomas (1986 [1776]) *Common Sense*, New York: Penguin.
"Panegyrical Oratory of Greece" (1822) in *Quarterly Review* 27, London: John Murray, 382–404.
Pastorius, Francis Daniel (1850 [1700]) *Umständige geographische Beschreibung der zu allerletzt erfundenen Provintz Pensylvaniæ*, trans. Lewis H. Weiss, *A Particular Geographical Description of the Lately Discovered Province of Pennsylvania*, in Memoirs of the Historical Society of Pennsylvania, vol. 4, part 2: 83–104.
Paz, Octavio (1973) "Invention, Underdevelopment, Modernity," *Alternating Current*, trans. Helen Lane, New York: Viking.
Pease, Donald E., and Robyn Wiegman (eds.) (2002) *The Futures of American Studies*, Durham, NC: Duke University Press.
Peirce, Charles Sanders (1931–66) *Collected Papers*, ed. Charles Hartshorne, Peter Weiss, and Arthur W. Burks, Cambridge, MA: Belknap Press of Harvard University Press.
Peraldi, François (ed.) (1982) *Psychanalyse et traduction*, special issue of *Meta* 27 (1) (March).
Pérez Firmat, Gustavo (1989) *The Cuban Condition: Translation and Identity in Modern Cuban Literature*, Cambridge: Cambridge University Press.
Picabia, Francis (1920) "Manifeste cannibale," *Dadaphone*, Paris (March): 7.
Picchia, Menotti del (1927) "Feira de Sexta," *Correio Paulistano*, 28 January.
Popovič, Anton (1976) *Dictionary for the Analysis of Literary Translation*, Edmonton: University of Alberta Press.
Pound, Ezra (1975) *The Cantos*, London: Faber and Faber.
Pratt, Mary Louise (1992) *Imperial Eyes: Travel Writing and Transculturation*, London: Routledge.
Rael, Juan B. (1977) *Cuentos españoles de Colorado y Nuevo México: Spanish Folk Tales of Colorado and New Mexico*, 2nd rev. edn., Santa Fe: Museum of New Mexico Press, 1977.
Rama, Ángel (1982) *Transculturación narrativa en América Latina*, Mexico City: Fundación Ángel Rama.
Reitzel, Robert (1913) *Des armen Teufel: Gesammelte Schriften*, Detroit: Reitzel Club.
Rémy, Henri (1854) *Histoire de la Louisiane*, in *La Journal St. Michel*, New Orleans: St James Parrish.
Rémy, Henri (1859) *Tierra Caliente*, N.P.
Renan, Ernest (1878) *Caliban, suite de La Tempête*, Paris: Calmann-Lévy.
Retamar, Roberto Fernández (1971) "Caliban: Notes toward a Discussion of Culture in Our America," *Casa de Las Americas* 68 (September–October); reprinted in

(1989) *Caliban and Other Essays*, trans. Edward Baker, Minneapolis: University of Minnesota Press, 3–45.
Ribaut, Jean (1927 [1563]) *The Whole and True Discovery of Terra Florida*, a facsimile reprint of the London edition of 1563, Deland: The Florida State Historical Society.
Ribiero, Darcy (1982) *Utopia selvagem: Saudades da inocência perdida*, Rio de Janeiro: Nova Fronteira.
Ripley, George et al. (eds.) (1838) *Specimens of Foreign Standard Literature*, vols. 1–14, Boston: Hilliard, Gray.
Rocha, Glauber (dir.) (1963) *Deus e o diabo na terra do sol* (Black God, White Devil).
Rodríguez, Luis Felipe (1937) *Ciénaga*, Havana: Trópico.
Romano-Sued, Susana (1999) "Duelo y melancolía en la traducción o la travesía imposible hacia la equivalencia" [Grief and Melancholy in Translation or the Impossible Voyage toward Equivalence], in Susana Romano-Sued (ed.) *Borgesíada*, Córdoba: Toppographía, 73–92.
Rosa, João Guimarães (1962) "O espelho [The Mirror]," in *Primeiras estórias*, Rio de Janeiro: Livraria José Olympio Editoria, 71–78.
Rowe, John Carlos (2002) "Postnationalism, Globalism, and the New American Studies," in Donald E. Pease and Robyn Wiegman (eds.) *The Futures of American Studies*, Durham, NC: Duke University Press, 167–82.
Salée, Daniel (1995) "Identities in Conflict: The Aboriginal Question and the Politics of Recognition in Quebec," *Ethnic and Racial Studies* 18 (2) (April): 277–314.
Salluste Du Bartes, Guillaume (1965 [1605]) *The Divine Weeks and Works*, trans. Joshua Sylvester, Gainesville, FL: Scholars' Facsimiles and Reprints.
Sandys, George (trans.) (1970 [1626]) Ovid, *Metamorphoses*, Lincoln: University of Nebraska Press.
Sarduy, Severo (1973) *Cobra*, Buenos Aires: Editorial Sudamericana; trans. Suzanne Jill Levine (1975) *Cobra*, New York: E.P. Dutton.
Schoenberger, Harold William (1924) "American Adaptations of French Plays on the New York and Philadelphia Stages from 1790 to 1833," PhD. thesis, University of Pennsylvania.
Schwartz, Roberto (1992) *Misplaced Ideas: Essays on Brazilian Culture*, London: Verso.
Schwartzwald, Robert (1997) "Of Deadly and Saving Sorrows: Three Observations on Criticism in Quebec," *Quebec Studies* 24 (Fall): 206–214.
Selvon, Sam (1952) *A Brighter Sun*, Stratford, Ontario: Wingate Press.
Selvon, Sam (1956) *The Lonely Londoners*, New York: St. Martins.
Selvon, Sam (1975) *Moses Ascending*, London: Davis-Poynter.
Shakespeare, William (1978) *Macbeth*, trans. Michel Garneau, Montreal: VLB.
Shell, Marc (ed.) (2002) *American Babel: Literatures of the United States from Abnaki to Zuni*, Boston: Harvard University Press.
Shin, Hyor B., and Rosalind Bruno (2003) "Language Use and English-Speaking Ability: 2000," *Census 2000 Brief*, Washington, DC: US Census Bureau.
Shorto, Russell (2005) *The Island at the Center of the World*, New York: Vintage.
Siemerling, Winfried (2005) *The New North American Studies: Culture, Writing, and the Politics of Re/cognition*, London: Routledge.
Silko, Leslie Marmon (1977) *Ceremony*, New York: Viking.

Simon, Sherry (1994) *Le Trafic des langues. Traduction et culture dans la littérature québécoise*, Montreal: éditions du Boréal.
Simon, Sherry (ed.) (1995) *Culture in Transit: Translating the Literature of Quebec*, Montreal: Véhicule Press.
Simon, Sherry (1996) *Gender in Translation: Cultural Identity and the Politics of Transmission*, London: Routledge.
Simon, Sherry (1999) "Translating and Interlingual Creation in the Contact Zone: Border Writing in Quebec," in Susan Bassnett and Harish Trivedi (eds.) *Postcolonial Translation: Theory and Practice*, London: Routledge, 58–74.
Simon, Sherry (2006) *Translating Montreal: Episodes in the Life of a Divided City*, Montreal: McGill-Queen's University Press.
Simon, Sherry, and Paul St.-Pierre (eds.) (2000) *Changing the Terms: Translating in the Postcolonial Era*, Ottawa: University of Ottawa Press.
Snell-Hornby, Mary, Franz Pöchhacker, and Klaus Kaindl (eds.) (1994) *Translation Studies: An Interdiscipline*, Amsterdam: John Benjamins.
Sollors, Werner (1997) "For a Multilingual Turn in American Studies," *American Studies Association Newsletter* 20 (2): 13–15.
Sollors, Werner (ed.) (1998) *Multilingual America: Transnationalism, Ethnicity, and the Languages of American Literature*, New York: New York University Press.
Souza, Eneida Maria de (1995) "Time of Postcriticism," in Bernard McGuirk and Else Ribeiro Pires Vieira (eds.) *Retranslating Latin America: Dimensions of the Third Term*, Nottingham: Nottingham Monographs in the Humanities.
Souza, Márcio (1977) *The Emperor of the Amazon*, trans. Thomas Colchie, New York: Avon.
Spiller, Robert E., Willard Thorp, Thomas H. Johnson et al. (eds.) (1974) *Literary History of the United States: Bibliography*, 4th edn, New York: Macmillan.
Spivak, Gayatri Chakravorty (1988) "Can the Subaltern Speak?" in Cary Nelson and Lawrence Grossberg (eds.) *Marxism and the Interpretation of Culture*, Urbana: University of Illinois Press, 271–313.
Spivak, Gayatri Chakravorty (1992) "The Politics of Translation," in Michèle Barrett and Anne Phillips (eds.) *Destabilitzing Theory: Contemporary Feminist Debates*, Cambridge: Polity Press; reprinted (1993) "The Politics of Translation," in *Outside in the Teaching Machine*, London: Routledge, 179–200.
Staden, Hans (1929) *Hans Staden: The True History of His Captivity, 1557*, trans. Malcolm Letts, New York: R.M. McBride.
Steiner, George (1975) *After Babel*, Oxford: Oxford University Press.
Strubberg, Friedrich [pseudonym Armand] (1862) *Sklaverei in Amerika; oder Schwarzes Blut*, Hanover: Carl Rümpler.
Strubberg, Friedrich [pseudonym Armand] (1863) *Carl Scharnhorst: Abenteuer eines deutschen Knaben in Amerika*, Hanover: Carl Rümpler.
Suárez, Constantino (1921) *Diccionario de voces cubanas*, Madrid: Imprenta Clarasó.
Suárez, José I., and Jack E. Tomlins (2000) *Mário de Andrade: The Creative Works*, Lewisburg, PA: Bucknell University Press.
Swann, Brian (1993) *Song of the Sky*, Amherst: University of Massachusetts Press.
Testut, Charles (1850) *Portraits littéraires de la Nouvelle Orléans*, New Orleans: Imprimerie des Louisianaises.
Testut, Charles (2004 [1858]) *Le Vieux Salomon*, Shreveport, LA: Les Cahiers du Tintamarre.

Thoreau, Henry David (1971 [1854]) *Walden*, Princeton, NJ: Princeton University Press.
Thoreau, Henry David (1973 [1849]) "Resistance to Civil Government" ["Civil Disobedience"], in Wendell Glick (ed.) *Reformed Papers*, Princeton, NJ: Princeton University Press, 63–90.
Thucydides (1843 [1629]) *The History of the Grecian War*, trans. Thomas Hobbes, in William Molesworth (ed.) *The English Works of Thomas Hobbes of Malmesbury*, vol. 8–9, London: John Bohn; trans. Charles Foster Smith (1956) *History of the Peloponnesian War*, 4 vols., Loeb Classical Library, Cambridge, MA: Harvard University Press.
Toury, Gideon (1980) *In Search of a Theory of Translation*, Tel Aviv: The Porter Institute for Poetics and Semiotics.
Toury, Gideon (1984) "Translation, Literary Translation and Pseudotranslation," in E.S. Shaffer (ed.) *Comparative Criticism 6*, Cambridge: Cambridge University Press, 73–85.
Toury, Gideon (1995) *Descriptive Translation Studies and Beyond*, Amsterdam: John Benjamins.
Tremblay, Michel (1972) *Les Belles-Soeurs*, Montreal: Leméac.
Tremblay, Michel (1985) *Le Gars de Québec*, Montreal: Lémeac.
Trudeau, Pierre (1962) 'The Conflict of Nationalism in Canada," *Cité Libre*, April.
Trudeau, Pierre (1968) *Federalism and the French Canadians*, Toronto: Macmillan.
Trudeau, Pierre (1992) *Towards a Just Society: The Trudeau Years*, trans. Patricia Claxton, Toronto: Penguin.
Tymoczko, Maria, and Edwin Gentzler (eds.) (2001.) *Translation and Power*, Amherst: University of Massachusetts Press.
United States Census (2003) "Language Use and English Speaking Ability: 2000" Brief, available online at http://www.census.gov/prod/2003pubs/c2kbr-29.pdf (accessed April 5, 2007).
United States Civil Rights Act (1964) Document Number PL 88-352, 88th Congress, H.R. 7152, available online at http://usinfo.state.gov/usa/infousa/laws/majorlaw/civilr19.htm (accessed April 5, 2007).
Valle-Inclán, Ramón del (1972) *Divinas palabras*, Madrid: Espasa-Calpe.
Vargas Llosa, Mario (1987) *El hablador*, Barcelona: Seix Barral; trans. Helen Lane (1990) *The Storyteller*, New York: Penguin Books USA.
Venuti, Lawrence (ed.) (1992a) *Rethinking Translation: Discourse, Subjectivity, Ideology*, London: Routledge.
Venuti, Lawrence (1992b) "Introduction," *Rethinking Translation: Discourse, Subjectivity, Ideology*, London: Routledge, 1–17.
Venuti, Lawrence (1995) *The Translator's Invisibility: A History of Translation*, London: Routledge.
Venuti, Lawrence (1998a) "American Tradition," in Mona Baker (ed.) *Routledge Encyclopedia of Translation Studies*, London: Routledge, 305–315.
Venuti, Lawrence (1998b) *Scandals of Translation: Towards an Ethics of Difference*, London: Routledge.
Vieira, Else Ribeiro Pires (1992) "Por uma teoria pós-moderna da tradução," Ph.D. thesis, Universidade Federal de Minas Gerais.
Vieira, Else Ribeiro Pires (1994a) "A Postmodern Translational Aesthetics in Brazil," in Mary Snell Hornby, Franz Pöchhacker, and Klaus Kaindl (eds.) *Translation Studies: An Interdiscipline*, Amsterdam: John Benjamins, 65–72.

Vieira, Else Ribeiro Pires (1994b) "A metáfora digestiva como representação de filosófia da apropriação na cultura brasileira pós 70," in Raúl Antelo (ed.) *Identidade e representação*, Florianópolis, Brazil: Pós-graduação em Letras/ Literatura Brasileira e Teoria Literária, 431–438.

Vieira, Else Ribeiro Pires (1995a) "Towards a Minor Translation," in Bernard McGuirk and Mark I. Millington (eds.) *Inequality and Difference in Hispanic and Latin American Literatures*, Lewiston, NY: Edwin Mellen Press, 141–152.

Vieira, Else Ribeiro Pires (1995b) "Can Another Subaltern Speak/Write?" *Renaissance and Modern Studies* 38: 96–125.

Vieira, Else Ribera Pires (1995–1996a) *"(In)visibilidades na tradução: Troca de olhares teóricos e ficcionais"* [(In)visibilities in Translation: Exchanging Theoretical and Fictional Perspectives], *Com Textos* (Mariana, Minas Gerais) 6:6, 50–68.

Vieira, Else Ribera Pires (1995–1996b) "El ser en 'visible': 'El espejo' en Guimarães Rosa [Being in "Visible": The Mirror in Guimarães Rosa], *Estudios* 6 (June 1995 – June 1996), Córdoba: Centro de Estudios Avanzados de la Universidad Nacional de Córdoba: 21–28.

Vieira, Else Ribeiro Pires (1999) "Liberating Calibans: Readings of *Antropofagia* and Haroldo de Campos' Poetics of Transcreation," in Susan Bassnett and Harish Trivedi (eds.) *Post-colonial Translation: Theory and Practice*. London: Routledge, 95–113.

Vizenor, Gerald (1981) *Earthdivers: Tribal Narratives on Mixed Descent*, Minneapolis: University of Minnesota Press.

Vizenor, Gerald (1998) *Fugitive Poses: Native American Indian Scenes of Absence and Presence*, Lincoln: University of Nebraska Press.

Vizenor, Gerald, and A. Robert Lee (1999) *Postindian Conversations*, Lincoln: University of Nebraska Press.

Waldo, Lewis Patrick (1942) *French Drama in America in the Eighteenth Century and Its Influence on the American Dramas of That Period 1701–1800*, Baltimore: Johns Hopkins Press.

Ward, Adolphus William, Alfred Rayney, William Peterfied Trent et al. (1907–1721) *The Cambridge History of English and American Literature*, 18 vols., Cambridge: Cambridge University Press.

Ware, Ralph Hartman (1930) *American Adaptations of French Plays on the New York and Philadelphia Stages from 1834 to the Civil War*, PhD thesis, University of Pennsylvania.

Warner, Rex (trans.) (1972) *Thucydides' History of the Peloponnesian War*, rev. edn., New York: Penguin.

Welch, James (1974) *Winter in the Blood*, New York: Harper and Row.

Whole Booke of Psalmes Faithfully Translated into English Metre, The (1640), Cambridge, MA: Stephen Daye.

Wilkens, Sir Charles, trans. (1849 [1784]), *Bhagavad Gita*, Bangalore: Wesleyan Mission Press.

Index

62: A Model Kit 139
1001 Nights 112–15, 117, 131

A Sociocritique of Translation: Theatre and Alterity in Quebec 1968–1988 46
à traduire 99, 168, 183, 187
acculturation 176, 177
African-American population of the US 9
After Babel 53
Akai, Joanne 174–5
Aleph, The 110, 118, 119
Alonzo, Anne-Marie 60
Ambassadors of Culture: The Transamerican Origins of Latino Writing 26–7
American Crossroads Project 37
American Scene, The 9
American Scholar, The 23–4
American Translation and Interpreting Studies Association (ATISA) 31, 40
Americas, the: boundaries of nation states in 5; Gómez-Peña's definition 159; hidden narratives of discovery and colonization 13–18; mistranslations of 5; namings 13; referring to the indigenous peoples of 6; translations in 5–7
Amerindians: "anti-imperial translation" 38; English and Spanish images of 17; extermination of 31; *Guatinaui World Tour* performance piece 161–5; identity 13; languages 16; misrepresentation of 163; mistranslation of 6, 13, 173; negotiating peace treaties with 12–13, 17, 22; one-way translation from colonizers 12–13, 18; storytelling 13; Van der Donck's descriptions of 16–17; *see also* Native Americans
Amour Bilingue 27

Amsterdam 15
Anaya, Rudolfo 148–50, 155, 184
Andrade, Joaquim Pedro de 100, 101, 105
Andrade, Mário de 84–5, 99–100, 109
Andrade, Oswald de 6–7, 77, 80–2, 84–5, 86, 100, 101, 106; critique of 103
"anti-imperial translation" 38
antitranslation 158
Anzaldúa, Gloria 150–7, 168
Apollinaire, Guillaume 4
Apter, Emily 3–4, 185
Argentina: identity formation in 110, 138, 141; Jewish women in 118–19; Arrojo, Rosemary 3, 109, 118, 137, 138
art: Benjamin on works of 131; Derrida's borders of 144
artists and translators 158–9
Ascher, Nelson 98–9, 109
assimilation policy 9, 183; resisting 7, 28, 47, 185
au féminin 57
author/translator binary 138
authorship 132
Averroës' Search 119
Awakening, The 26

back-translations 113
Bary, Leslie 80
Bassnett, Susan 1, 2, 37, 64, 109, 174, 180
Bay Psalm Book, The 18–19
Bellei, Sérgio 104–5, 106
Beloved 181, 182
Benjamin, Andrew 186
Benjamin, Walter: *The Storyteller: Reflections on the Works of Nikolai Leskov* 130–2; *The Task of the Translator* 68, 90, 95–6, 132–4,

170; translation theory 38, 70–1, 130–4, 137; *The Work of Art in the Age of Mechanical Reproduction* 131
Bersianik, Louky 60
Bhabha, Homi 4, 7, 145
Bhagavad Gita 22, 38–9
Bible: Derrida on translations of 170; Haroldo de Campo's translation of 86–7; translation into Algonquian 18; translation theory 128
Bickerton, Derek 166
bilingual audiences 161
bilingual writing 147, 148, 153, 157, 178
bilingualism and translation 27
binary opposites 72, 145; of author and translator 138; of fiction and translation 109; of global politics 85, 92–3; of translation theory 52, 53–4, 68
Blake, William 98
Blanchot, Maurice 70–1, 168, 169, 170, 171
Bless Me, Ultima 148–50, 155, 184
Blow-Up 139
Bly, Robert 32, 33
border culture 38, 145, 148, 151–2, 153
border writing 143–79; Calibanization 171–4; in the Caribbean 165–8; deconstruction and 168–71; Gloria Anzaldúa 150–7; *la frontera* 146–57; *Living On/Border Lines* 70, 144, 168–71; *New World Border* 157–65; nontranslation 153, 161; translation studies 164–5, 167, 174–9; translators of 146
Borderlands/La Frontera 151–7
Borges, Jorge Luis 97, 110–19, 136, 138, 141; *Death and the Compass* 118; *Emma Zunz* 118–19; *Garden of the Forking Paths, The* 117; *The Library of Babel* 116–17; on "original" texts 34, 132; *Pierre Menard, Author of the Quixote* 34, 35, 115–16, 141; on translations of *1001 Nights* 112–15; on translations of Homer 111–12; writings on translation studies 110
Braithwaite, Edward Kamau 176
Brazil: Cannibalist Manifesto 80–2, 100, 101; cannibalist movement in 6–7, 77–107; concrete poetry 80, 84, 86, 91, 93, 98, 103; critiques of the cannibalist movement 101–7; identity formation in 78, 79–80, 85, 99, 103, 106–7; intellectual elite in 103, 104; power dynamics in relationship with European culture 101–2, 104, 105; translation and cannibalism in 82–92, 97–101, 102, 107; translation studies association in 6; "Tropicalismo" movement 101
Brighter Sun, A 167
Brisset, Annie 46, 48, 49, 50
Brossard, Nicole 56, 61–5, 66, 67, 109
Burrow, The 138
Burton, Richard Francis 112, 113, 114

Cabrera Infante, Guillermo 34–5, 66
Cajuns 29
Caliban and Other Essays 172
Caliban: Notes towards a Discussion of Culture in Our America 171–4
Caliban, suite de La Tempête 173
calibanization and translation 171–4
Campos, Augusto de 77, 82, 83, 97–9, 101, 103, 104
Campos, Haroldo de 3, 77, 84–92, 95–7, 102–5
Can the Subaltern Speak? 182
Canada 32, 40–76; comparison of translation services with the US 40; feminist translation in Quebec 51–4, 65–72; history of 41–3; immigration 43; languages of 42, 44, 46, 48–9, 70; multiculturalism in 73–6; Native Americans 42, 74–5; Quebec feminism 56–61; separatist movement in Quebec 43–5, 74–5; studies on psychoanalysis and translation 186; theatre translation in Quebec 45–51, 73; translation histories in 41–2; translation studies associations in 6; a translational culture 2, 45
Canada Council Translation Grants 40, 45
Canadian Association for Translation Studies (CATS) 40
Canadian Confederation 42
Canadian Play, A/Une plaie canadienne 47
Candido, Antonio 104, 106
Cannibalist Manifesto 80–2, 100, 101
cannibalist movement 77–107; critiques of 101–7; in European translation traditions 114; links with postmodern and postcolonial theory 92, 101, 102; metaphors 83, 86, 105, 107; translation and 82–92, 97–101, 102, 107
"cannibals" 172–3
canonical texts, translating 46, 86, 134
Caribbean: border writing in 165–8;

caliban texts 171–4; Cuba 172–8; translation studies in 6; *see also* Creole language
Carpentier, Alejo 178
Cart, the Tram and the Modernist Poetry, The 103
Cartier, Jacques 14, 42
Catechism in the Massachusetts Indian Languages, A 18
Cather, Willa 25
Césaire, Aimé 3, 171, 172
Chamberlain, Lori 53
Chamberlain, Paul 50
Champlain, Samuel de 14, 42
Cheyfitz, Eric 185
Chicano language 152–3, 161
Chinese 8
Chopin, Kate 26
Choreographies 71–2
Cienaga 178
Civil Disobedience 22–3, 39
Civil Rights Act 1964 8
Cixous, Hélène 41, 52; on writing 54–6
Clément, Catherine 52, 54, 55
colonial culture 18–19, 30–1, 78, 165
colonist agendas 162–5
Columbus, Christopher 172, 173
Common Sense 21
Como era gostoso o meu frances (How Tasty was my Little Frenchman) 79, 100
Comparative Literature: A Critical Introduction 37
Constructing Cultures 1
"contact zone" 38, 164
Contemporary Translation Theories 128
Corrêa, José Celso Martinez 100
Cortázar 139–40
Creole culture 165–6
Creole language 25–6, 165–6, 167; in Cuba 176; Haitian Creole 8; "nation language" 176; translating the oral language into written English 166, 174–5
"critical criollism" 176, 177, 178
Cronin, Michael 180
cross-cultural/temporal communication 39, 106
Cuba 172–8
Cuban Condition, The: Translation and Identity in Modern Cuban Literature 175–8
cultural assimilation 9, 183; resisting 7, 28, 47, 185
cultural evolution 2, 84–5, 109, 132
cultural identity: feminist destabilizing of 52, 60–1; participation of translation in 31–2
cultural immersion 128
cultural studies 1–2
culture: border 38, 145, 148, 151–2, 153; colonial 18–19, 30–1, 78, 165; cross-cultural/temporal communication 39, 106; European 5–6, 37–8, 78, 100, 101–5; flows between source and target 102; hidden 149; "hybrid" 7, 144, 158, 159; of Latin America in the modern world 85–6, 103; *mestizo/a* 150–7; monolingual 9–10, 158, 160, 161; New American Studies 5, 37–9; new theories of 7, 91–2; popular 35; representations in museums 163–4; translational 2, 7, 45, 145, 175; understanding through translation 123; *see also* minority culture
Culture in Transit 67

Dabydeen, Cyril 174
Dadaist movement 77
Danish 23
de-translation 184
Death and the Compass 118
Death Sentence 70–1, 168, 171
Declaration of Independence 19
Declaration of the Rights of Man and the Citizen 21
deconstruction 92, 93, 94, 130, 136, 168–71
deculturation 177
"deep time" 22
Delle Navigationi et Viaggi 14
democracy in translation 19–22, 95
Derrida, Jacques: concern with borders 144; deconstruction 92, 93, 94, 130, 136, 168–71; *Des tours de Babel* 68, 134–5, 187; "fictional turn" in translation studies 134–5, 136; hidden cultures 149; on language in Quebec 70; *Living On/Border Lines* 70, 144, 168–71; *Monolingualism of the Other* 9–10, 27, 29–31; multilingualism of 170; *Nacionalidad y nacionalismo filosófico* 92–5; original texts "living on" in translation 134, 169–70, 187; *Roundtable on Autobiography* 68–9; *Roundtable on Translation* 68, 130, 134, 135; on translation 68, 71, 96, 134–5, 137; translation theory 68, 71, 96, 134–6; translator's note 169; on women in writing 69, 70, 71–2

Des tours de Babel 68, 134–5, 187
Description of New Netherlands, A 16–17
Descriptive Translation Studies and Beyond 53
descriptive translation studies (DTS) 2
Deus e o Diablo no Fausto de Goethe 87–92, 97
dictionaries 176
Difference in Translation 68
Dimock, Wai Chee 22–3, 38–9
Donne, John 101
Dos Santos, Nelson Pereira 79, 100
Du Bartas, Guillaume de Salluste 18
Duffy, William 33
Dwight, John Sullivan 23

Ear of the Other, The 68, 69, 71
écriture au féminin 57
écriture féminine 54, 55, 56, 57
Edwards, Jonathan 18–19
Eliot, John 18
Emerson, Ralph Waldo 22, 23
Emma Zunz 118–19
English: Caribbean 176; male coding of 60; on the Mexican/US border 148, 152; speakers in the US 8; translations in Québécois theater 46, 47
English colonies in the US 15, 17, 18–19
English-only policy in the US 11–12, 24, 27, 29, 31, 32
European culture: in Brazil 78, 100, 101–5; domination of 37–8; idealized belief of 185; translated in the Americas 5–6
Even-Zohar, Itamar 2, 53

Faust 3, 87–9, 91, 102
Federalist Papers 11, 19, 20–1
feminism: French 52, 54, 57, 58; Québécois 56–61
feminist translation: in Quebec 51–4, 65–72; theorizing 65–8
feminist writing 54–6
Fichte, Johann Gottlieb 94
"fictional turn" in translation studies 108–42; Arrojo on 109, 118, 137, 138; Borges 110–19, 136, 141; Derrida 134–5, 136; González on 110, 141–2, 182; Larkosh on 110, 117–18, 137–8, 140–1; Márquez 119–23, 136, 141–2; Pagano on 109–10, 137, 139–40; Vargas Llosa 124–30, 135–6; Vieira on 108–9, 136–7

fidelity in translations 111, 115, 116, 137, 164
Fifties, The 33
Finnish 24
Firewords 60
Firmat, Gusatvo Pérez 175–8
fragmentation 158
Franklin, Benjamin 11, 19
Free Trade Art Agreement/El tratado de libre cultura 159–60
Freefalling toward a Borderless Future 158–9
French Enlightenment thinkers 19, 21
French feminism 52, 54, 57, 58
French language 8, 11, 24; Canadian 42, 44, 49; early texts on the "discovery" of America 14; *joual* 46, 48; male coding of 58–9, 60; in New Orleans 29; translations in Québécois theater 46, 47, 48
French literature in the US 25–6
French Revolution 21, 94
French theater in the US 26
Freud, Sigmund 36, 170, 184, 186–7
Fuller, Margaret 23
Fusco, Coco 161–5

Galland, Jean Antoine 112, 113
Galvez, imperador do Acre/The Emperor of the Amazon 100
Gandhi, Mahatma 23
Garden of the Forking Paths, The 117
Garneau, Michel 48, 49–50
Gehring, Charles 17
Gender and the Metaphorics of Translation 53
Gender in Translation: Cultural Identity and the Politics of Transmission 52
Gentzler, Edwin 32, 128, 137, 168, 182, 187
geographical space of translation 3–4
Germain, Jean-Claude 47
German Ideology, The 95
German language: eradication in the US 27; in Pennsylvania 11–12, 24; speakers in the US today 8; translations in Quebecois theater 46–7
German literature in the US 24–5
German nationalism 94–5
German theater in the US 25
ghettoization 9
Gil, Gilberto 101
Godard, Barbara 3, 56, 66–8
Goethe, Johann Wolfgang von 3, 23, 87–9, 102

Gogol, Nikolay 48
Goldman, Emma 71
Gómez-Peña, Guillermo 157–65, 171
González, Anibal 110, 141–2, 182
Graham, Joseph 68, 134–5
Grandmont, Eloi de 47
Greek: etymologies 170; texts 19, 20; translations in Québécois thater 46
Gruesz, Kirsten Silva 26–7
Guadalupe 153–4
Guatinaui World Tour, The 161–5
Guillén, Nicolás 178–9

Haitian Creole 8
Hamlet 87–8
Harris, Wilson 181–2
Heath Anthology of American Literature 26
Hebrew/Yiddish tradition 23–4
Hinojosa, Rolando 146–8
Hispanic population of the US 9
history and translation 111, 139, 140
Hobbes, Thomas 19, 20
Holland 14, 15, 24, 25
Holmes, James 117
Homer 111–12
Homeric Versions, The 111, 112, 141
hybrid cultures 7, 144, 158, 159
hybrid language 158, 161, 165, 176
hybrid texts 105, 117
hyphenated identities 31, 145, 159

Icelandic 23
identity: Amerindian 13; in a borderless future 159; hyphenated 31, 145, 159; language 69–70; loss of women's 59; national 93
identity formation 36–7; acquisition of language and links to 184; affect of translation on Levine's 36–7; in areas of difference 99; in Argentina 110, 138, 141; in border spaces 145; in Brazil 78, 79–80, 85, 99, 103, 106–7; Caribbean translations and 159, 175, 179; effect of male coding of language on 59; language as a tool in minority 76; Québécois 45–8, 76; suppression on the Mexican/US border 151; translation studies and 2, 4, 7, 31–7, 84–5, 109, 111, 186; in the US 31–7
In Search of a Theory of Translation 2, 25
intertextualisation 88, 92
intra-translation 98
intradução 98, 99

intralingual translation 63
Iraq war 185
Irigaray, Luce 41, 52, 58–9, 109
Island at the Center of the World, The 15
Italian: early texts on the "discovery" of America 13, 14; translations in Québécois theater 46
Itwaru, Arnold 174

James, Henry 9
Jay, John 11
Jefferson, Thomas 11, 19
Jewish exiles 118–19
Johnson, Barbara 56, 107
Johnson, Jeremiah 16
Johnson, Randal 105
joual 46, 48
journals 23, 84
Jouve, Nicole Ward 64
Juan Crillo 178

Kafka, Franz 138
Khatibi, Abdedkebir 27–9, 30
King, Martin Luther 23
"kinship of languages" 132
Kleptomaniac Translator, The 138
Kline, Nancy 55–6
Kosztolányi, Dezsö 138
Krupat, Arnold 38

La folie du jour (The Madness of the Day) 168
La frontera 146–57
revered hybrid-border-translational figures 154–5
La lettre aérienne 56
La Llorona 155
La Malinche 154–5
L'Afficheur hurle 50
Lamy, Suzanne 57
Lane, Edward 112, 113, 114
language: discrimination against minority 12; hybrid 158, 161, 165, 176; identity 69–70; "kinship" of 132; lost 181; on the Mexican/US border 152; national 93, 171; of philosophy 93; "pure" 90, 95, 96, 132; resexualizing 72; subverting the dominant 28–9; survival battles 3
Laplanche, Jean 4, 99, 183–4
Larkosh, Christopher 110, 117–18, 137–8, 140–1
L'Arrêt de mort 70–1, 168, 171
Latin America 108–42; Borges 110–19, 136, 141; criticism of the "fictional

turn" in 136–42; culture in the modern world 85–6, 103; ideas exchange with Europe 137; Márquez 119–23, 136; mistranslations of 5; nation building in 137; translation studies in 6, 108; Vargas Llosa 124–30, 135–6; *see also* Argentina; Brazil; Mexico
Laugh of Medusa, The 55
Le Desért mauve 61–5, 109; Godard on 67; translating 56
Le Gars de Quebec 48
Lefevere, André 1, 2, 174, 180
les belles infidèles 53
Les Voyages de la nouvelle France 14
Lévesque, Claude 69–70
Lévesque, René 43
Levine, Suzanne Jill 31, 33–7, 51
L'Homme rapaillé 50
Lianeri, Alexandra 19–21
Library of Babel, The 116–17
literary criticism 170, 171
Littmann, Enno 112, 113
Living On/Border Lines 70, 144, 168–71
Locke, John 19, 20
Los pasos perdidos 178
Lotbinière-Harwood, Susanne de 56–7, 60, 66
Loveira, Carlos 178
Luciferian translators 89–90, 96, 97
Lukács, Georg 95–6

Macbeth 48, 49–51
Macunaima 99–100, 105, 109
Madison, James 19, 20–1
magic realism 120
Maier, Carol 3, 31, 32
Manifesto Antropofago 80–2, 100, 101
"manipulation school" of translation studies 2
Manual for Manuel, A 139–40
Mardrus, J.C. 112, 113, 114
Marlatt, Daphne 67
Márquez, Garcia 119–23, 136, 141–2
Marvell, Andrew 97, 98
Marx, Karl 95
Marxism 92–3, 95, 182
Más allá del principio de la nostalgia (Sehnsucht) 95–7
McDonald, Christie 68, 69, 70; *Choreographies* 71–2
McGuirk, Bernard 118
Mehrez, Samia 28
mestizo/a culture 150–7
metalepsis 183, 184

metaphors: cannibalist 83, 86, 105, 107; of construction and architecture 137; for the translation process 86, 87, 90, 102, 134, 137; in translation theory 53; in women's writing 55
metaphysical thinking 54, 90, 97, 99
Mexico 12; border with the US 146–57; hybrid-border-translational figures 154–5
Michaud, Ginette 186
migration and translation 7, 142, 159
minority culture: assimilation of 9, 183, 185; avoiding assimilation in the dominant culture 7, 28, 47, 185; repression of the remainder in 9, 10; translation as a tool in 76
Miron, Gaston 50
Misplaced Ideas: Essays on Brazilian Culture 102–4
mistranslation: in the Afghan and Iraq wars 185; of "America" 5; of "cannibal" 172–3; of "Latin America" 5; of Native Americans 6, 13, 173; revealing "truths" through 99, 145–6, 164; to reverse power relations 158, 160, 161
modernism 92, 95
Möllhausen, Heinrich Balduin 24
monolingual cultures 9–10, 158, 160, 161
monolingual policy in the US 11–12, 24, 27, 29, 31, 32; failure of 185–6
monolingualism/multilingualism binary 9–10, 29–30
Monolingualism of the Other; or The Prosthesis of Origin 9–10, 27, 29–31
Morrison, Toni 181
multiculturalism: in Canda 73–6; the new norm 156; in the United States 8–39
multilingual: hybridization 105; writing 28, 157, 160, 166
museums 162–5
music 101
My Antonia 25

Nacionalidad y nacionalismo filosófico 92–5
Naipaul, V.S. 174
names in Europe and Latin America 129
nation building 137
"nation language" 176
national identity 4, 9, 93, 94, 106
nationalism 92–5
Native Americans: assimilation of 185; attitudes to women 152; in Canada

42, 74–5; cannibalism among 79; mistranslation of 6, 13, 173; reconstructing the image of 106; translation issues in Quebec 75–6; Tupinambá Indians 78, 79; *see also* Amerindians
Nature 23
Neate, Wilson 9
Négritude 172
neoculturation 177
New American Studies 5, 37–9
New Amsterdam 14, 15
New Netherlands colony 14–17
New Netherlands Project 15
New North American Studies, The 38
New Orleans 25–6, 27, 29
New World Border, The 157–65; *Free Trade Art Agreement/El tratado de libre cultura* 159–60; *Freefalling toward a Borderless Future* 158–9; *Prophecies for the End of the Century* 160
New York 15, 17, 18
Newly Born Woman, The 52
newspapers 23–4, 26, 27, 84
Nida, Eugene 128
Nietzsche 90, 170
Noigrandes 84, 92
nontranslation: in border writing 153, 161; in the poems of *Borderlands/La Frontera* 157; policy in the US 12; policy towards Native Americans 185; to resist monolingual language policies 28, 143, 158
North Africa 28–9, 31
Norwegian 23
novelists 131

O homem do Pau-Brasil (The Brazilwood Man) 101
O Pioneers! 25
O rei da vela (The Candle King) 100
Ocampo, Victoria 137–8, 140–1
Odyssey, The 111–12
Office of Civil Rights 8
Official Languages Act (Canada) 43, 45
Oncle Vania 48
One Hundred Years of Solitude 119–23, 136, 140, 141–2, 182
oral histories 13
oral literature 131, 146; translated into written English 166, 174–5
original texts: Borges' questioning the existence of 34, 132; "living on" through translation 68, 90, 133–4, 169–70, 187; occuring simultaneously 158, 160; parodying 82, 115, 116, 136; retranslations of 161; rewriting of 97, 174; self-translations of 157, 174; target and 38, 102, 113; and translations in border spaces 145, 161, 167–8, 175
Ortiz, Fernando 4, 5, 144, 176–8
"Other", the: accessing 130; monolingualism and 9–10; repression of 35, 54, 186; translating 150, 164
Otis, James 21

Pachuco 152
Pagano, Adriana 109–10, 137, 139–40
Paine, Thomas 21
parodying original texts 82, 115, 116, 136
Parti Québécois 42, 43–4, 45, 46, 74
Pastorius, Francis Daniel 24
Pau-Brazil movement 80
Paz, Octavio 85, 86
Pennsylvania 11–12
Peru 124
Picture Theory 56; translating 67
Pierre Menard, Author of the Quixote 34, 35, 115–16, 141
Poetics of Imperialism: Translation and Colonization from The Tempest to Tarzan 185
poetry: Augusto de Campos on 97–8; in *Borderlands/La Frontera* 151, 156–7; concrete 80, 84, 86, 91, 93, 98, 103; German 25; Guillén's sonnets 178–9; John Donne in translation 101; New England 18; Provençal poets in translation 97; Québécois 50, 60; *The Triumph of Life* 168, 169; *Zone* 4
political zone of translation 4
Politics of Translation, The 149, 180–1
Polysystem Studies 53
popular culture 35
postcolonial theory 4, 78, 82, 144, 172, 173; cannibalist movement and 92, 101, 102
Postmodern Translational Aesthetics in Brazil, A 101–2
postmodernism 92, 101, 102, 104, 105
Postnationalism, Globalism, and the New American Studies 37–9
poststructuralism 3, 4, 78, 103, 132, 145, 182
Póstudo 103
Pound, Ezra 84, 90, 97–8
power: changing balance of 164; dynamics in European versus

Brazilian culture 101–2, 104, 105; mistranslation to reverse relations of 158, 160, 161; of translation 1, 20, 32
Pratt, Mary Louise 164
presidential elections 21
Prophecies for the End of the Century 160
Provençal poets 84, 97
psalms 18–19
psychoanalysis 36, 183–4, 186; *à traduire* 99, 168, 183, 187
psychological zone of translation 4
"pure" language 90, 95, 96, 132
Puritan colony 15, 17, 18–19
Pygmalion 47

Quebec: feminism 56–61; feminist translation in 51–4, 65–72; history of 42; Hydro-Quebec 75; independence movement in 43–5, 74–5; language 42, 48–9, 70; multiculturalism in 73–6; Parti Québécois 42, 43–4, 45, 46, 74; theater in 45–51, 73; translation issues with the Native Americans 75–6; translational culture in 2, 45

racism 162–5
Rama, Angel 4
réécriture au féminin 41, 54, 56
Reitzel, Robert 24
religious translations 18–19 *see also* Bible
rememory 181, 184
Renan, Ernest 172, 173
representation of culture 163–4
repression: of the "Other" 35, 54, 186; of the remainder 9, 10; translators' implication in 9, 51
Retamar, Roberto 144, 172–4
Rethinking Translation: Discourse, Subjectivity, Ideology 3, 186
retranslation 161
rewriting, translation as 97, 174
Ribaut, Jean 14
Riberio, Darcy 101
Rights of the British Colonies Asserted and Proved, The 21
Ripley, George 23
Rituel 60
Rodriguez, Luis Felipe 178
Romano-Sued, Susana 119
Roosevelt, Theodore 11
Rosa, Guimarães 136, 137
Roundtable on Autobiography 68–9

Roundtable on Translation, The 68, 130, 134, 135
Rousseau, Jean-Jacques 21
Routledge Encyclopedia of Translation Studies 18
Rowe, John Carlos 37
Russian 8, 46

Salée, Daniel 75
Sandys, George 18
Scandals of Translation 31–2
Schwarz, Roberto 102–4, 105, 106
self-translation 157, 174
Selvon, Sam 166, 167, 168, 174
Senghor, Léopold 172
Sepmaines, Les 18
sermons 18
sexuality 72, 117–18
Shakespeare, William: Caliban 172; first translations in a culture 49; *Macbeth* 48, 49–51; parodying 82; plagarisation of 87–8; *The Tempest* 3, 171
Shaw, Bernard 47
Shelley 168, 169, 170, 171
Shorto, Russell 14–15, 16, 17
Siemerling, Winfried 38
Simon, Sherry 2–3, 41, 52, 67, 73
simultaneous translations 158, 160
Sixties, The 33
slang expressions 35
"slow translation" 22
Smith, Charles Foster 20
social-psychological turn 180–1, 184–5, 186
sol/soleil 55
Sollor, Werner 37
source texts 102, 113, 115, 133; ephemeral 132; in self-translation 157; *see also* original texts
Sousândrade, Joaquim 91
Souza, Márcio 100
space of the translator 54, 64–5
Spanglish 148, 158
Spanish 8, 24; Chicano 152–3, 161; early texts on the "discovery" of America 13–14; on the Mexican/US border 152–3; standard 158; translations in Québécois theater 46
Spanish writing in the US 26–7
Specimens of Foreign Standard Literature 23
Spivak, Gayatri 4, 145, 149, 180–3
Squanto 12–13
Steiner, George 53

Storyteller, The 124–30, 135–6; style of narrative 128–30
Storyteller, The: Reflections on the Works of Nikolai Leskov 130–2
storytelling 13, 131
Strubberg, Friedrich 24
Suárez, Constantino 176
subaltern consciousness 182, 183
subject-effects 183
subversion in translation 28–9, 33–7
Subversive Scribe: Translating Latin American Fiction 33–7
Swedish 23, 24

Tagalog 8
Taliaferro, Lawrence 22
target texts 102, 113, 114, 157; importing the foreign into 38
Task of the Translator, The 68, 90, 95–6, 132–4, 170
Taylor, Edward 18
Tempest, The 3, 171
Tessera 40, 66
texts: *see* original texts; source texts; target texts
theater: French 26; German 25; *The New World Border* 157–65; translation in Quebec 45–51, 73
Theorizing Feminist Discourse/Translation 66
Theory of the Novel 95–6
"Third World" 85
This Sex Which is Not One 58
Thoreau, Henry David 22–3, 38, 39
Through Other Continents: American Literature across Deep Time 22, 38–9
time, translations across 38–9, 70
Toury, Gideon 2, 25, 53
Toward a Theoretical Practice for Cross-cultural Translation 32
Towards a Minor Translation 102
trans-position 137
transcreation 90
"transculturation" 4–5, 103, 106, 143, 144, 176, 177, 178, 180
Transformance 67
Translating Montreal: Episodes in the Life of a Divided City 2–3, 73
Translating Origins: Psychoanalysis and Philosophy 186
Translation and Democracy in Nineteenth-Century England 19
Translation and Identity 180
Translation and Power 32, 137
Translation and the Postcolonial Experience: The Francophone North African Text 28
Translation as Testimony: On Official Histories and Subversive Pedagogies in Cortázar 137
Translation, Counter-culture and the Fifties 32–3
Translation, History and Culture 1
Translation, Poststructuralism, and Power 182
translation studies: associations 6, 40; border writing and 164–5, 167, 174–9; Borges on 110; challenging traditional theories 171; "cultural turn" in 1–2; defining 2–3; descriptive translation studies (DTS) school 2; an emerging discipline 6, 108; expanding 165; fidelity in 111, 115, 116, 137, 164; identity formation and 2, 4, 7, 31–7, 84–5, 109, 111, 186; representation and 164; social-psychological turn 180–1, 184–5, 186; in the US 6, 31–7, 40; *see also* "fictional turn" in translation studies
translation theory: Benjamin's 38, 70–1, 130–4, 137; Bible 128; binary opposites in 52, 53–4, 68; in border spaces 145, 153; Borge's fiction as a source for 117–18; cultural immersion 128; de Campos brothers' 84–92, 104–5; Derrida's 68, 71, 96, 134–6; Levine's 33–7; metaphors in 53; parodied in Borge's fiction 115, 116, 136; Québécois feminist 65–72; repression of the remainder 9, 10; "satanical" element in 89–90, 96, 97; traditional versus cannibalist 99
Translation Zone, The: A New Comparative Literature 3, 185
translational culture 7, 145, 175; of Quebec 2, 45
Translator of 1001 Nights, The 112–15
translators: in the 50s and 60s in the US 32–3; Amerindian 12–13, 22; author/translator binary 138; in border spaces 146; Canada Council Translation Grants 40; cannibalistic 102; Derrida's notes for 169; Gómez-Peña's links to artists 158–9; implicated in exclusionary policies 9, 51; in-between space of 54, 64–5; in *Le Desért mauve* 62–3; Luciferian 89–90, 96, 97; making visible the creative process 33–4, 56–7, 66, 67, 102, 109; personal identity 36–7;

Québécois feminist 51–4, 65–72; Québécois theater 47–51
Translator's Invisibility, The 174
transluciferation 90, 103
transtextualistation 86
treaties 12–13, 17, 22, 76
Tremblay, Michel 48
Trinidad 166–7
Triumph of Life, The 168, 169
"Tropicalisimo" movement 101
Trudeau, Pierre 43
TTR 186
Tupinambá Indians 78, 79
Tupy or not Tupy 105
Turn to the Native: Studies in Criticism and Culture 38
Two Undiscovered Amerindians Visit (name of city) 161–5
Tymoczko, Maria 2, 31, 32, 137
typography, altering 60

Une tempête: Adaptation de "La Tempête" de Shakespeare pour un théâtre nègre 171
United States 8–39; African-American population 9; American Revolution 19–22; assimilation policy 7, 9, 183, 185; border with Mexico 146–57; British colonial religious translations 18–19; Constitution 11, 19, 20; Declaration of Independence 19; development of democracy in 19–22, 95; English colony in 15, 17, 18–19; English-only policy 11–12, 24, 27, 29, 31, 32; *Federalist Papers* 11, 19, 20–1; German language eradication 27; hidden narratives of discovery and colonization 10–18; Hispanic population 9; identity formation 31–7; languages spoken in 8–9, 24, 29; monolingual policy failure 185–6; multicultural society in the 19th century 22–7; New American Studies 5, 37–9; New Netherlands colony 14–17; New Orleans 25–6, 27, 29; New York 15, 17, 18; newspapers and journals 23–4; presidential elections 21; reactionary nationalism in 95; repression of the remainder 9, 10; translation laws in 8; translation studies in 6, 31–7, 40; unwritten policy of nontranslation 12
untranslatable stories 149, 181, 184
Unwelcome Remainders, Welcome Reminders 9
Utopia selvagem: Saudades da inocencia perdida (Savage Utopia: Longings for a Lost Innocence) 100–1

Van der Donck, Adriaen 14–18
Vargas Llosa, Mario 124–30, 135–6
Veloso, Caetano 101
Venuti, Lawrence 3, 9, 18, 31–2, 33, 38, 53, 54, 109, 129, 174, 186
Verde-Amarelo 77, 82, 83
Verso, reverso, controverso 97
Vieira, Else 3; on the cannibalist movement 83–4, 85, 101–2, 107; on the "fictional turn" 108–9, 136–7
Vietnamese 8
Virgin Mary, representations of 153–4
Vizenor, Gerald 13
Voyages 14

war and translation 4, 185–6
Whitman, Walt 12
Whole and True Discovery of Terra Florida, The 14
women: in Argentina 118–19; Derrida on 69, 70, 71–2; on the Mexican/US border 151–2
women's writing 54–6, 57, 58, 119
Work of Art in the Age of Mechanical Reproduction, The 131
writing: bilingual 147, 148, 153, 157, 178; fragmentary 169; translations from oral literature 166, 174–5; *see also* border writing; original texts

Yale School of Deconstruction 169, 171

Zone (poem) 4
"zones", Apter's 3–4